# THE
# ULTIMATE
# INVESTOR

# THE ULTIMATE INVESTOR

## THE PEOPLE AND IDEAS THAT MAKE MODERN INVESTMENT

**DEAN LeBARON & ROMESH VAITILINGAM**

CAPSTONE

First published 1999 by
Capstone US
Business Books Network
163 Central Avenue
Suite 2
Hopkins Professional Building
Dover
NH 03820
USA

Capstone Publishing Limited
Oxford Centre for Innovation
Mill Street
Oxford OX2 0JX
United Kingdom
http://www.capstone.co.uk

British Library Cataloguing in Publication Data
A CIP catalogue record for this book is available from the British Library

ISBN 1-84112-006-5

Typeset in 11/14 pt Plantin by
Sparks Computer Solutions Ltd, Oxford
http://www.sparks.co.uk
Printed and bound by
T.J. International Ltd, Padstow, Cornwall

This book is printed on acid-free paper

Substantial discounts on bulk quantities of Capstone books are available to corporations, professional associations and other organizations. If you are in the USA or Canada, phone the LPC Group for details on (1-800-626-4330) or fax (1-800-243-0138). Everywhere else, phone Capstone Publishing on (+44-865-798623) or fax (+44-865-240941).

# Contents

# Preface

Is the volume you are holding in your hands – or reading on a screen – really ultimate? Well, of course not. But it is our intention to come as close as we can to getting to the key ideas in modern investment and the people who have them and use them. And to make it as comprehensive as we know how.

We only know the ultimate after the fact. And then new features come along, yet to be time-tested, which might prove to be part of a new ultimate. So, like the trace of a particle in a cloud chamber, by the time we see it, the particle has passed by. Our view of ultimate has to be colored by our times. The role of the observer determines the experimental outcome, another thought taken from the physical sciences.

We have tried to approach a moving target as best we can, treating thirty ideas and thirty-plus people. The ideas are not neatly bounded so that they exist without important and active relations with other elements. Rather, they are part of the market soup, boiling and vibrant, which is constantly evolving in the interplay of mathematics and personalities. We can pretend that each element is distinct only for the purpose of descriptive analysis. But, in the end, each market instant and each investor has to reassemble the pieces to grapple with our task of forecasting imponderable outcomes.

We have tried to simplify the ideas, at times borrowing from the writings of the personalities or *gurus* who are associated with the ideas – and borrowing from the ideas of others. None of us as investment students and practitioners lives in isolation: we are all part of the mosaic being analyzed, shard by piece.

At times, we may seem glib and cavalier. It is merely in our attempt to be concise about things that defy precision.

So now that we have started with our limitations, what will we be doing to merit your attention? Answer: give you a grounding in the ideas and people who have brought us to today's market understanding. These people have also shaped tomorrow's market. They might not know it yet but they – and others we have omitted or do not know – set the base for innovation. You need to know them and their work. They are your investment future – at least your future in ways we try to understand for you.

Ours was a seamless collaboration despite living an ocean apart. We had two *in corpus* (face-to-face) meetings and a daily dozen email iterations. We could have been sitting at adjoining desks swapping papers and marker pens back and forth. Instead, it was done electronically. And we posted the chapters on Dean's website in nearly finished form for comment by gurus, potential readers and the publisher. It was possible for us and others to see the book arise in its entirety as it neared completion. And we hope this openness will promote more sales of the hard copy. We would do it again just the same way.

In our discussion of investment ideas, we talk equally about people because it is the people who have the ideas. The best investment ideas, in our opinion, are consistent with the psyche of the people who have them. The cliché, "managers do not pick markets, markets pick managers" refers to the possibility that it is the style of the day that plucks some investors for greatness rather than the other way around. The managers who succeed are most often confident of their views to the limits of arrogance, hate to see their ideas diluted in the interest of diversification (unless diversification was their idea) and are eager to display their market wit. Mostly they are colorful characters, most known and liked by at least one of us.

In each chapter, we describe an idea. Then we talk about one or two people associated with the idea. We also introduce the counterpoint: the downside and limitations of the idea. And we have asked each person discussed (where, as in most cases, they are still around) to react and comment if they wish: many of our gurus have kindly taken up the challenge. Each chapter concludes with suggestions for the next steps, if any – ideas for application and research – and recommendations for further reading whether in print or online.

In addition to our main chapters, we have two introductory pieces: one by Peter Bernstein on the history of the markets over the past fifty years, which he has kindly allowed us to reprint; and another by Dean on changing investment styles across time and space. We have also included a selection of ten investment classics by James Fraser, and a discussion of ten key issues related to the world of investing plus ten broader, more global questions. Finally, there is a *webliography*, a list of recommended investment websites for further study and sometimes fun reading.

Numerous people have contributed to our thinking about these ideas over the years and we would like to thank them all. In Dean's case, he learned from clients who became friends, among them Gordon Binns, David Feldman, Robert ("Tad") Jeffery and William Wirth, all investment gurus. Particular thanks go to our friends, family and colleagues who helped directly with the writing of this book: our gurus, of course – plus Mark Allin, Richard Burton, Annemarie Caracciolo, Donna Carpenter, Stephen Eckett, Tom Fryer, Steve Gage, Kate Holland, Blake LeBaron and Marilyn Pitchford.

We very much hope you enjoy reading this book and would be delighted to receive any comments.

Dean LeBaron – *deanlebaron@compuserve.com*
Romesh Vaitilingam – *romesh@compuserve.com*
March 1999
*www.deanlebaron.com* – Dean's website

# *Prolog*

## *A Conversation about Business and Investment*

C apstone Publishing has many important books on business but this is the first to deal with investment. Of course, the two are intimately connected. Business needs investment to thrive. Investment is the assessment of business success and, by rating different businesses with different returns, acts as the arbiter of who gets how much money and when.

To help explain the symbiosis between business and investment, we invited two friends who are also Capstone authors to have an electronic conversation with us. One is Robert Monks, who is profiled in our chapter on *Corporate Governance*. The other, Christopher Meyer, is a fellow trustee of the Santa Fe Institute with Dean and the head of Business Innovation for Ernst & Young. In a sense, they cover the two extremes of the business market with Bob identifying companies that need restrengthening and Chris working with the best of companies trying to be better.

Bob and Chris generously responded with an exchange of email messages, which underlines the importance of remembering that behind all the investment ideas and styles we discuss in this book, some of which may seem very exotic, there are real businesses. Much of the book deals with the external influences on companies: the shareholders and the mechanisms by which they value companies and make investment decisions. But ultimately, the key determinant of whether the market walks or stays is internal to a company: the actions and quality of management.

The conversation with Bob and Chris touches on many of the key issues in the interaction of business and investment:

- How do individual and institutional investors decide which stocks and other assets they should own and what do they do with that ownership?

- Do investors treat their stocks simply as pieces of paper in the hope that they will provide good short-term returns?
- Or do they want to get truly involved in the companies, perhaps as shareholder activists, pushing for better economic performance and hence better returns?
- Might some investors actually take a longer-term view than managers, perhaps even demanding more attention to broader social goals?
- And can the short- and long-term interests of owners, corporate managers and society really become better aligned?

## Chris Meyer

It is demonstrable that investors value non-financial characteristics of firms. Our *Measures That Matter* research shows that about 34% of buy-side analysts' valuations are driven by variables like perceived quality of management, R&D effectiveness, etc. These can be interpreted as proxies for business actions that will create future cash flows. But it seems likely that individual investors will stay away from the securities of companies they do not like, for whatever reason. Some of those reasons will be *green-ness*; some will be people who do not like particular chief executives. In any case, they will reduce the market for the security and thus, presumably, the market value of the company. So there is a connection between a company's social stance and the financial outcome.

But I would guess that pension funds, in general, are more likely to believe that their constituencies are demanding the highest possible return rather than a balanced scorecard. CALPERS (the California Public Employees Retirement System) is a notable exception, which, I think, proves the rule: this pension fund makes political and social judgments as part of its investor behavior. Nonetheless, I think the difference in multiples between Coca Cola and Philip Morris has more to do with the financial decline of the cigarette business than investors' distaste for nicotine-stained profits.

## Bob Monks

In the UK, there is endless debate between *the City* and industry with corporate managers taking the position that they are inhibited by the *short-termism* of the investing community. Actually, the real shareholders – the defined benefit pension plans and the index funds – have the longest perspective, far longer than the tenure of any generation of managers. What is the perspective of these defined benefit plans? Is it not to take such steps as are necessary for their pensioners to retire into a civil, clean, well-policed world with adequate money to maintain a desired living standard? Thus, the real agenda for the real owners necessarily involves subjective value judgments.

## Chris goes deeper into the alignment of management and shareholder interests

The short-term earnings complaint is a sign of weak management. Senior executives get paid and are appointed to do things that are too subtle to measure. The price of the stock – a construct of what analysts and investors say to each other – is the one measurement they see – so some respond too strongly to it. Powerful managers feel that it is only important to be able to raise capital when necessary, and our *Measures That Matter* research suggests that access is not only a function of what you do in the short term. Those who bow to the pressures of Wall Street are as craven as the MIS managers who chose the palpably inferior DOS computer operating system because IBM told them to. GE, for example, does not seem to be very concerned about short-term investor sentiment.

## Bob points out a few weak spots

Within the corporate constituency, everyone – managers, arbitrageurs, long-term owners – has an interest in controlling the time frame within which their own compensation will be determined. Only the long-term owner has an interest that is harmonious with that of society as a whole. The activist shareholder must involve himself sufficiently in corporate affairs to ensure first that employment contracts precisely align management incentives with enhanced ownership values. Second, he should monitor board functioning to ensure independence and appropriate "self criticism." Finally, the assurance of his legitimacy is the fact of continuing ownership of the stock.

## Dean comments

As far as aligning employment contracts precisely with ownership values to achieve interests "harmonious with that of society as a whole"... good luck. Too many of the interests of society are not denominated in any way that would be accepted as a part of employment contracts (for example, the well-being of employees) and each individual is motivated differently by compensation and such other factors. As Bob points out, only the long-term investors even approach representing such interests; the traders and arbitrageurs do not take harmony to the bank.

It is the difficulty of avoiding the effects of short-term financial market forces that provides incentives, even for those management teams with_shareholders' interests at heart, to be less than forthcoming with plans they fear will not be understood by the financial markets, regardless of their long-term value creation potential.

## Coming to possible solutions, Dean suggests

An investor running for the board and proposing a different plan represents a wake-up call, indicating that the board must assess whether or not it is governing the company in accordance with investor as well as corporate interests. As such, it should be seen as an opportunity for the board either to consider new points of view or to articulate its rationale to shareholders and other constituencies. If the board cannot meet this test, it will ultimately collapse. The situation is analogous to trying to sustain pegged currency prices in the face of mobile capital and aggressive traders – those who use all the available information will win in the end. The ever-increasing ease of publicizing issues to the shareholder body makes the "running for the board" strategy eminently feasible.

## Bob discusses his role as an activist director candidate

Running as a self-nominated board candidate has certain unique virtues. When you call on shareholders, you do not leave the meeting with a warm – glowing but muddled – view as to their intentions. Supporting my candidacy is the ultimate way for shareholders to communicate a message of urgency to management. There are only a few live bodies – those big shareholders who are willing *publicly* to voice their displeasure with management – in the whole institutional investor world. But remember I do not have to get elected to win: serving on boards is like being a delegate to a National Political Convention: everyone should do it once, a second time maybe, but any more is evidence of a serious character flaw. What I have to do is to make management understand that they do not have the choice of doing nothing, nor do they have the choice of "following our game plan."

## And Chris concludes

If shareholders truly value the future, agree on what the future should be and express this in their investments, there would be no market failures and hence no need for government in an economic sense.

And hence this new part of the Capstone *Ultimate* series aims to bring the best of market understanding to assist investors today.

*Chris Meyer*
*Bob Monks*
*Dean LeBaron*
*Romesh Vaitilingam*
*March 1999*

## Read on

### In print

- Stan Davis and Chris Meyer, *Blur: The Speed of Change in the Connected Economy* (Perseus Books/Capstone Publishing, 1999)
- Bob Monks, *The Emperor's Nightingale: Restoring the Integrity of the Corporation* (Perseus Books/Capstone Publishing, 1998)
- Hilary Rosenberg, *A Traitor to His Class: Robert AG Monks and the Battle to Change Corporate America* (John Wiley, 1999).

### Online

- *www.businessinnovation.com* – Ernst & Young website with links to the *Measures That Matter* study
- *www.santafe.edu* – website of the Santa Fe Institute.

# The Promises Men Live By

*by Peter L Bernstein*

T he title resonates from college days, although memory of the subject matter it refers to has faded out. The title resonates today as well, but for reasons that may not be immediately apparent.

The meaning will emerge from history. The history we relate here is familiar, but the focus and perspective are different from the customary approach. Our purpose, in fact, is to offer a hypothesis that might explain the history of this extraordinary bull market.

## From the beginning of time to the 1960s

For most of financial market history, bonds were owned by institutions and trusts, while stocks were owned largely by wealthy individuals. Public speculation came and went, and wealthy people also owned bonds, but the stock market was, for the most part, a domain of the wealthy.

When I started out as an investment counsel in the early 1950s, this structure was still very much in place. All our clients were rich individuals; institutional accounts were scarce as hen's teeth. The institutional business in the equity market would remain in the minor leagues for another decade at least. Insurance companies, endowments, and trusts were still working under old-fashioned restraints and held minimal amounts of equities. Not-so-wealthy individuals were still on the periphery, as most of them did not yet have enough to start playing in the market while those that did have some money did not yet have the courage. The first ten years or so after V-J Day were a risk-averse era, socially, politically and economically. From 1949 to 1954, the dividend yield on stocks averaged 365 basis points over the yield on Treasury bonds – more than double the spread during the decade of the 1920s.

As the conviction gradually faded that the return of the Great Depression was just around the corner, the environment began to change. The shift got under way during the latter half of the 1950s and became increasingly visible in the course of the 1960s. In those years, the shell-shocked veterans of the 1930s were beginning to disappear from the scene, due either to retirement or death – a development that contributed to the acceptance of a more hopeful view of the future. Money now came into the market in the expectation that maybe this was a place that could make you rich, not just a place for the already-rich to park their assets. That was quite a switch.

## The pension fund impact

At the same time, the swelling flow of pension fund money into the stock market during the course of the 1960s, and more rapidly in the 1970s, injected a fundamental change into the process of equity investing. The whole purpose of investing had always been to make money, but precisely how much money an investor should earn in the market was a matter that only a tiny minority of people had ever stopped to consider. Actuaries in Wall Street? An oxymoron! The defined benefit pension funds, however, could not function without calculating a required rate of return. They had made a set of contractual promises, promises on which they could welch only at their peril. After the near-catastrophe in the early 1970s, in fact, ERISA came into being with the aim of keeping those promises honest.

Charitable foundations were the next group of institutional investors to join in this process. Like most investors, the foundations had given little thought to the matter of required returns; they aimed simply to do their best under whatever circumstances presented themselves. Most of the funds I encountered in the 1970s – and we built up a significant consulting business in the area – were managing their investments via committees of Wall Street luminaries but without any full-time professional staffs.

A large number of foundations at that time were exploiting a glaring loophole in the tax system. These miscreants typically held mostly donor stock, which enabled the donors to continue to control their companies while simultaneously sheltering their shares from estate taxes and the dividends from income taxes. Doing good works was a secondary objective, often ignored altogether as the flow of dividends piled up tax-free in the coffers of the foundation.

By the 1970s, Congress had slammed the loophole shut. Foundations were ordered to distribute annually at least 5% of their assets or all of their income, whichever was greater. That was a murderous requirement in the inflationary 1970s until the government relented and limited the requirement to 5% of assets. Nevertheless, as most foundations believe that they have a mandate to exist into perpetuity, earning 5%-plus-inflation became an obligatory investment objective. Soon after, the educational endowments started to think like the pension funds and foundations, setting forth explicit investment objectives and establishing systematic spending rules to govern transfers of assets from the endowment to the university budget.

The promises were growing. By the time the 1980s rolled around, increasing numbers of people were being promised something, and usually more than had been promised in the past, which meant new investment groups dependent upon required returns were making their appearance. Meeting those promises during the 1980s turned out to be easier than people had expected, with high coupon bonds from the inflationary days still in the portfolios and with a bull market in stocks that moved forward with impressive energy. Figuring out the least risky method to keep promises was never simple, but the calculations were not yet colored by a sense of urgency in the objective.

Solutions create problems. The enemy is us. In order to fulfill all these promises, investors piled into assets with high expected returns. This process in and of itself propelled the bull market onward, quite aside from improvements in the economic environment. Welcome as rising prices of stocks and long-term bonds may have been after the dark days of the 1970s, the soaring asset values that investors were inflicting upon themselves complicated the task of meeting required return objectives for the future. The beautiful fat bond coupons were reaching maturity or disappearing due to call. The average yield on long Treasury bonds fell from an average of 10.5% during the 1980s to 8.7% during 1990–94. The average yield on stocks sank from 4.2% to 3.0%.

Now the only way to meet required returns – to keep those promises – was to take on even greater risk. Conventional government and high-grade corporate bond exposure in institutional portfolios shriveled, while cash turned into trash. Foreign markets with brief histories became irresistible, bonds of dubious quality sold at diminishing premiums over Treasury yields, and the accumulation of a wide variety of exotic and less liquid assets was rationalized. The latter appeared to reduce portfolio risk because of low covariances, but that appearance hid substantial and costly specific risks within the group and correlation coefficients whose stability was a matter of debate. Nevertheless, if required returns were to be earned, there seemed to be no choice but to shift out toward the further limits of the efficient frontier.

## Welcome to the individual investor

Into the midst of that process came the 401(k) phenomenon, at first no smaller than a man's hand against the sky but then with burgeoning momentum. The most powerful impetus came from the swelling cohort of baby boomers, now finally reaching forty years of age. Once upon a time, people told you that life begins at forty, but in the 1990s, forty is where you begin worrying about retirement. Suddenly a huge number of novice investors were being told to think about investment in terms of required returns. It was the turn of the baby boomers to start making promises, only in this case the promises were to themselves rather than someone else. Yourself is the last person you would want to disappoint.

Financial planners proliferated, brokerage houses doused their prospects with seminars, and the financial press added to the cacophony of advice about how to prepare for that terrible day of judgment, now only about twenty years away and coming closer with every hour of the day and night. Fears about job security in the private sector and about Social Security in the public sector only contributed to the sense of crisis and to the magnitude of the promises that individuals were convinced they had to make to themselves.

As a result, individuals joined the institutions in succumbing to the inevitability that taking on risk was the only choice. To many investment neophytes, however, "taking on risk" has meant investing in stocks, but the decision was so fashionable and acceptable that the expression "taking on risk" has had no substance, appearing to have little to do with the possibility that the assets might end up well below that promised return. People were persuaded that they could ignore volatility, because in the long run, in the long run, in the long run, in the long run, everything would come out roses. Even though the rising stock market in fact diminished the probability that these individuals would be able to keep their promises to themselves, rising prices felt so good that the negative implications of higher prices for prospective returns carried little weight. Anyway, what other choice was there?

Two related points are worth mentioning as a brief digression. Both of these items provide telling evidence of the state of mind of the individual investors.

First, I recently appeared on a panel with three financial planners plus Martin Leibowitz of TIAA/CREF. We addressed a relatively unsophisticated audience. After several people in the audience had used the word *fun* in describing their investment activities, Leibowitz felt compelled to sound off, reminding these individuals that they would be well-advised to approach this matter in cold-blooded fashion rather than as a vehicle for entertainment.

Second, the public still believes that picking a few winners in a bull market, especially risky high-tech stocks, is a certificate of brilliance in investing. One thing leads to another. The *Wall Street Journal* for 16 November 1998 has a graph showing that block trades had shrunk from 56% of total NYSE volume in 1995 to only 48% through October 1998. Most of this loss, the *Journal* reports, is due to day trading by individual investors whose heads are buried deep inside their computers and whose transactions costs are minimized by the use of discount brokers. Fun indeed!

## Not the end of history, by any means

All of this history is familiar, but the emphasis here is on the pressure placed on the capital markets over time by the growing volume of promises by investors large and small. The process has colored investing, and risk-taking, with a sense of urgency that represents a distinct break with earlier economic history.

If the hypothesis is valid, it explains more about market patterns than simplistic notions like the effect of *buy-on-dips*. Why is buying on dips a great idea in the 1990s when it never was before? Yes, the 1987 experience was a demonstration of how well you can do if you buy on dips, but so was 1958 or 1962 or 1970. Stepping up to the plate after a steep sell-off is scary under any circumstances. Our point is that investors are now convinced they have no choice but to keep plugging away, and it is that sheer determination rather than pure and simple courage that drives the buy-on-dips strategy.

We have to face the possibility that there is indeed only one god in the stock market – the beneficent view of the long run – and that Jeremy Siegel is its prophet. The whole business could turn out to be self-fulfilling, with so many believers convinced through thick and thin that only the stock market can make their promises come true. In such a world, where decision-making is on automatic pilot, it is possible that the careful calculations of valuation and probable expected returns that firms like ours produce will provide amusing intellectual recreation but will be irrelevant for the execution of successful investment strategies.

There is, somewhere, a shock massive enough to shake loose this set of beliefs. We would be naive to deny that. The shock that can turn the tide under these conditions, however, will have to be substantially larger and more sustained than any of the disturbances that have attacked the economic and financial environment over the past twenty years.

*This article originally appeared in Peter Bernstein's newsletter* Economics & Portfolio Strategy, *December 1, 1998 (© 1998 by Peter L Bernstein, Inc.). It is reproduced here by kind permission of the author.*

# Investment Insights: Changing Styles Across Time and Space

*by Dean LeBaron*

## Style radiation

T he spread of investment insights may be visualized as waves radiating outwards in concentric circles from pebbles falling into water. The source of these investment pebbles is the United States. The dynamic force behind the rise of post-World War II equity markets has been academic research coming out of US universities. The availability of cheap computer time, cheap graduate student labor and creative senior professors (six of whom have now received the Nobel Prize in Economics) has contributed to the development of concepts like the capital asset pricing model, the efficient market hypothesis and performance measurement, as well as the growth of derivatives markets.

Not every investment technique is appropriate at every place around the world at the same time. Ideas radiate, interfere with one another and produce new patterns, then reach the periphery at the same time as new stimuli occur at the origin. Technology and communications accelerate the speed of ideas radiating outwards until, finally, the impact reaches emerging markets. As the process is repeated, it is accelerated further.

We can divide the investment world into three parts – the United States, developed (ex-US) markets and emerging markets. Most US institutional investors have dedicated teams covering each of these segments. In some cases, they have specialized teams within each team segmented by geography.

The investment world was reshaped immediately after World War II. In fact, if we go back farther, we can gauge the present long-wave bull market from the Battle of Midway in 1942. If we look at equity styles since then, we see that there have been two major waves, each lasting one or two decades. And a third may have begun.

## *1945-70*

Right after World War II, a widely anticipated global depression was expected – a common occurrence after nearly every major world conflict. Surprisingly, in the United States, a major interest in equities prompted the success of a handful of companies that became known as the *nifty fifty*. These companies dominated in managerial skills, product R&D and financial resources. Investors remained skeptical about economic progress throughout this growth era, and markets faced the traditional wall of doubt, the trellis up which green investment ivy must climb.

"Buy high, sell higher" dominated investment styles over this period. Supply and demand for equities became the watchword more than underlying valuation. To adapt a phrase from a quantum physicist, "there appeared to be an underlying price spin tilted in the direction of the positive" – other things being equal, something that had gone up would go up more. Another description might be the *economics of increasing returns*. Eventually, the era ended with the shock of 1967 and the subsequent decline of growth funds in the sharp market downturn in the United States during the 1973–4 period.

The developed (ex-US) markets – essentially those of the advanced countries that were the major protagonists in World War II, whether victor or vanquished – during this period were dominated by international reconstruction programs. The Marshall Plan in Europe and its counterpart under the administration of General MacArthur in Japan and Asia led the way. These programs were typically centered around infrastructure improvement and, with the exception of the UK, did not produce much in the way of private equity development until the second half of the period, when government programs became directly supportive of private development activities.

What we know now as emerging markets were, in the immediate post-World War II period, dominated by programs for subsistence largely to stave off famine and disease and to provide other necessities of basic living. At that time, these nations were not worried about the development of market economies but rather about how to eat and clothe and shelter themselves.

## 1970–90

The post-World War II era and its corollary in other markets of the world ended after a generation, almost simultaneously, with academic studies on efficient markets achieving prominence in the United States. Firms capitalized on this phase shift by introducing index products and popularizing valuation shifts and new valuation techniques that are all price-related. As the dictum shifted to "buy low, sell high," it was characterized by the emergence of new investment folk heroes like Warren Buffett. A few firms, Batterymarch among them, popularized valuation techniques for institutional investors, giving voice to this newly emerged market style in the United States.

In Europe and Asia, internationally dominant companies, which looked very much like the nifty fifty, appeared popular for investing. Siemens, Hitachi, Sony, Philips, Bayer and their counterparts became components of more venturesome US institutional portfolios and appeared as the first equity holdings of some of the more fixed-income-oriented institutional holdings outside the United States.

And exactly the same pattern seen in the United States during 1945–70 was repeated, except in different places, in different markets.

Development institutions then shifted their attention from the devastated areas of World War II to the poorer countries suffering from population explosion. In many cases, these were agrarian-based economies with little ability to soften the shocks and cycles inherent in farming. These markets that had previously been worrying about subsistence began to establish the basis for market economies. Largely influenced by government programs, some of these countries began developing market structures.

## *Since 1990*

For the United States today, characterizing the investment style is somewhat more speculative. In my view, the appropriate investment style is far more flexible, eclectic, and quick – almost trading-oriented. These are the very skills that large institutions find almost impossible to exploit for organizational reasons. Institutional investors are organized around consultants and the need for extensive documentation, preventing, almost completely, the flexibility that is demanded to make money by today's market responses to external shocks.

Today's institutional investors are like the medieval troops standing in line wearing bright uniforms, waiting to be slaughtered by the drably clad guerrillas standing behind trees. Which would you prefer to be in today's market climate: a British Redcoat or a member of Ethan Allen's Green Mountain Boys? We know the outcome from the Revolutionary period and Vietnam and Tito's Yugoslavia, and I think we can predict the outcome for US investment styles.

Value, the watchword of the US market in the preceding twenty years, has now shifted to Japan and Europe. Japan and Japanese investors characteristically adopt the same investment style, all at the same time. In Europe, the development is a bit slower because investors are maintaining a traditional stock-picking investment practice. We do know, however, that the establishment of quantitative research groups in almost all the major investment institutions – and their attraction to indexing – clearly is an exact replication of earlier, successful investment practices in the United States.

Again, several decades intervened, and the initial US phase moved over one step. Now, emerging markets reflect the nifty fifty period – or at least, they did until the start of the Asian crisis in July

1997. Global enterprises can be found in the most unlikely places and the investment goal is to find world-class companies in unexpected places at unexpected prices. It is still possible: those enterprises that are strong in emerging markets tend to get stronger, because management resources and externally provided finance tend to be in short supply and limited in those markets.

Old growth stock managers from developed markets who see such companies can feel instantly at home. They know what it was like, because they have been there before. They have the opportunity to live a third professional life, seeing the nifty fifty again, in a new market.

## The right venue, the right style

It is an old adage of investment cynics that "managers do not pick markets, markets pick managers." This attitude suggests that brilliance is about evenly distributed, but that markets select their own heroes rather than vice versa.

With the construction of investment styles according to the radiation approaches I have described, that limitation is not quite true. Rather, managers can freely roam the world looking for an investment style that suits them – a growth manager could have a period of successful investing in the United States, become a non-US manager, and then find a suitable venue in emerging markets: three investment lives all engaged in approximately the same principle. One can invest in all traditional ways and change location, or one can change investment techniques and invest in the same location.

How did you know a growth company in the 1945 and later period? I knew it when I saw it. When I see it again, now, in an emerging market, I say, "this company can compete on a worldwide basis, regardless of the fact that it is ... wherever."

The US style is now flexible, fast and fuzzy. The developed (ex-US) market style is structured, systematic and suited to individual customization. And despite the global economic crisis, emerging markets are the places where there is the greatest potential for growth if we hark back to the high-quality investment styles of yore.

Market students must look geographically outwards to see familiar, repeated patterns – and inwards to see what is next.

*A version of this article originally appeared as "A Universal Model of Equity Styles: Style Predictability by Geography and Time" in the* Journal of Portfolio Management *twentieth anniversary issue (volume 21, number 1, Fall 1994).*

# Investment Ideas and Their Gurus

# Active Portfolio Management

s it possible to outperform the market? This is one of the most important questions any investor should ask. If your answer is no, if you believe the market is efficient, then passive investing or indexing – buying diversified portfolios of all the securities in an asset class – is probably the way to go. The arguments for such an approach include reduced costs, tax efficiency and the fact that, historically, passive funds have outperformed the majority of active funds (see *Market Efficiency* and *Indexing*).

But if your answer is yes, it is possible to beat the market, then you should pursue active portfolio management. Among the arguments for this approach are the possibility that there are a variety of anomalies in securities markets that can be exploited to outperform passive investments (see *Investor Psychology*), the likelihood that some companies can be pressured by investors to improve their performance (see *Corporate Governance*), and the fact that many investors and managers have outperformed passive investing for long periods of time.

But the active investor must still face the challenge of outperforming a passive strategy. Essentially, there are two sets of decisions. The first is asset allocation, where you carve up your portfolio into different proportions of equities, bonds and other instruments (see *Global Investing* and *Investment Policy*). These decisions, often referred to as market timing as investors try to reallocate between equities and bonds (see *Fixed Income*) in response to their expectations of better relative returns in the two markets, tend to require macro forecasts of broad-based market movements (see *Economic Forecasting* and *Politics and Investing*). Then there is security selection – picking particular stocks or bonds. These decisions require micro forecasts of individual securities underpriced by the market and hence offering the opportunity for better than average returns.

Active investing involves being *overweight* in securities and sectors that you believe to be undervalued and *underweight* in assets you believe to be overvalued. Buying a stock, for example, is effectively an active investment that can be measured against the performance of the overall market (see *Performance Measurement*). Compared with passive investing in a stock index, buying an individual stock combines an asset allocation to stocks and an active investment in that stock in the belief that it will outperform the stock index.

In both market timing and security selection decisions, investors may use either technical or fundamental analysis (see *Technical Analysis, Value Investing* and *Growth Investing*). And you can be right in your asset allocation and wrong in your active security selection and vice versa. It is still possible that an investor who makes a mistake in asset allocation, perhaps by being light in equities in a bull market, can still do well by picking a few great stocks.

There are arguments for both active and passive investing though it is probably the case that a larger percentage of institutional investors invest passively than do individual investors. Of course, the active versus passive decision does not have to be a strictly either/or choice. One common investment strategy is to invest passively in markets you consider to be efficient and actively in markets you consider less efficient. Investors can also combine the two by investing part of a portfolio passively and another part actively.

## Guru of active portfolio management: William Miller

It is hard to be the best performing manager for the past five years out of a field of more than five hundred. Not just that it is so difficult to be there – and it is – but also difficult to maintain one's mental balance. The temptation is to be too cocky and believe the publicity one receives. Or one could become too concerned with the inevitable stumble that lies ahead: old Bill has just lost it, some will say.

One way Bill Miller of Legg Mason's Value Trust keeps his head is to stress the intellectual side of investment. And he concentrates his investment attention so that extraneous contemporary PR does not distract him. His job is to outperform and every instinct he has is brought to bear on that objective. Over and over, he can repeat his lessons from profits and losses. His shareholders' glories and pains are his own. He takes the lessons, structures them into principles and keeps improving.

Miller is rather liberal in defining the details of his tactics when it suits him. He is not bothered by people who say that Czech bonds, for example, or go-go technology stocks trading at sky-high price-to-earnings ratios are not value investments: if they go up, they were and that is what counts. The definitional straitjackets of others are their problems, not his.

Miller is reaching out to complexity and the Santa Fe Institute, where he is a trustee and has a house, to teach him how to break today's investment bronco. Few others have the patience to deal with the ambiguities inherent in any emerging science. And it lets him contemplate the future of investment styles with a catholic perspective, a dogged determination to triumph and in the company of physicists ready to humble anyone wasting a good mind on one of the soft sciences, for money.

## Counterpoint

Nobel Laureate William Sharpe makes a simple yet powerful case against active management in his article "The Arithmetic of Active Management:"

> *If active and passive management styles are defined in sensible ways, it must be the case that: (1) before costs, the return on the average actively managed dollar will equal the return on the average passively managed dollar; and (2) after costs, the re-*

*turn on the average actively managed dollar will be less than the return on the average passively managed dollar. These assertions will hold for any time period. Moreover, they depend only on the laws of addition, subtraction, multiplication and division. Nothing else is required.*

Sharpe continues:

*This need not be taken as a counsel of despair. It is perfectly possible for some active managers to beat their passive brethren, even after costs. Such managers must, of course, manage a minority share of the actively managed dollars within the market in question. It is also possible for an investor (such as a pension fund) to choose a set of active managers that, collectively, provides a total return better than that of a passive alternative, even after costs. Not all the managers in the set have to beat their passive counterparts, only those managing a majority of the investor's actively managed funds.*

Rex Sinquefield of Dimensional Fund Advisors is more brutal. He says there are three classes of people who do not believe that markets work: the Cubans, the North Koreans and active managers.

Yet investment managers are competing hard to manage institutional and individual investors' money and it is not surprising that they make claims about their market-beating potential – usually using active strategies – and, where possible, their market-beating performance records. And social norms of prudence, investor anxiety and anticipation of regret over flawed decisions contribute strongly to the demand for supposed financial expertise. Of course, if you believe in active investing, it is best not to judge a manager by their past performance indicators but rather by the plans by which they expect to add value through outperformance in the future.

Ambitious investors and investment managers almost all want to beat the market, but it is worth asking why they should want to beat it for you. Why should precious insights into the nature of the market be available for sale to the general public, either directly through a fund or indirectly, perhaps through a book advocating a particular investment technique as the route to outperformance? If an investment technique is so good, it would seem to make more sense to keep its secrets to yourself.

It does seem to be the case that an investor who tries to predict short-term changes in share prices has to be right about 70% of the time to beat the market. Peter Jeffreys of S&P Fund Research, a London-based fund-rating company, has screened 4,800 funds since 1982 to see if past winners repeat their success in the future. He finds that the probability of that comes down to "almost pure random chance:" using three-year rolling average performance as a measure, it turns out that of funds that beat the average six years running, only just over a half did so the next year.

## Guru response

Bill Miller comments:

> *Is active management just a loser's game, and passive indexing the only viable investment strategy? Not at all. Just as poorly performing companies can often improve their results by studying winning competitors, active managers can improve theirs by deconstructing the sources of competitive advantage of the index, in our case the S&P 500.*
>
> *The first and most important feature of the S&P 500 is that it does not employ a passive investment strategy. Managers of index funds employ such a strategy since they engage in no active stock selection. But the S&P 500 is an actively managed portfolio. Its stocks are selected from the nearly 9,000 publicly traded securities on the New York, American and NASDAQ markets by a committee using specific investment criteria.*
>
> *The returns of the S&P 500 are the best evidence of the long-term advantage of active portfolio management. It has consistently beaten broader, passively constructed indices such*

*as the Wilshire 5,000, the Russell 2,000 and the NYSE Composite. That it has also beaten other active money managers is not an argument against active management; it is an argument against the methods employed by most active managers.*

*The S&P 500 is a long-term oriented, low turnover, tax efficient portfolio employing a buy-and-hold investment strategy. It lets its winners run and selectively eliminates its losers. It never sells a successful investment no matter how far up the stock has run, and it does not arbitrarily impose size or position limits on holdings, either by company or industry. Size is fixed at five hundred names, and new names usually come into the portfolio because of the merger or acquisition of existing holdings. Periodically, new names are added and others eliminated in an attempt to replace companies that are marginal with those whose position in the economy or in an industry are deemed more important.*

*The overall portfolio is positioned to represent the broad sweep of the US economy. The stock selection committee at S&P consists of nine analysts, and new names are meant to be seasoned companies with a history of profitability, financially sound, leaders in their industry or market, with a probability of being in business over the next ten to twenty years. Portfolio turnover averaged twenty-five to thirty names in the 1980s but has picked up to forty or so in the past few years.*

*The contrast with the typical active manager is stark. The average mutual fund is short-term oriented, has high turnover, is tax inefficient and employs a trading-oriented investment style. Most funds systematically cut back winners or rotate out of stocks that have done well into those expected to do better. Position limits and industry weightings are usually rigidly maintained in the name of either investing discipline or risk control. The number of holdings is usually well over a hundred, but may vary significantly, both among funds and within the same fund over time. The overall portfolio is constructed in accordance with some style the manager erroneously believes is likely to outperform the long-term, low turnover approach of the S&P 500.*

*What is the source of the S&P's superiority over other active management styles? I think it comes back to market efficiency. The market is pretty well aware of the information that may affect the prospects of its constituent companies for the next year or so. New information arrives unpredictably. Beyond the next year, the complexities, uncertainties and vagaries are such that no one is vouchsafed any special insight into the future. Most of the activity that makes active portfolio management active is wasted; it adds no value since it is engendered by the mistaken belief that the manager possesses information the market is unaware of or that the market has mispriced. It does impose costs: trading costs, market impact costs and taxes. It is also often triggered by ineffective psychological responses, such as overweighting recent data, anchoring on irrelevant criteria and a whole host of other less than optimal decision procedures currently being investigated by cognitive psychologists.*

*Money managers often wrongly decry the growth of indexing and complain that it is a mindless strategy. While they may be right that pure factor-based indexing strategies, for example, buy all companies with characteristics xyx, are unlikely to add value over time (the evidence is not clear on this); they are surely wrong to bemoan either the desire of investors for S&P 500 index funds or their own inability to compete with the results of such funds. Investors are rationally selecting an active money management style that is sensible, tax efficient, has a long history and works.*

## *Where next?*

The latest research in financial economics seems to confirm that markets are not strictly efficient and that there are *pockets of predictability*. This offers some hope to "disciplined" active managers if they can come up with innovative techniques to achieve superior long-term returns (see *Financial Engineering*).

But it is very important for any investor to watch closely for changing market drivers. For example, the market drivers until late 1998 were easy credit, moderating inflation, lower interest rates, rising earnings and the wide publicity of nearly an eighteen-year bull market in equities – by some counts, a fifty-year bull market. The 1990s have seen a 16% compounded rate of growth for equities versus 6% historically, so it is not surprising that strong momentum keeps everyone in the game.

But we are beginning to face a different set of market drivers and it is hard to tell where they will drive us. The kind of financial concerns we face are rather novel in all of our lifetimes. There is illiquidity; wealth has been destroyed in many parts of the world; and inflation has turned to disinflation, to lower inflation and now to deflation. Deflation is destructive, especially for debt, which has led to a quality preference on debt where only the highest quality can pass muster and the ability to borrow is probably the only thing that counts in analyzing securities (see *Value Investing*).

What about the impact of news on portfolio management decisions? It is worth noting that precisely the same evidence may be used to support a good market tone or a bad market tone – a bull market or a bear market. For example, the absence of rising prices could be good for continued growth and low unemployment, or it could be bad because deflationary forces are building up and, as the experience of Japan indicates, they are extremely destabilizing. Interest rates are attractive for borrowing and money is plentiful, which is very good for business; but it may well be bad because it means that a great deal of money is flowing in from overseas to the United States as the last fortress of capital.

Similarly, the public continues to buy IPOs (see *Initial Public Offerings*), almost every single one. Is that good because it means confidence or bad because it means that there is such a strong psychological undertone to the market that when it cracks, nothing will bring it back? What is more, the quality stocks have done much better for the last several years than the broad market averages. Good because it suggests leadership? Or bad, meaning that there really is a low level of confidence, and this is just speculation in well-known names?

Also, we have continued concerns about what will happen in the year 2000 with our computer systems. Good – if nothing happens – or bad – because the year 2000 is only months away? Finally, earnings are good, but on the other hand, the majority of the surprises are on the downside: there appears to be a deterioration in terms of buildup of disappointments. So the same news can be seen as good or bad.

## *Read on*

### In print

- Roger Ibbotson and Rex Sinquefield, *Stocks, Bills, Bonds, and Inflation*
- Doug Henwood, *Wall Street: How it Works and for Whom* (Verso Books, 1997)
- Bill Sharpe, "The Arithmetic of Active Management," *Financial Analysts Journal*, 1991
- Romesh Vaitilingam, *The Financial Times Guide to Using the Financial Pages* (Third edition, Financial Times Pitman Publishing, 1996).

### Online

- *www.santafe.edu* – website of the Santa Fe Institute.

# Contrarian Investing

Confusion abounds about what contrary thinking is. Any mother would consider it an insult were someone to suggest that her baby was contrary. What mother wants to have a contrary child? In the investment world, the word generally has more complimentary connotations, though there is still little clarity on what it precisely means.

Many think that *contrary* means always going against the majority – that a contrarian investor is automatically acting in counterpoint to the current market trend. In a long bull market, this implies being like Cassandra, who made doleful predictions that were met with scorn, and while ultimately proved right, was never believed at the time. Similarly, on this view, contrarians bet against the common wisdom in the hope of making a killing.

Another angle contrasts the contrarian with the fundamental or value investor, who buys and sells on the basis of assets' prices relative to their *intrinsic value* (see *Value Investing*). Instead, a contrarian trading strategy is based on the assumption of negative serial correlation of prices: a predictable pattern such that if prices have gone up, they must come down, and vice versa. This view of contrarians focuses on the important role of fads: rather than acting independently, investors exhibit herd-like behavior, following waves of mass optimism and pessimism (see *Investor Psychology*).

To a third group, contrarian investing is the reverse, a steadfast adherence to value- or asset-based investing. David Dreman, for example, who has written two widely read books on contrarian investing, writes a regular column for *Forbes* and manages a successful investment firm, describes it as "buying stocks that are out of favor according to some well-defined, fundamental measures such as low price-to-earnings (p/e) ratio, low price-to-book, or high dividend yield."

Dreman is attracted to stocks that have declined in price on the assumption that a price return to something like the mean will give him a profit. He uses traditional ratio analysis of yield, p/e and book to screen his list. This is more the strategy of a traditional value investor than a contrarian, though in some sense, Dreman is still being a contrarian to the *nifty fifty* growth stock era of his apprenticeship in investments (see *Growth Investing*).

In reality, contrarian investing is none of these: though the tactics of a contrarian may resemble one or more of these naive descriptions, they miss the point and seriously so. Contrary thinking is most like intellectual independence with a healthy dash of agnosticism about consensus views. While it is true that if a consensus grows to be a *herd* or *crowd*, the contrarian will flee. But not necessarily to the exact opposite. Instead, identification of a herd charges the contrarian to be more rigorous in independent thinking. And the contrarian is more likely to be attracted to a point of view that has not yet been thought of – the *empty file drawer* idea – than one that has been considered and rejected.

Contrary ideas usually guide broad strategies rather than specific investments. For example, in the late 1990s and early 2000s, Russia might be seen as providing excellent contrary opportunities in the aftermath of its 1998 debt default and currency devaluation and the subsequent flight of capital.

Timing is not usually indicated by a contrary approach. And because true contrary ideas are not an automatic knee-jerk reaction away from the consensus, there can be a number of different, good, contrary reactions to the same challenge. All may be appropriately contrary.

## *Contrarian investing guru: James Fraser*

Contrary thinking is as old as philosophy. More recently, Charles Mackay's book *Extraordinary Popular Delusions and the Madness of Crowds* placed the emphasis of independent thinking clearly on investments. And the late Humphrey Neill, known as the Vermont

Ruminator, developed the modern approaches of contrary thinking, founded on the simple yet powerful idea that "when everybody
thinks alike, everybody is likely to be wrong."

Neill's appointed successor, James Fraser, has extended his
work: continuing to write newsletters, *The Contrary Investor* and
*The Fraser Opinion Letter*; managing funds in the style; organizing
an annual conference – a blend of investment professionals and
individuals burying their bags of silver coins in the backyard; and
running a publishing house that specializes in reprinting various
investment classics, such as the Mackay book. (At the back of this
book is a list of ten of his favorites.) Fraser's Fall conferences at the
century-old Basin Harbor Club resort on the shores of Lake
Champlain bring out new ideas and attract the best of the US investment world.

Fraser's descriptions of his newsletters' aims neatly sums up
his approach to investing. The aim of *The Contrary Investor* is to: "1.
Watch and report popularity in shares. 2. Report on neglected shares.
3. Give psychological overbought early warnings, when we detect
them. 4. Comment on Crowd approach to market. 5. Guide subscribers away from the Crowd. 6. Endeavor to ferret out an occa-
sional contrary vehicle for a small portion of your funds." *The Fraser
Opinion Letter* offers: "Thoughtful analyses upon: 1. prevailing po-
litico-economic conditions, 2. crowd psychology, and 3. popular
opinions and predictions, wherein fundamental and human approach opposes mechanistic methods of forecasting."

## Counterpoint

If contrary thinking is so good, why doesn't everyone do it? In the
first place, if everyone did it, then it would not work because there
would be fewer panics and speculative orgies. Second, it can be
very uncomfortable to be wrong and contrary at the same time: the
humiliation of going against the crowd when the crowd is right –
and that can happen – is devastating. And third, much of our training and socialization teaches us that the majority is right, or at least,

that it rules: contrarians are out of step or did not get that message when they were growing up.

Is contrarian strategy profitable? There is some indication that former *loser* stocks perform better than *winners*, but is this because they are riskier? And what about the transactions costs of a short-run contrarian strategy? The quantitative evidence on these questions, as in most investment documentation, seems to depend on the case the researcher wishes to support more than the case itself. Nowhere is the adage, "if you torture the data long enough, it will confess to anything," more clearly observed than in the examination of investment techniques. But a mixture of contrary instincts and investment skills seems to be a part of most investors we admire.

Finally, is contrarian strategy inconsistent with the concept of market efficiency (see *Market Efficiency*)? The efficient market hypothesis (EMH) in its strong form contends that security prices are always correctly assimilating information. Today, investors generally expect that the weak form of EMH is operative, which means that sometimes it is possible, with generally available information, to gain an advantage over other investors. Contrarians look for these small opportunities by noting where the consensus seems to be clustered and they examine the other, independent alternatives.

## Where next?

Contrary thinking can be a challenge to assumptions that are so deeply embedded in our understanding of the world that we often do not even realize they are there. Three contrary questions in particular may be helpful in guiding us to contrary answers. Contrarians should ask questions like these that are often not even being considered.

The first is, why do investment markets assume that growth should be the sole objective of economic enterprise? Primarily, because of a fifty-year expansion in bull markets, but in most cases, the pursuit of growth comes with the possibility of volatility and risk. Stability and survivability can also, under some conditions, be worthwhile objectives. Contrarians are likely to value these features, which are considered valueless by other investors. Corporate control through proxy voting, for example, is often considered valueless and even a potential conflict for a manager in his client relations. And yet, in a merger or acquisition environment, proxy power is quite valuable: some studies have estimated it at about 15% of total share price. Contrarians might be quicker to identify these underlying mispricings.

Second, we are raised on the notion of continuous time. Nobel Laureate Robert Merton (see *Risk Management*) wrote a fundamental text with that idea in the title. We learn that time is a horizontal axis on a time chart with each unit of time connected to its neighbor and all units of equal space and importance – time is continuous, time flows, time moves on, time in any one period is connected with any other period, time reveals trends. But in the physical world, time may be discontinuous and unconnected with any other time period – sometimes coming in bursts, separate packets of information, unique in themselves. And investment time could be like that: Humphrey Neill wrote "sudden events quickly crystallize opinion." Our assumptions about time having a root in the past leading to clues about the future may be wrong.

Third, there is the built-in notion of an equity premium. After a fifty-year period of expansion, we take it for granted that equities produce higher returns, and we think that this is because they have higher degrees of risk. Are we prepared for the time when risk produces lower returns for equities? Or that on closer examination, risk itself becomes something other than volatility but risk of loss and risk of being knocked out of the game?

## Read on

### In print

- David Dreman, *Contrarian Investment Strategies: The Next Generation*

- James Fraser's newsletters, *The Contrary Investor* and *The Fraser Opinion Letter*
- Charles Mackay, *Extraordinary Popular Delusions and the Madness of Crowds* (Reprinted by John Wiley, 1995)
- Steven Mintz, *Five Eminent Contrarians: Careers, Perspectives and Investment Tactics* (Fraser Publishing, 1995)
- Humphrey B Neill, *The Art of Contrary Thinking* (Reprinted by Caxton Press, 1985).

## Online

- *www.deanlebaron.com* – website of one of this book's co-authors – "dedicated to exploring the changing world of global investing, with particular emphasis on the emerging markets in the former Soviet Union, China and elsewhere, and the newly developing investment tools being made possible by the internet."

# Corporate Governance

Shareholders demand high returns on their equity investments, while executives of public companies typically want a peaceful life with good remuneration and minimal outside intervention. These conflicting interests and how to achieve some kind of alignment between them – to give corporate managers the incentives to act in the best interests of corporate owners – are the central questions of corporate governance. They have become increasingly important in the 1990s as instead of choosing *exit* – simply selling their holdings in underperforming companies – investors are beginning to exercise their *voice* – telling managements to change their ways.

In the 1980s, the most powerful external pressure on executives for stock market performance was the threat from corporate raiders, poised to bid for companies with underperforming shares. Latterly, challenges have come more from institutional investors, the activist shareholders who demand long-term value creation from the companies whose shares they own. This activism has been most dramatic in the United States, and has been supported by regulation: for example, the SEC has mandated the reporting of value creation in the proxy statement.

In the UK too, the pressures have shifted from the threat of takeovers to shareholder activism, often around the subject of top managers' pay and its weak relationship to corporate performance. For example, guidelines on remuneration published by the investing institutions' professional bodies (the National Association of Pension Funds and the Association of British Insurers) demand a clearer link between performance and pay. In turn, many UK companies now explicitly target the creation of shareholder value.

# Corporate governance guru: Robert Monks

The 1970s and 1980s saw the growing dominance of institutional shareholders with an ability and propensity to trade away their unhappiness with the way their assets are employed. Meanwhile, Bob Monks was Assistant Secretary of Labor, the federal official responsible for supervising the public interests of pension funds – exactly the right place to observe the lack of interest of institutional investors in taking part in corporate decision-making, effectively enfranchising managements whose stewardship of assets was questionable.

When Monks left public service, he applied this lesson to develop a profitable investment management style resuscitating slack companies. In early 1990, he launched LENS, a fund that takes active equity positions in companies whose management needs shaking up. He appealed to shareholders and directors to function as they were legally charged, to monitor and, as a last resort, remove hard-of-hearing managements who forget that they are employees, not owners. The investment record of LENS has been outstanding, surpassing the S&P 500 every year since 1990.

In 1991, Monks electrified the investing world by running a credible race for director of Sears Roebuck as a unique way of calling attention to that company's failed strategies. Sears changed, as did Eastman Kodak, Westinghouse, American Express and several other companies in which Monks and LENS have asserted their rights as shareholders. It helps that as a candidate for an activist board seat, Monks is well qualified as a successful business person and public leader. He is not a single-issue advocate with nothing else to offer, but a fully skilled manager that any board would be privileged to have on its roster.

LENS describes itself as an activist money manager, buying stock in a limited number of companies that meet two investment criteria: they must be underperforming in the light of strong underlying values and susceptible to increased value through shareholder involvement. Once the fund has established its position, it approaches company management and directors, with the goal of enhancing value for its clients and other shareholders. Creating value requires specialized knowledge, hands-on involvement and vigilance. It is the fund's activism, coupled with expertise in law, corporate governance and business, that gives it a measure of control in its investments beyond that available to passive managers (see *Indexing*).

Physically and intellectually imposing, Bob Monks puts his stamp on any activity in which he engages. A successful investor for over 40 years – the founder of Institutional Shareholder Services, the world's premier proxy advisory firm, and former chairman of the Boston Company, a prominent institutional investor – Monks has an unrivaled understanding of how to lead shareholders in cost-effective initiatives to increase value.

After leading the charge to wake up US shareholders to their stake in corporate affairs, Monks has been taking the message to Europe and Asia in response to the increasing globalization of capital markets. Markets outside the United States are following his lead in examining rules for shareholder participation and giving new energy to its firms. The 1998 strategic alliance between CALPERS (the California Public Employees Retirement System) and Hermes (the UK pension fund for British Telecom and the Post Office) is a good example of such international shareholder activism, as is the role of LENS and Hermes in removing the chief executive of the UK's Mirror Group in early 1999.

Like growing numbers of people in the business and investment community, Monks has adopted the new tools of adaptive complexity and computer simulations to demonstrate his points about shareholder activism. His book *The Emperor's Nightingale*, describes how corporations behave through the stages of their life cycles, and shows that synergy really does exist – not as a single burst of energy but as a continuous, healthy adaptation to business conditions. He does not condemn corporate managers for their ironclad budgets, rigid forecasts and attempts to control the uncontrollable. Rather, he provides informed support for the view that business must consist of smaller independent units, which pursue their own aims but collectively achieve what is beyond their individual capability.

## Counterpoint

The corporate and investing worlds are typically constituted of interconnected networks of trustees, executives and managers. These create a wide variety of conflicts of interest that can make corporate governance less effective than it should be.

Bob Monks comments:

> *The question of the ineffectiveness of institutional investors is most important, particularly as it relates to "conflict of interest." Even the best chief executive of a fiduciary organization is not going to be willing to be activist, or to be perceived as activist, because "my customers don't like it." Until the government enforces the fiduciary laws respecting conflicting interests, there has been an attitude of benign neglect in the Anglo-American world. Thus, we have the irony that among institutional investors, only those least qualified by education, training and outlook are free to be activist.*

The concept of corporate governance has its roots in the legal structure giving companies unique status with an allocation of powers among owners, managers, customers and society. But do many advocates of shareholder activism go too far, pushing the interests of shareholders too strongly to the exclusion of other "stakeholders"? After all, a firm is not just a bunch of shares but a collection of relationships between its owners, managers, employees, customers, suppliers and society as a whole. Thinking of the firm as a social institution rather than a capital market vehicle has important implications for corporate governance.

Bob Monks comments:

> *I don't think of the firm so much as being social as being a question of* power: *who has the power to create reality, whose standards will prevail?*

Stock option plans have become increasingly popular among UK and US corporations, as they are generally regarded as effective tools of corporate governance, rewarding executives for enriching their shareholders. But such corporate compensation plans are due for a major overhaul and reform. At present, they are a travesty and may become a source of litigation and anger on the part of workers and shareholders: not only has executive pay increased the gap between lower-level workers and senior executives, but these executives have given themselves attractive golden parachutes that pay off handsomely in the event they are let go for incompetence or any other reason.

Furthermore, executive pay is increasingly tied to stock incentives or stock options. On the surface, this seems fine except that if the stock price goes down, options are nearly always rewritten to the lower stock price. This is a compensation scheme that cannot lose for the executive. Compensation by this technique is not typically a deduction in income and does not reduce reported earnings per share, though it should as it is a regular part of the compensation package. But in the United States, the Business Roundtable has bullied the accounting profession and the US Senate to the extent of creating an accounting practice that does *not* take the current cost of options into the profit-and-loss account.

Another concomitant of executive remuneration increasingly tied to stock prices is that companies and investors are accused of short-termism. There is a very simple solution if we want long-term ideas and focus on the part of our companies. Instead of having executives paid with bonuses or stock options related to current results, we could change the time frame to three to five years hence. In other words, a chief executive would be paid according to the results of the company three to five years from the time in which the bonus or option was set.

In the event of a sustained market decline, executive compensation could become a critical issue with potentially big payoffs for lawyers: when shareholders lose money in an absolute sense and then find that executive compensation has been high; when options have been ratcheted upwards to be more attractive and adjusted when the stock price goes down so that it is always a winning strategy for the executive; and when executive compensation includes very large payments for severance. Executive compensation could be the touchstone for the next market decline.

## Where next?

Corporate governance is all about the relationship between investors and the companies in which they invest. But what does investor relations really mean? To the practitioner, it means a craft of communication striving to be a profession. To a shareholder receiving its output, it is a necessary way to understand markets and companies. To corporate officials, it is a convenience to fend off the time-consuming quest for information that is often a distraction from running a business. All these views are correct but they are far from the story of investor relations today.

An unprecedented eighteen-year bull market has multiplied all financial service tasks. Abby Joseph Cohen of Goldman Sachs notes that compensation for financial service workers has been the only area of wage inflation in the present business cycle. And many others note that financial assets are the only inflating assets in a deflationary economy. It is reasonable to look at the macro-influence of a bull market creating the need for ever more competent and ever more highly paid investor relations people. But that is not the whole story either.

At its base, investor relations is about communication of fact. Usually, it is what is today called "push" through releases, attractive venues and targeted sources. Investor meetings and lunches have given way to conference calls and internet group emails in turn to global videoconferences. Facts are still distilled by lawyers but, curiously, with the most important facts withheld during blackout periods when the most significant developments are taking place.

With computer databases and search capabilities, remarkable things can be done to turn masses of data into information. Most of the innovations have already taken place in the corporate world, especially in comparative retail sales. Now, they are finding their way into finance: for example, screening of the type used at *www.fortuneinvestor.com* can survey sixteen thousand securities on six hundred variables; and charts of historical activity on almost anything are available at *www.bigcharts.com* and *www.yardeni.com*. Hundreds of tools like these are converting the "push" from investor relations into a "pull" by users in control of what they want, what they do with it and the conclusions to be reached.

Investor persuasion is moving to the user through the empowerment of technology. The nub of judgment remains in an elusive corner of agency finance, behavioral sciences and computation. But each single user has access to machinery to do the chores, which is low-cost, readily available, global and instantaneous. Like Microsoft endorsing the internet, which may ultimately be its downfall, so the alert investor-relations person will provide these tools to make the user's job easier and better.

The next steps for investor relations are straightforward:

- First, companies, funds and countries that wish to inform their constituency should maintain and publish *FAQs* (frequently asked questions), a common practice in industry. All questions with whatever favorable or unfavorable answer can be made available on a bulletin board. It is the next step to the ultimate in transparency, the ultimate being when the answers are created automatically regardless of the questions asked.
- Second, companies should actively trade their own shares with open disclosure of transactions on an instantaneous basis. Companies would reveal their own interplay between business conditions, availability of capital and their assessment of prospects by their actions.
- Third, and in the same vein, insiders would be encouraged to trade with no reservations on when, except that they would have to be identified as an insider.

Technology makes all these possible, and investor relations would be advanced, providing the user with live, real and significant information individually customized for each. It is possible today. But no one has done it.

## Guru response

Bob Monks comments:

> *I would add a fourth bullet point to your summary of the next steps for investor relations: as "institutional" ownership approaches the 50% level in the OECD world, the question arises repeatedly,* quis custodiet ipsos custodes *– who is watching the watchers?*
>
> *I believe that internet technology will allow trustees to communicate with pension beneficiaries, mutual fund operators with the beneficial owners, and union trustees with the membership. The mechanics of communication and consent will need to be worked out over the next fifty years. What is important is to require that there be some obligation on the trustees to take into account the fact that they are acting for others. Modern technology provides a relatively cheap and reliable means for doing this.*

## Read on

### In print

- Bob Monks, *The Emperor's Nightingale: Restoring the Integrity of the Corporation* (Perseus Books/Capstone Publishing, 1998)
- Bob Monks and Nell Minow, *Watching the Watchers: Corporate Governance for the Twenty-First Century* (Blackwell Publishers, 1996)
- Bob Monks and Nell Minow, *Corporate Governance* (Blackwell Publishers, 1994)
- Bob Monks and Nell Minow, *Power and Accountability*

- Hilary Rosenberg, *A Traitor to His Class: Robert AG Monks and the Battle to Change Corporate America* (John Wiley, 1999).

## Online

- *www.ragm.com* and *www.lens.com* – Bob Monks' websites
- *www.hitachi.com* – an example of a corporate bulletin board
- *www.fortuneinvestor.com, www.bigcharts.com* and *www.yardeni.com* – examples of websites with various historical data and investment management tools.

# Corporate Restructuring

O ne of the most high profile features of the business and investment worlds is corporate restructuring – the mergers and acquisitions (M&A), leveraged buyouts, divestitures, spin-offs and the like that are contested in the "market for corporate control." These recombinant techniques of corporate finance often have an impact on the financial markets far beyond the individual companies and sectors they involve and, in theory, all return real control of companies to shareholders. Virtually without exception, stock prices of participating companies rise in response to announcements of corporate restructuring. But are such events good for investors beyond the very short term?

The late 1990s have seen yet another wave of M&A activity. Indeed, the number and value of mega-mergers in 1998 set new records, a 50% increase on activity in 1997, itself a record year. This has reawakened the populist cry that such mergers do not create new wealth, that they merely represent the trading of existing assets – rearranging the deck chairs on the Titanic. What is more, it is argued, the threat of takeover means that managements take too short-term a view, bolstering stock prices where possible, investing inadequately for the future and, where a company has been taken over in a leveraged buyout, perhaps burdening it with excessive debt.

On the other side of the debate, the primary argument in favor of M&A is that they are good for industrial efficiency: without the threat of their companies being taken over and, in all likelihood, the loss of their jobs, managers would act more in their own interests than those of the owners. In particular, this might imply an inefficient use of company resources, overinvestment, lower productivity and a general lack of concern about delivering shareholder value. Feeble supervision of corporations often leads to mismanagement, it is argued, and while increased shareholder activism is one option (see *Corporate Governance*), takeovers are a more radical solution for remedying poor performance and safeguarding against economic mediocrity.

Certainly, a takeover bid is frequently beneficial to the shareholders of the target company in terms of immediate rises in the stock price (though acquisitions often have a negative effect on the profitability and stock price of the acquirer). And managements that resist takeover may be doing it for their own interests rather than those of their investors. Senior executives may use such bizarre devices as *shark repellents* and *poison pills*, which make it extremely costly for shareholders to replace the incumbent board of directors.

## Guru of corporate restructuring: Bruce Wasserstein

In the mid-1980s, there was an avalanche of takeovers of underperforming companies, the targets of institutions and arbitrageurs who suspected that, with the help of plentiful leverage, they could increase corporate values by *mobilizing assets*. Often that term meant disposal of non-performing assets. In this earlier age of corporate restructuring, Bruce Wasserstein was an *enfant terrible*. M&A deals were being done at premiums of 30–40% above market prices and Wasserstein would be in the middle designing strategies to make them happen.

This was also the heyday of shark repellents and poison pills. Often, the other side would be lawyers and PR people trying to set defenses against shareholders who had corporate control in mind, artfully removing shareholder rights whenever they might be exercised to change corporate control. But the SEC formed an advisory committee to evaluate many of these activities and concluded that the market mechanisms must be left unimpeded.

Wasserstein's youthful energy tapped intensity suited to the pulsing business of deals. Always very well prepared, he worked with arbitrageurs, lawyers, accountants and regulators to move business combinations forwards over institutions dedicated to thwart combinations, which, in the light of hindsight, seemed to favor one group of investors over another. He went on to found his own successful investment banking firm, his personality skills leading him on the correct path.

In his 1998 book *Big Deal*, Wasserstein surveys "the battle for control of America's leading corporations," including his own role in the past two decades or so. He describes five waves of mergers beginning in the mid-1800s: the first involved the building of the railroad empires; the second, in the 1920s, saw merger mania fueled by a frothy stock market and rapid industrial growth; the third happened during the go-go years of the 1960s and featured the rise of the conglomerate; the fourth occurred with the hostile takeovers of the 1980s, driven by names such as Icahn, Boesky and Milken; and finally, a fifth wave happening today. Wasserstein attributes the explosion of M&A activity at this turn of the century to the need for companies to reposition themselves in today's ever changing competitive environment:

> *The patterns of industrial development through mergers, like those of economic activity, are crude and imperfect. However, there do seem to be elemental forces, Five Pistons, which drive the merger process:*
>
> - *Regulatory and political change: many of the most active M&A sectors over the past few years – media and telecommunications, financial services, utilities, health care – have been stimulated by deregulation or other political turmoil. Before deregulation, a number of industries owed their very existence to regulatory boundaries.*
> - *Technological change: technology creates new markets, introduces new competitors and is intertwined with regulatory change. Changes in technology make old regulatory boundaries obsolete and sometimes silly.*
> - *Financial change: financial fluctuations have a similar catalytic effect. A booming stock market encourages stock deals.*

*A low market with low interest rates can have an especially strong effect after a period of high inflation in which the cost of hard assets has increased more rapidly than stock prices. In this environment, it may be cheaper to buy hard assets indirectly by purchasing companies on the stock market. Falling interest rates and available capital lubricate the process.*

- *Leadership: of course, corporate combinations do not occur in a mechanistic fashion. A human element is involved – the man on horseback who leads a company to seminal change.*
- *The size-simplicity vortex: scale matters, and bigger seems to mean better to most managers. Maybe it's critical mass, or technology and globalization, or integration, or sheer vanity and ego, but there is a natural imperative towards scale. However, just as some companies keep getting bigger, others shed their skin and become smaller. The imperative towards focus and simplicity is as strong as that for size. The two competing elements create a vortex of change.*

## Counterpoint

Why so many mega-mergers? The evidence seems to be very clear, at least on the academic side, that mergers ultimately do not pay off for buyers or sellers. Economically, they equalize themselves out in the normal process of bidding so that the gains do not accrue to one side or the other. Similarly, there is a tendency now to have smaller business units, which, because of the new computer tools, are as functional and more motivational than larger business units.

In the 1980s, the deals were adversarial and there were not enough goodies to go around. Now, they are not adversarial: they are friendly and there are plenty of goodies to go around. The reasons seem to lie first in a compliant US anti-trust division – which is strange under a Democratic administration – but even more in the payoffs that go to the agents involved. Executives get their stock options written up and then reissued after they are able to exercise their old options in advance in order to keep the managements around under the new corporate structure.

In addition, merger accounting allows for a great deal of flexibility of accounting for goodwill and burying old mistakes. A fresh slate is often good and a merger provides that opportunity. And, of course, there are the agents, brokers, lawyers, accountants and so on, who form part of the transaction costs of a merger and act as an incentive to keep it going. It is the agency function that makes it go plus the high price. That is the characteristic of mergers now, and it does not necessarily bode well for efficient business in the future.

Is the creation of new behemoths really what should be going on? Computer technology is empowering individuals to do marvelous things. Projects are taking the place of process. No longer do we have permanent constabularies of process administrators keeping the wheels of business moving. Instead, we have projects, where the *administration* may include customers, employees, suppliers and temporary consultants to complete a project and then split apart. Business management of the future is very similar to movie production: bringing people together to engage in a creative function and then split. People can be members of several creative teams at the same time. But in each one, there has to be someone who has the "fire-in-the-belly" to make it happen.

Yet companies do want to merge and become larger, perhaps propelled by the results of management consultant studies that say that is the thing to do. But everything that we know is on the empowerment of smaller and smaller groups, the behavior of smaller units of organizations, which pulls against exactly these structures towards higher and higher, larger and larger units of consolidation. Companies in the United States, at least, have learned that instant gratification comes from mergers, while operations come from smaller and smaller units. So we are shifting to having to feed our own financial greed with more and more artifices.

M&A activity seems to be at its highest at the top of bull markets when borrowing is easy. It is probably no accident that the merger waves Wasserstein describes have tended to occur at moments of the greatest optimism and the highest valuation of financial markets. A hundred years ago, there was talk of a new era. Similarly, in the 1920s and the 1960s, and again in the 1990s, the higher the stock market, the more intense the optimism, the greater the tendency towards consolidation. These are cyclical features of markets.

## Where next?

Among investment styles and techniques, one is hardly ever mentioned but it is the one that is being used prominently today: event investing. Markets today are looking for events like earnings surprise anticipated – the so-called *whisper number*; stock promotions – the stocks that are mentioned on news broadcasts; merger news that allows companies to rewrite history in their accounting statements and write up options for the management; and deals – deals between companies for strategic alliances and deals on sales.

Events and anticipation of events are what drives markets in very short-term environments, and that is what is happening today. Yes, we have momentum investing, but much more directly we have event investing, fueled by the communications on the internet, chats and even the old-fashioned way of your friendly broker calling you with a tip. But our communications have become much faster, more sophisticated and widespread, more popular – so event investing is what is ruling the day.

While mergers dominate as the millennium dawns, demergers may offer the best business and investment prospects for the future. For example, British management consultant Andrew Campbell and his colleagues calculate that there is one trillion dollars worth of shareholder value locked up waiting to be released by the breakup of multi-business corporations in the United States and the UK. They claim that breaking up these firms into far more focused businesses will create enormous improvements in company performance and, along with it, vastly increased shareholder wealth. And they describe potential investment strategies to gain from it:

- Speculate ahead of a breakup: work out which companies may break up and invest in them before other investors have driven the price up and before an official breakup announcement is made.
- Avoid breakup candidates: a converse strategy involves avoiding potential breakup candidates altogether and instead investing in those companies which are already focused – they will outperform companies with value-destroying corporate centers.
- Invest in a broad portfolio of breakups: breakups release value so invest in a broad range of breakups immediately after each breakup is announced.
- Invest selectively in particular breakups: identify those companies which will increase in value most once broken off. These are likely to be those companies which are likely to be subsequently acquired by another focused company.

## Read on

### In print

- David Sadtler, Andrew Campbell and Richard Koch, *Breakup: When Large Companies are Worth More Dead than Alive* (Capstone Publishing/Free Press, 1997)
- Bruce Wasserstein, *Big Deal: The Battle for Control of America's Leading Corporations* (Warner Books, 1998).

### Online

- *www.sternstewart.com* – website offering access to the *Journal of Applied Corporate Finance*, edited by Don Chew, a good source of recent research and writing on corporate restructuring.

# Economic Forecasting

A lmost every financial services firm has an extensive economic forecasting effort. It is usually part of a so-called *top-down* investment process, which starts with an outlook for the economy and monetary conditions, continues to the strongest industries, follows with detailed company study for stock selection and may include an overlay of technical analysis to provide a timing dimension. Some would add analysis of social and political conditions even before economic studies (see *Politics and Investing*).

Economic forecasts derive from models – usually of the aggregate national or global economy, but sometimes of parts of those economies: particular industrial sectors, regions of the world or even single products or firms. Basic approaches to forecasting simply extrapolate the past; more sophisticated models attempt to understand the sources of past changes and build them into their forecasts. The latter requires knowledge of economic history and economic principles, though, even then, forecasting is by no means an exact science. But while the accuracy of economists' predictions is frequently a target of jokes, forecasting remains a popular pursuit.

Forecasts for the macroeconomy are published regularly by academic institutions, thinktanks, governments, central banks and international organizations like the OECD and the IMF. In these places, modeling can, to a certain extent, be conducted free of the constraint of producing quick and usable data on a daily basis. But in the investment world, forecasts are required to be done *early and often*. A relatively short-term outlook is normally the limit of their aspirations – what will happen to interest rates within the next month? – with decision-makers demanding rapid output that they hope will be directly relevant to their immediate problems.

Much of the output of financial market models is naturally closely guarded in the hope that it may bring advantage to its owners and their clients. But, at the same time, investment economists like to maintain a public profile for marketing purposes, and are often called on by the media to give their opinion on the latest macroeconomic developments. Their interpretations of economic data may give some clues as to how the financial markets will react, though more often than not, they are explaining why the markets have already reacted as they did. Invariably too, there are disagreements about what various indicators mean, depending on different beliefs about the economy, and whether the firm is taking an optimistic or pessimistic view of the markets.

Each month, the *Economist* polls a group of financial forecasters and calculates the average of their predictions for real GDP growth, consumer price inflation and current account balances in a variety of countries. More specialized services like Consensus Economics survey over three hundred economists each month and offer details on average private sector predictions.

## Economic forecasting guru: Peter Bernstein

Despite the pressures for *early and often* forecasts, a number of Wall Street and City economists do as good a job as any forecasters, among them Abby Joseph Cohen, Stephen Roach and Edward Hyman. Most such investment economists are good students of market conditions – careful keepers of useful data, and on occasion creative in extracting some kind of signal out of the noise. Ed Yardeni, for example, the chief economist at Deutsche Bank Securities, turns his website into a cyber-chart room. If you want to access data and view charts, Yardeni's site is an essential stop. He also makes his commentary available in a section for clients that is password protected, but a substantial amount of the content is openly accessible.

One economic commentator stands amid the few that many of us would class as the best: Peter Bernstein. He grew up heading his father's investment firm, Bernstein MacCauley, in New York. He was the first editor of the *Journal of Portfolio Management*, founded by Gilbert Kaplan, and has received many awards, among them the highest honor granted by the investment management industry's professional body, the Association of Investment Management & Research.

Bernstein is able to walk on both streets – with practitioners and academics. He writes a newsletter, *Economics and Portfolio Strategy*, to test and disseminate his analyses. And writing is one of his main strengths: his two books on the history of risk and on how capital ideas came to Wall Street have been regulars on the business best-seller lists during the 1990s.

Like a good academic, Bernstein marshals all the arguments, especially those that are counter to his own position. His mid-February 1998 letter, for example, examined the case for exuberant stock prices in the United States, giving particular emphasis to the market's reliance upon an all-knowing Federal Reserve for economic management. Bernstein concluded that "stocks are a risky investment and should be managed accordingly." Since that analysis was approximately the same as his November 1997 conclusion, he was ahead of the wave and for the right reasons. Bernstein is also faster than most to admit where he has been wrong and to try to examine what led him astray – or, as he jokes, "what led the market astray when it failed to act the way I thought it would."

## Counterpoint

Financial analysts are professional forecasters. But why study the economy, a traditional lagging indicator, if you want to forecast investment measures? The investment record of this process is only rarely better than random – and when you take account of the expenses of achieving these results, they come out a little bit less than chance. Why do it at all with that unconvincing record of success?

Economic forecasts are supposed to be meaningful. But if you believe that asset prices reflect a forecast of future outcomes, it would seem quite difficult to use a technique that reaches back into the past to get an idea of the future. But that is what economic forecasting does. It is teased for forecasting three recessions for every one that actually happens. No wonder it is called the dismal science.

*Financial Times* economics columnist Sir Samuel Brittan makes a pointed reflection on the practice of forecasting: "The golden rule for economic forecasters is: forecast what has already happened and stay at the cautious end. Forecasts tell us more about the present and the recent past than about the future."

Poor methods, bad models and inaccurate data are all blamed for the recurrence of serious forecast errors. But according to Oxford economics professor David Hendry, these are not the primary cause of systematic mistakes. Rather, unanticipated large changes within the forecast period are the culprit. The primary fault of economic forecasting is in not rapidly adjusting the forecasts once they go wrong.

Hendry uses an analogy from rocket science: a rocket to the moon is forecast to reach there at a precise time and location, and usually does so. But if it is hit by a meteor and knocked off course – or destroyed – the forecast is systematically badly wrong. That outcome need not suggest poor engineering or bad forecasting models – and certainly does not suggest that Newtonian gravitation theory is incorrect.

## Guru response

Peter Bernstein comments:

> *For better or worse, economic forecasting is an essential ingredient in investing because earnings and interest rates are both conditional on economic conditions. So you have to do it or use it in some fashion. Furthermore, although a forecast of next quarter's GDP or even next year's earnings per share may be wrong, the kind of forecasting I do – and really that Abby Cohen does too – is to try to define the basic environment – inflationary or not, fast growth or not, competitive or not, and so on. That kind of thing is most helpful and has paid the biggest dividends over the years, not just in this cycle.*

At the front of this book is further commentary from Peter Bernstein: a grand sweeping history of the markets reprinted from the 1 December 1998 issue of his newsletter.

## *Where next?*

Forecasting is a key task in financial institutions because of the profound effects economic developments can have on potential profits. And while leading economic indicators might provide a hint as to what the economic future holds, they do not anticipate what the additional effects of powerful economic agents like government policy and the financial markets themselves might be. To try to get ahead of the competition, companies will aim to model more accurately, and with more consideration of possible discontinuities in the markets.

One way to make forecasts more useful – though not necessarily better – might be to follow the principle of *truth-in-labeling* used on food packages and elsewhere. We could describe the kind of forecast we are making more accurately. For example, if we are using backtesting, we should say that that is exactly what we are doing and which of two varieties.

One form of backtesting is *momentum*: the forecast is derived from a view that the past momentum will continue in roughly the same direction – often straight line – as it has in the past. The other form is *regression to the mean*: we think things will not go back or up or down, but return to average conditions. This is like a series of coin flips that goes ninety-nine times in one direction, and we think the next event is related to the preceding one.

Alternatively, we can say that our forecast comes from our own insight or novelty, and label it that way so it is known as essentially out of our head and our own creativity – or lack of creativity, which will be known in time. Sometimes different techniques like high-frequency forecasting come from this. Or it can come from news and our response to new news. This is not necessarily insider information but news that is not necessarily generally recognized by others – a form of forecasting derived from information.

Finally, the most common form of forecasting is waffle: we do benchmark investing or stick to the middle because we do not know what else to do. That is perfectly all right, but we should label it as such. Let us say that is what we are doing, so people can understand what they are getting when they listen to us. Most of the time, a waffle is the right thing to do, but at all times, we can make our forecasts better by correctly labeling them.

## *Read on*

### In print

- Peter L Bernstein, *Against the Gods: The Remarkable Story of Risk* (John Wiley, 1996)
- Peter L Bernstein, *Capital Ideas: The Improbable Origins of Modern Wall Street* (Free Press, 1992)
- Peter L Bernstein's newsletter *Economics and Portfolio Strategy*
- Reports from *Consensus Economics.*

### Online

- *econwpa.wustl.edu/EconFAQ/* – Bill Goffe's "Resources for economists on the internet", one of the best entry points on the internet for economic information
- *www.economics.ox.ac.uk/hendry/Frontpage.htm* – David Hendry's research project on the econometrics of macroeconomic forecasting
- *www.economist.com* – website of *The Economist*
- *www.ft.com* – website of the *Financial Times*
- *www.yardeni.com* – Ed Yardeni's website.

# Emerging Markets

"*E*merging markets* may be a euphemism but it is also a declaration of hope and faith," Mark Mobius has said. "Although some of the stock markets of developing nations may sometimes seem 'submerged,' they are generally emerging into bigger and better things."

Such a definition of emerging markets expresses the typically optimistic view of people specializing in this branch of equity investment. Certainly, this relatively new focus of investor enthusiasm is always exciting with something happening all the time, somewhere in the world, with the opportunity for huge profits. Investment returns in some emerging markets have the potential to exceed those in the developed world.

But equally, for the dedicated emerging market investor, there are considerable challenges: the frequent frustrations of a lack of common standards and a lack of information, grueling travel schedules, language problems and cultural suspicions. And, of course, as the Asian crisis and subsequent global economic events have confirmed, stock markets and currencies in the developing and formerly communist worlds can be highly volatile, reacting strongly to international investor sentiment and economic and political changes.

Investments in emerging markets can result in spectacular returns, positive or negative. But picking potential winners, at the level of either country or company, is very difficult. There are frequently problems in comparing the relative merits of companies across markets: financial reporting and accounting standards vary, and indicators such as price-to-earnings ratios are often unreliable for international comparisons. Countries employ a variety of accounting conventions in their treatment of corporate profits.

It is clear that emerging markets carry considerable risks, including illiquidity, lack of transparency and sharp swings in prices. Individual investors seeking a stake in these markets should be either thinking long-term or prepared to take substantial risks. They should also consider carefully what proportion of their portfolios they can reasonably afford to commit to such markets.

## Emerging markets guru: Mark Mobius

As a category of equity investment, emerging markets may be considered to have begun in 1986 under the sponsorship of the International Finance Corporation (IFC), an arm of the World Bank. David Gill, then head of its Capital Markets Division, convinced the IFC to invest in equities in some of the strongest countries the World Bank was financing with debt, initiating private involvement in what had largely been a public domain. The Emerging Market Fund, which Gill started, gave its investment mandate to Capital Group in Los Angeles, a firm that now manages $75 billion in these markets. David Fisher has successfully managed this group since the early days.

But no one epitomizes the emerging market manager better than Mark Mobius of the Templeton Emerging Markets Group. Mobius meets the requirement for physical stamina of an emerging market investment guru. Now in his sixties, he is in top physical shape to maintain the pace of fifteen-hour days, seven days a week. From a childhood in the United States, he has been based in Hong Kong since the 1960s and travels on a German passport. His scope is global with more emphasis on the fast-growing economies, like Asia, that especially challenge an investor when reminded that volatility is two-way.

Mobius is a hard-headed investor in markets that do not usually inspire confidence. His tough valuation bottom-up discipline demands that investments sell at no more than five times earnings five years hence. And the cheaper the better for him. He is a fundamental investor who visits companies and studies the businesses, while fretting little over the country's macro issues (see *Value Investing*, *Economic Forecasting* and *Politics and Investing*). Since his techniques are common to the well-schooled analyst, he has to find different markets and different industries from other analysts. He is often out of step, buying investments that look like they may continue to decline. It is discipline – the old-fashioned kind.

Mobius is a frequent commentator on emerging market investing and has written a well-received book, *Mobius on Emerging Markets*, which summarizes his keys to success:

- Hard work and discipline: the more time and effort put into researching investments, the more knowledge will be gained and wiser decisions will be made.
- Common sense: the clarity and simplification required to integrate successfully all the complex information with which investors are faced.
- Creativity: looking at investments from a multi-faceted approach, considering all the variables that could negatively or positively affect an investment. Creative thinking is also required to look forward to the future and forecast the outcome of current business plans.
- Independence: when making investments, it is most unlikely that committee decisions can be superior to a well thought-out individual decision.
- Risk-taking: investment decisions always require decisions based on insufficient information. There is never enough time to learn all there is to know about an investment and even if there were, equity investments are like living organisms undergoing continuous change. There always comes the time when a decision must be taken and a risk acquired.
- Flexibility: it is important for investors to be flexible and not permanently adopt a particular type of asset or selection method. The best approach is to migrate from the popular to the unpopular securities, sectors or methods (see *Contrarian Investing*).

Mobius also describes five central investment attitudes:

- Diversification: this is particularly important in emerging markets where individual country or company risks can be extreme. Global investing is always superior to investing solely on the investor's home market or one market. Searching world-wide leads an investor to find more bargains and better bargains than by studying only one nation (see *Global Investing*).
- Timing and staying invested: as Sir John Templeton says, "the best time to invest is when you have money." In other words, equity investing is the best way to preserve value rather than leaving money in a bank account. As a corollary, an investment should not be sold unless a much better investment has been found to replace it.
- Long-term view: by looking at the long-term growth and prospects of companies and countries, particularly those stocks that are out of favor or unpopular, the chances of obtaining a superior return are much greater.
- Investment averaging: investors who establish a program from the very beginning to purchase shares over a set period of intervals have the opportunity to purchase at not only high prices, but also low prices, bringing their average cost down.
- Accepting market cycles: any study of stock markets around the world will show that bear or bull markets have always been temporary. It is clear that markets do have cyclical behavior with pessimistic, skeptical, optimistic, euphoric, panic and depressive phases (see *Manias, Panics and Crashes*). Investors should thus expect such variations and plan accordingly.

In assessing emerging market investments, Mobius stresses the importance of constantly being aware of influences and biases. These are strongest in the places where you spend most of your working and leisure hours and from where you obtain most information. For this reason, the emerging market investor must continually visit all the countries in the emerging market areas and read news and research reports originating from all over the world. (However, as a counterpoint, the internet now makes available a wealth of information on individual markets and countries – perhaps better and less costly in time and effort than that obtainable on the ground.)

For wise portfolio decisions, Mobius suggests, two important perspectives are necessary:

- the global outlook and experience that comes from having invested in many countries
- the more detailed and intimate knowledge that comes from a local presence.

It is important to combine both perspectives by having local and country-specific information collated, digested and compared with other global data. This kind of analysis yields much more powerful results, which enhance the locally gathered information by, for example, providing insights into a particular company as a consequence of comparisons with similar companies in another country. The end results are much more valuable insights that must yield far better long-term investment returns.

Mobius also outlines the five types of risk involved in emerging market investment:

- political – instability, regulation, foreign investment restrictions
- financial – remittance/exchange control, convertibility, currency devaluation
- investment – disclosure, ownership, minority shareholder culture
- transactional – brokers, fees, computerization, settlement, custody/certificate exchange
- systemic – liquidity, regulatory enforcement, transparency, operational structure of stock exchange.

## Counterpoint

It is no accident that Mobius describes "perspiration more than inspiration" as one of the most important features of his investment approach, starting from there with a strong dash of independent thinking. But where does it break down and how can it go wrong?

The ability to move from market to market assumes that investments and their environments are disconnected, that market movements are not strongly correlated. But in these days of global banking and instant communication, that condition is less likely. Markets and investments in those markets may be increasingly synchronized.

In the past two decades, as emerging market investment grew dramatically, globalization permeated our financial systems. Now there are some clues of a cyclical return to local and national interests. If so, investments by foreigners in any market may be treated harshly.

For example, some now argue that the rapid expansion of emerging stock markets in recent years is likely to hinder rather than assist faster industrialization. According to this view, while stock markets may be potent symbols of capitalism, paradoxically, capitalism often flourishes better without their dominance. The inherent volatility and arbitrariness of stock market pricing in developing countries make it a poor guide to efficient investment allocation. Portfolio capital inflows from overseas lead to interactions between two inherently unstable markets: the stock and currency markets. Such interactions in the wake of unfavorable economic shocks may exacerbate macroeconomic instability and reduce long-term growth.

Emerging market investment depends on steadily growing liquidity to be able to pay back investors at higher levels in a foreign currency. This works when the market is going up and money is coming in. But in the reverse, liquidity is tight; the ability to pay foreign creditors is lacking and confidence plummets.

Thus, emerging market investing may be a long-term cyclical phenomenon and not a steady, one-way path to riches. Certainly, the emerging market investment phase of more than the last decade is over. Not only has capital been destroyed and confidence shattered, but the idea of capital flows for superior return from developed countries to needy, developing ones is gone. The latter do not want the funds on anything like the terms that would be required.

A common theme of this book is that investment success is most often observed where the market requirements and investor personality are one. The old shibboleth that "investors don't pick markets, markets pick investors" is more true in emerging markets than elsewhere. And Mark Mobius's style, hard work and tough mind are exactly what was needed in emerging markets. These markets may undergo a change. Will he?

## Guru response

Mark Mobius comments on the future of emerging markets in 2010:

> When we started our first emerging markets fund in 1987, we had no idea how significant emerging markets would become. After all, that fund was only about $100 million in size. But it seemed like an enormous amount of money because we then only had six markets in which to invest: Hong Kong, the Philippines, Thailand, Malaysia, Singapore and Mexico. Today, the picture has changed dramatically. We now manage $10 billion, a hundred times more than we were managing in 1987, and from one small office in Hong Kong, we've grown to ten offices around the world on every continent.
>
> More critically, globalization has overwhelmed countries all over the world. In 1987, most emerging countries were adhering to a closed door economic framework with rigid state controls on foreign exchange, the flows of funds in and out, industry, and a whole range of economic straitjackets formulated in a panoply of isms, with communism and socialism the most pervasive. Soon after, however, a new economic philosophy began to take hold as the failure of communism, socialism and statism began to become apparent. More importantly, accelerating technical achievements in telecommunications and mass communications (most importantly, television) began to

*break down psychological barriers between nations, weakening the ability of governments to erect barriers between people and markets.*

*The new economic philosophy said that private investment was good and better than government investment. It said that foreign investment should be encouraged because it not only swelled the reserves of the recipient nations but because it brought know-how and technology. It said that the private sector's guiding hand would best allocate resources and that capital markets were the best way to speed the flow of information so that money could best be allocated to the deserving – read profitable – enterprises. But there were booms and crashes along the way, not only because they are a natural part of human existence, but because many of the emerging nations were not ready for the new philosophy. They didn't have the institutional framework in place to create a level playing field for all market participants. In some cases, there were no stock markets and if there were, they were not liquid. There were no securities laws and regulations and if there were, they were not properly enforced. There were no central depositories for shares and if there were, they were not used by all companies. In other words, the markets were not fair, efficient, liquid or transparent.*

*The rest, as they say, is history. There was a big 1994 crash in Mexico with the spark lit in the bond market tinder and spreading to other emerging markets. More recently, the fire started in Thailand and spread throughout the world. So we enter the millennium with a battered and bloodied emerging markets environment. Currencies have crashed, stock markets have crashed, bond markets have crashed and ... governments have crashed.*

*Given this scenario, what can we expect? First, we know that there is no turning back. The information and capital flows speeding throughout the world are not decelerating but accelerating. Governments can't close the doors because they know they will be left behind. Banks are in temporary retreat but they are being replaced with strategic investors from the ranks of multinational firms and private equity funds eager to take advantage of the many investment bargains now uncovered by the crash. More, not fewer, emerging markets will upgrade their capital markets and will compete for equity and fixed income funds from all over the globe. In the process, they will attract the capital of their own compatriots who have been keeping their money offshore in an effort to escape their investor-unfriendly governments and markets made risky by the lack of law and order.*

*In the new millennium, there will be more emerging markets and larger emerging markets. We will go from forty nations active in the emerging market investment picture to over eighty countries. Very few countries will move from emerging status to developed status because the developed countries will be moving ahead as well, albeit at a slower pace, so that the general water level will rise. The hundred times increase we experienced in the last decade will be realized again in the next decade. The internet miracle will enable much more cross-border trading.*

*Perhaps more importantly, the success of the euro will set a benchmark for regions all over the world to emulate that success. In Africa, a new currency union will evolve in sub-Saharan Africa with South Africa at its core. In Eastern Europe, most countries will join the European Union and Russia will also move in that direction. In Latin America, another currency union will emerge from Mercosur, tying Brazil, Argentina, Chile and other countries together in a currency, which will then merge with a North American union encompassing the United States, Mexico and Canada. In Asia, a currency union will be formed by Southeast Asian nations at first. Then agreements will be reached by China and Japan to join their currencies. These developments will not only be driven by the necessity to avoid the currency volatility of the past but also because nations around the world will move towards currency board systems, where currencies are strictly linked to a standard and currency adjustments by governments and central banks will not be allowed. In addition, the spread of internet commerce will require a single currency and simplified payments transfers.*

*As regards specific markets and where they will be placed in the overall emerging markets scheme, it is most likely that twelve countries will dominate: India, China, Indonesia, Brazil, Mexico, Argentina, South Africa, Nigeria, Egypt, Turkey, Poland and Russia:*

- *India will go through an unexpected transformation. Privatizations will be speeded up and the government's role in the economy will be reduced to the more important position of umpire rather than player in the economy.*
- *China will first experience a severe economic shock as a result of the necessity to reform the banking system by holding them accountable for the loans they make. The privatization of all the major state enterprises will result in massive bankruptcies. But then a new vibrant, efficient and open economy will emerge and the latent economic power of China will be apparent.*
- *In Indonesia, a new pluralistic government will buttress a diversified and decentralized economy, which will surpass the economic booms of the past.*
- *Brazil will lead the rest of Latin America out of economic stagnancy as the results of the massive privatization programs begin to feed into the economic system through dramatically increased productivity.*
- *Argentina and Chile will also experience the same phenomena and will augment and enhance Brazil's boom, bringing the rest of Latin America along with them.*
- *Mexico's special relationship with the United States will mean that, more and more, the Mexican economy will be merged with that of the United States, to the benefit of both nations, particularly Mexico.*
- *In South Africa, a new generation of black leaders will emerge and enhance the excellent South African infrastructure with*

> *policies that draw all parts of that nation and other sub-Saharan nations together in a new economic partnership and capital market mergers.*
>
> - *Nigeria will return to the international fold and represent a hitherto neglected but substantial capital market potential.*
> - *Egypt's current accelerating privatization program will be bearing fruit by the time 2010 rolls around. Former government-owned enterprises will no longer be a drag on the government budget but will add productivity and new wealth to the economy.*
> - *Turkey will extend its capital market operations not only to the Middle East but also eastwards to Central Asia.*
> - *Poland will be the most significant part of East European capital markets.*
> - *Russia will be the big surprise. Reforms on the back of significant efforts to wipe out corruption and crime will accompany economic reforms, including increased capital markets focus.*
>
> *In sum, in the coming years we will wake up to a remarkably improved emerging market day. More markets, more liquidity, better regulation, fairer markets and enormously expanded opportunities. This new environment will bring untold benefits not only to the people living in emerging markets but to the investors who were willing to accept the risks of emerging markets investing.*

## *Where next?*

Is the emerging market phenomenon really the free market initiative and glorious triumph of John Locke that Mobius describes? Perhaps rather it was a natural consequence of the modern portfolio theory taught in the United States, to diversify and take higher risks, coming on the back of what wsa then a ten-year-old bull market. From the developing countries' position, private investors were offering capital at no annual interest rate (we called it equity; they called it free, without management strings), which was more attractive than bank or government lending. It was a meeting of lovers and there was a love fest. And now, they have matured with all of the obligations and responsibility that come from the next age level.

Mobius selects the largest countries as the ones with best future potential presumably for the attractiveness of their domestic markets. The first rush of emerging markets was for export sales and that is now over. He is right to emphasize places like Nigeria and Egypt. And he is right in the sense that if he is wrong, these overpopulated countries will not tolerate a world with such huge disparities of communications and living standards.

But before we get to 2010, we must deal with the traumas of the late 1990s. Since the beginning of the Asian crisis in July 1997, there has been an approximately 50% decline in emerging markets. It started in Asia, became most visible and most illustrative in Russia, with about a 90% decline, approximately the same as in Indonesia, the fourth largest country in the world in terms of population. And pressure built up in Latin America.

Think of a swamp fire, or a fire in a coal mine, where underneath the ground there is a common smoldering heat source, which every once in a while flares up to the surface where it must be put out. Firemen come in and douse it with water and fire extinguishers and that flame goes away. Six months later, it comes up again.

This is what the conditions are today in emerging markets. In Indonesia, South Korea, Thailand, Malaysia, Brazil, Russia, Mexico – one after another – we get a flare-up. But it is all the same thing. It is a preference for risk-averse investing. It is a preference for guaranteed returns. And it is an aversion to the downside risk of a free market that extracts a penalty for over-exuberance. We have to treat the basic fire, rather than just the flare-ups.

Each emerging market considers itself unique in attempting to solve its own problems. But the problems are quite common. In order to rebuild their economies, most emerging markets have borrowed heavily in dollars in this capital-plentiful period. Investors have also invested dollars in those economies and now plan, at higher rates, in higher markets, to take them out. And even if not at higher levels, they take them out anyway because emerging markets on the whole look like a considerably less attractive place to invest than they did five years ago. This is a world-wide phenomenon, not just limited to Indonesia, Russia and Latin America.

What is it all about? The mixture of rising nationalism and deflation is very potent negative medicine for emerging markets. Reform of banking systems means banks have to recognize bad loans. Interconnectivity means that when something happens in one part of the world, the rest of us all feel it. This is not necessarily a dramatic buying opportunity except for those people who can watch the hourly news. And yet, we are setting up the conditions by which the long struggle of the workout period can take place. It is probably some distance into the future, but the early dramatic decline has certainly been felt.

In the meantime, there will be continual turmoil in these countries, promoting more nationalism, more separation from the international community and yet more necessity on the part of the developed nations, especially the United States, to support them.

China may be different in the sense that it has a high surplus of dollars with its very positive trade balance with the United States, and it may come out of this phase as the dominant emerging market. Mobius is right about the necessity for structural reform but this country seems destined to dominate its region and possibly to be the next sole superpower. It is a tremendously powerful force in the region and in the world, and the group that is running China now – and in the next decade – is very competent. We should pay careful attention to them.

Meanwhile, the United States itself looks increasingly like an emerging market. As with most emerging markets, it depends entirely on an inflow from outside its own borders in order to survive. There is a negative savings rate, and debt cannot be liquidated on its own but only rolled over, a characteristic of an emerging market. And it is very much an overbought emerging market having extended a very great boom for essentially the last 18 years.

But more than that, the United States is an emerging market that has turned over its financial responsibility to the rest of the world. The degree to which the country borrows in dollars is helpful. But the degree to which dollars are held by foreigners is harmful since foreigners can start liquidating those dollars in order to meet their own demands. As an emerging market, it is not clear that the United States would meet the IMF requirements for borrowing, a strange concept given the extent to which it is perceived to be the safest.

## Read on

### In print

- Mark Mobius, *Mobius on Emerging Markets* (Second edition, Financial Times Pitman Publishing, 1996).

### Online

- *www.capgroup.com* – Capital Group's website
- *www.emgmkts.com* – a "companion" to emerging market research
- *www.deanlebaron.com* – website of one of this book's co-authors.

# Financial Engineering

**F**inancial engineering is, in essence, the phenomenon of product and/or process innovation in the financial industries – the development of new financial instruments and processes that will enhance shareholders', issuers' or intermediaries' wealth. In the *New Palgrave* finance dictionary, John Finnerty lists countless recent financial innovations – from adjustable rate preferred stock to zero-coupon convertible debt – but these all can be classified into three principal types of activities: securities innovation; innovative financial processes; and creative solutions to corporate finance problems.

All these innovations are implemented using a few basic techniques, such as increasing or reducing risk (options, futures and other more exotic derivatives – see *Risk Management*), pooling risk (see *Mutual Funds*), swapping income streams (interest-rate swaps), splitting income streams (*stripped* bonds), and converting long-term obligations into shorter-term ones or vice versa (maturity transformation). But to be truly innovative, a new security or process must enable issuers or investors to accomplish something they could not do previously, in a sense making markets more efficient or complete.

Finnerty describes ten forces that stimulate financial engineering. These include risk management, tax advantages, agency and issuance cost reduction, regulation compliance or evasion, interest and exchange rate changes, technological advances, accounting gimmicks and academic research.

The emergence of financial engineering has also been influenced by the realization on Wall Street in the early to mid-1990s that there was a need for a new kind of graduate training. The financial institutions wanted people with heavy mathematics skills and some finance training, but had previously been fed from a haphazard network of different programs. Universities began to respond to the demand by setting up masters programs in financial engineering – and they were helped by the fact that the physics job market was at an all-time low due to the end of the Cold War.

## Financial engineering guru: Andrew Lo

Where else but the Massachusetts Institute of Technology (MIT) would you expect to find a course track called Financial Engineering? For a while the Sloan School of Management was not really accepted at MIT though its graduates were among the most sought-after in the job market for newly-minted MBAs. But within the science-oriented faculty, business education was hardly taken as seriously as Alfred Sloan, the donor of the facilities, hoped it would be.

Now that has changed. Finance has gone quant: higher mathematics is a regular feature of security pricing, risk management and business strategy. Professor Andrew Lo is one of the key people responsible. He is a first-rate scholar who, like others in this volume, can straddle academe and business. His research output is huge, often in collaboration with other leading lights who appear in the *Journal of Finance*, the *Journal of Financial Economics*, the *Journal of Econometrics*, the *Review of Financial Studies* and the many other publications still being added to the reading lists of professors and practitioners.

The burgeoning field of financial economics has produced a group of young professors who now hold endowed chairs. Just a decade or so ago, they were pre-tenured stars full of research ideas sprung from the basic efficient market hypothesis. They were going on to the next level or two, testing and applying these theories to specific valuation, portfolio strategy and risk problems. They showed their students, who were to become the star practitioners in institutions, how to do investments the modern way. Many of this group won a coveted Batterymarch Fellowship for research when little other funding was available. Andrew Lo, of course, was one of the most promising of that group as a winner in 1989.

Lo's research interests run the gamut of today's financial interests and his papers are among the most thoroughly researched of the field. Students call him an inspired teacher, perhaps because he believes in the worth of his subject matter. And in addition to his heavy teaching load, he carries an administrative burden as the director of the Laboratory for Financial Engineering, in fact its founder, at MIT. Somehow, he also finds time to help leading investment firms through consulting projects as well as steadily maintaining active parenting of a young toddler.

In addition to being the co-author of the first major financial econometrics textbook, Lo has a book published in early 1999 entitled *A Non-Random Walk Down Wall Street*, an obvious counterpoint to Burton Malkiel's classic book of almost the same name (see *Market Efficiency*). As his title suggests, Lo's research indicates that there are some elements of short-term predictability in stock returns and that it may be possible for disciplined active managers to seek them out, exploit them and "beat the market."

Financial engineering is the key to superior performance. Lo uses the analogy of the exceptional profitability of a pharmaceutical company, which may be associated with the development of new drugs via breakthroughs in biochemical technology. Similarly, even in efficient financial markets, there can be exceptional returns to breakthroughs in financial technology. Of course, barriers to entry are typically lower, the degree of competition much higher and most financial technologies are not as yet patentable – so the *half-life* of profitability of financial innovation is considerably smaller.

Clearly, it is difficult to beat an efficient market but, according to Lo, not impossible. So what are the sources of superior performance an active manager can draw on:

- better mathematical models of the markets?
- more accurate statistical methods?
- more timely data in a market where minute delays can mean the difference between profit and loss?

All can contribute, as Lo concludes:

*By better understanding the sources of value-added of active managers, rather than focusing purely on past performance, the chances of obtaining consistently superior investment returns can be increased dramatically.*

## Counterpoint

Counterpoints to financial engineering include traditional market efficiency arguments against active management, such as Bill Sharpe's arithmetic (see *Active Portfolio Management*). And even if it is possible to beat the market, and notwithstanding the fact that past performance should not be the sole criterion for judging investment managers, the riskiness of active strategies can be very different from passive strategies (see *Indexing*). Such risks do not necessarily average out over time, and investors' risk tolerance should be part of the process of selecting an investment strategy to match their goals (see *Investment Policy*).

A second counterpoint is the set of arguments against quantitative investing, and notably its reliance on backtesting and *data mining* (see *Quantitative Investing*). Engineering, by the very nature of its development and application, builds on whatever is accepted theory at any given stage of the cycle. Investment theories tend to lurch forward in leaps, usually after the disappointment of a prolonged bear market. New theories emerge, correcting the ills exposed by a calamitous decline and engineering applies the new wisdoms.

It should not surprise us that the applications of today's financial engineer seem internally consistent, sound and almost unassailable. That would always be found after decades of reconfirmation of market and portfolio theory. But we should not be lulled into complacency by a catechism built on data of only a few decades. Nor should we imagine that portfolio theory, as we know it today, is the end of investment knowledge. There will be new theory and new engineering to apply it. But it may have a different label than the contemporary *financial engineering*.

Finally, one of the consequences of the development of computer and financial technologies (as well as the long bull market) is the incredible growth in electronic trading. This has both good and bad implications for ordinary investors. On the positive side, the tools developed by cutting-edge financial institutions over two decades ago are now available to the individual household. Yet as with most technologies, the tools are more advanced than the general population's understanding of how to use them properly. Although trading costs have come down dramatically for the individual investor, the possibility of doing serious damage to one's nest egg is even greater.

## Guru response

Andrew Lo comments:

> These are exciting times for financial engineering, a discipline that has coalesced only within the last decade or so. Despite the recent turmoil in financial markets, or perhaps because of it, quantitative methods have become indispensable to even the most hardened fundamental investment manager. Indeed, the distinctions between fundamental, technical and quantitative have become blurred – all three approaches to financial decision-making are now subsumed by the term financial engineering.
>
> The enormous popularity of financial engineering can be attributed to three factors. The first is the simple fact that the financial system is becoming more complex over time, not less. This is an obvious consequence of general economic growth and development in which the number of market participants, the variety of financial transactions, and the sums and risks involved also grow. And as the financial system becomes more complex, financial technology must develop in tandem to keep pace with such complexity.
>
> The second factor is, of course, the set of breakthroughs in

*the quantitative modeling of financial markets, pioneered over the past three decades by the giants of financial economics: Black, Cox, Lintner, Markowitz, Merton, Modigliani, Miller, Ross, Samuelson, Scholes, Sharpe and others. Their contributions laid the remarkably durable foundations on which all of modern quantitative financial analysis is built.*

*The third factor is an almost parallel set of breakthroughs in computer technology, including hardware, software, and data collection and organization. Without these breakthroughs, much of the financial technology developed over the past thirty years would be irrelevant academic musings, condemned to the moldy oblivion of unread finance journals in university library basements. The advent of affordable desktop microcomputers and machine-readable real-time and historical data have irrevocably changed the way financial markets function. The outcome is nothing short of an industrial revolution in which the old-boys network has been replaced by the computer network; where what matters more is what you know, not who you know; and where graduates of Harvard and Yale suddenly find themselves less employable than graduates of MIT and Caltech. It is, in short, the revenge of the nerds!*

*Of course, this is not to say that technology will replace human judgment altogether. As with other successful technologies, financial technology will succeed by* leveraging *human abilities, allowing us to do far more efficiently what we have been doing all along and liberating us from the more menial tasks that can be readily automated and delegated. But this suggests that the biggest challenges over the next few decades for financial engineering will not lie in improving existing technologies, but rather in focusing on aspects of human judgment that are now considered impossible to mimic computationally: fear, greed and other emotional aspects of decision-making. Recent advances in the cognitive sciences, neurobiology and computer science may provide some clues to solving these tantalizing problems in financial contexts.*

*In this respect, financial engineering is following a path not unlike those of the engineering disciplines in their formative stages: applications tend to drive the technology, yet research and development are characterized by an intellectual entrepreneurialism that cuts across many different methodologies. Although some of the mathematical and statistical machinery displayed at the cutting edge of the field may seem foreign to the financial community, rest assured that if they prove their worth, they will quickly become absorbed into the mainstream of financial practice.*

*No one has illustrated this entrepreneurialism more eloquently than Harry Markowitz, the father of modern portfolio theory and a joint winner of the 1990 Nobel Prize in Economics. In his Nobel address, he described his experience as a PhD student on the eve of his graduation: "When I defended my dissertation as a student in the Economics Department of the University of Chicago, Professor Milton Friedman argued that portfolio theory was not Economics, and that they could not award me a PhD degree in Economics for a dissertation which was not Economics. I assume that he was only half serious, since they did award me the degree without long debate. As to the merits of his arguments, at this point I am quite willing to concede: at the time I defended my dissertation, portfolio theory was not part of Economics. But now it is."*

## Where next?

Andrew Lo's research results and the implication that there are pockets of predictability in the stock market lend support to contrarian strategies of buying *losers* and selling *winners* (see *Contrarian Investing*). But he is less convinced by investment strategies based on the insights of behavioral finance into psychological biases inherent in human cognition, which aim to take advantage of individual "irrationality" (see *Investor Psychology*).

As financial engineering attempts to define itself as a field with connections closer to the engineering disciplines than more traditional finance, associations are being set up, and the general engineering community does not quite know what to do. Patenting is becoming a big issue. Recent changes in patent laws and interpretations, along with encouragements for universities to do more patenting have led to an explosion of new patents. Some of these are in financial engineering but it is not clear which can be defended. Certainly, financial patents will have an impact on the efficiency of markets and the rate of financial innovation.

Financial engineering is also having an impact on banking. Innovation in combination with electronic technology is creating a world in which maturity transformation – turning short-term deposits into long-term loans, the central function of banks – is unnecessary. Economic agents – individuals, households, companies – will no longer require this service. Their portfolios of assets and liabilities will be broadly matched in maturity terms: short-term assets will match short-term liabilities, longer-term liabilities will offset longer-term assets. As a result, as Peter Martin of the *Financial Times* suggests, "traditional banking is dying. But the grieving throng around the deathbed face a long and expensive vigil."

Finally, what about market innovations? Financial innovations have been fast and furious over the past two decades. But why are market innovations so slow in coming? We have known for a long time what to do: integrate global markets electronically; pay shares in decimals not fractions; open the specialist books and stock exchanges like the New York Stock Exchange; record and display publicly the questions and answers exchanged by companies and analysts. Indeed, we could even go further and encourage insider trading, bringing insiders' wisdom into the market sooner rather than holding out, waiting for culprits to take advantage of us. It could be done, merely by identifying fewer insiders and letting them trade, at which point they would identify themselves. All of these things and more could be done in a stroke.

## Read on

### In print

- John Campbell, Andrew Lo and Craig Mackinlay, *The Econometrics of Financial Markets* (Princeton University Press, 1997)
- Andrew Lo and Craig Mackinlay, *A Non-Random Walk Down Wall Street* (Princeton University Press, 1999)
- Burton Malkiel, *A Random Walk Down Wall Street: Including a Life-Cycle Guide to Personal Investing* (Seventh edition, WW Norton, 1999)
- Peter Newman, Murray Milgate and John Eatwell, *The New Palgrave Dictionary of Money and Finance* (Stockton Press, 1992).

### Online

- *linux.agsm.ucla.edu/dir/* – an international directory of financial economists
- *web.mit.edu/lfe/www* – website of the Laboratory for Financial Engineering.

# Fixed Income

ixed-income securities or bonds are generally thought of as safe rather boring investments, lacking the risks associated with equities. After all, no one seems to worry about the US government defaulting on its debt and US Treasuries make up a significant proportion of the bond market. In practice, though, it is possible to lose vast amounts of money by getting the bond markets wrong. Because bonds appear to have a more definable risk profile than equities, leverage tends to be more easily obtainable. And high confidence in understanding fixed-income relationships may lead to excessive leverage and unexpected outcomes, as the case of Long-Term Capital Management (LTCM) in the late summer of 1998 vividly illustrates.

Bonds are debt instruments, securities sold by governments, companies and banks in order to raise capital. They normally carry a fixed rate of interest, known as the coupon (usually paid every six months), have a fixed redemption value (the par value) and are repaid after a fixed period (the maturity). Some – deep-discount and zero-coupon bonds – carry little or no interest, instead rewarding the buyer with a substantial discount from their redemption value and hence, the prospect of a sizeable capital gain.

As Michael Lewis explains in *Liar's Poker*, his entertaining account of life among Salomon's bond traders in the 1980s, the one thing you need to know about bonds is the relationship between their prices and interest rates. In short, as one goes up, the other goes down. This is because the fixed income paid by a bond – which when calculated as a percentage of its market price is its current yield – is equivalent to the rate of interest. If rates go up, the relative attractiveness of newly issued bonds over existing bonds increases. And since coupons are fixed, for yields to be comparable to those on new bonds, the price of existing bonds must fall.

In most developed countries outside the United States, government bonds issued in the domestic market have traditionally dominated fixed-income investors' portfolios. But with the opening of markets around the world, the range of choices has increased enormously in recent years. There are now markets not only in the government bonds of developing and transition countries (see *Emerging Markets*) but also for numerous other debt instruments: corporate bonds, junk bonds, stripped bonds, mortgage-backed securities, convertibles, and so on. In the United States, the Treasury bond market is now significantly smaller than the mortgage and corporate bond markets.

Credit quality has become a key issue. For example, emerging market and corporate bonds generally carry a risk premium over US government bonds, with higher yields to reflect the more variable creditworthiness of their issuers and the greater risk of default. Periodically, bonds of an entire category – sovereign debt, real estate, junk – become nearly worthless. Under these conditions, there is a preference for liquidity and quality, making refinancing difficult or impossible for less than top quality issuers.

Interest rates and credit risks are crucial considerations in fixed-income investing but perhaps most important of all is the expected future path of inflation. Inflation is bad for bonds, eroding their value as prices and yields, unless index-linked, fail to keep pace with rising prices. What is more, higher inflation or the prospect of higher inflation is usually associated with higher interest rates, as policy-makers tighten monetary conditions in order to try to contain inflation or protect a weakening currency (see *Foreign Exchange* and *International Money*). This makes cash more attractive, pushing down bond returns.

The yield curve is a means of comparing rates on bonds of different maturities, as well as an indication of the tightness of monetary conditions. Longer term yields are usually higher because of the greater degree of time and inflation risk. They are a good indicator of expected trends in the rate of interest and the rate of inflation. When short-term rates are higher, there is an inverted yield curve.

It is vital for active fixed-income investors to look for changes in expectations about the future rates of interest and inflation. Key indicators of these are the strength of the economy and the framework of fiscal and monetary policy (see *Economic Forecasting* and *Politics and Investing*). Bond markets tend to like signs of economic weakness since strong growth might trigger inflation. They also like fiscal policies that dampen the economy, squeezing out inflation.

Indeed, bond traders have become increasingly effective in preventing governments from introducing policies that may reignite inflation, hence driving interest rates higher and bond prices down. Their actual or implied threat to flee the markets in response to such policies has led to them being called *vigilantes*, and to presidential adviser James Carville's famous remark, "I used to think that if there was reincarnation, I wanted to come back as the President or the Pope. But now I want to be the bond market: you can intimidate everybody."

Steven Mintz uses a good analogy to describe the way to approach the bond markets in his book *The Art of Investing*. He writes:

*Investing in bonds requires attention to more than one event at a time. Driving a car requires a foot on the gas, hands on the wheel, and eyes on the road. Navigating the bond market requires a foot on interest rates, a handle on the prospects of being repaid, and an eye on inflation.*

## Fixed income guru: Andrew Carter

"If Andy Carter did not invent active fixed-income management, he is one of its very earliest practitioners," comments Peter Bernstein, someone well qualified to observe fixed-income history. And perhaps nothing epitomizes the development of investment management more than the changes in fixed-income practice in the last 30 years.

Classic investment finance reserves the function of providing funds to run a business to equity. Borrowing, whether short-term or long-term, is matched to the payment flows of specific projects for interest and repayment of principal.

We have come a long way since this basic early understanding. Today, fixed-income instruments have rather little to do with specific projects but are another device, like equity, to raise permanent capital. As such, bonds are expected to be refinanced and bond quality is as much a measure of the likelihood of new investors to step forward to replace those who wish to move on to other investments as it is a measure of the profitability of business projects.

Bonds in the 1950s and 1960s were purchased by institutional investors for the major part of their portfolios and were normally held to maturity. These investors might have occasionally altered their quality preference, using rating agencies to attest to bond quality and covenants, but the modest changes they made were almost entirely through their selection of new issues. It was a slow, deliberate process. And expected bond returns were likely to be the coupon return to maturity and the repayment of principal. Many fixed-income portfolios were carried on an institution's accounts at par or purchase price, unadjusted for fluctuations in market value. After all, there was unlikely to be a sale before maturity so recognition of market fluctuations by changes in interest rates or creditworthiness was immaterial.

But then came the emergence of active fixed-income management. Sometime around the bull market excesses of the late 1960s and the collapse of equities in mid-1970s, the thought occurred to Andy Carter and a few others that bonds presented an opportunity for swaps. By studying the underlying characteristics of one bond, it might be possible to find a comparable instrument at a cheaper price. And with the knowledge that a trade could be done with someone who lacked this insight, perhaps a small but promising gain could be captured. Thus, the bond trading business and bond capital gain business were born.

Andy Carter looks like a flashy, dour Scot. Wearing a signature bow tie, he is totally immersed in the full range of fixed-income active management, having been there from day one. It tells us much about Carter that he followed his father as the top student at Loomis School and donated a residence hall there in his family's name.

Carter started in the investment business at Irving Trust in 1964. But his exploration into active fixed-income management began with the Harvard University endowment in the mid-1960s. Just as interest rates began a huge rise, the opportunity was available to show how a bond portfolio could be energized by trading compared with the historic strategy of buy-and-hold.

Carter took active bond management to a new firm, Thorndike, Doran, Paine & Lewis in Boston and then started his own operation in 1972. At both places, he collected a blue chip roster of institutional clients who expected, and received, a different style of bond management and paid equity-like fees for the service. He collected mandates of billions from demanding clients for management. Currently, he is chief executive officer of Hyperion, a bond management firm based in New York City.

Today, fixed-income management is the most quantitative of investment disciplines, incorporating the most extensive use of sophisticated derivatives and advanced statistical techniques of risk management (see *Quantitative Investing* and *Risk Management*). However, the well-publicized near demise of LTCM was active fixed-income management carried to its extreme. And Andy Carter can take the credit – or blame – for starting it all.

## Counterpoint

One of the major disadvantages of investing in bonds is that they seem to underperform equities over the long term. This conventional wisdom is strongly expressed by Wharton finance professor Jeremy Siegel, who argues for the vast superiority of the equity markets as an investment vehicle. Siegel calculates that a dollar invested in a representative group of US stocks in 1802 would have grown to $559,000 in 1997 after adjustment for inflation (which reduced the value of the dollar to seven cents over that period). In contrast, a dollar invested in long-term government bonds, short-term bills or gold would have grown after inflation to $803, $275 and $0.84 respectively.

So while bonds are usually thought to be less risky than equities, in terms of inflation-adjusted returns, they have actually been more risky for most of the nineteenth and twentieth centuries. Siegel estimates that the real return on equities over almost two hundred years was 7% a year compounded, compared to 3.5% for bonds and 2.9% for bills. What is more, the superiority of stocks grows and their riskiness falls the longer they are held: they outperform bonds and bills 60% of the time over a single year, 70% over five years, 80% over ten years and 90% over twenty years.

The credit risk of bonds is a further downside, particularly during bull markets as investors become more willing to accept risk, which tends to reduce the spread or risk premium that poorer risks pay. When the market is jolted by bad news, the spread invariably widens again dramatically, causing the poorer risks to fail. Notorious recent examples include the aftermaths of the December 1994 Mexican devaluation and the August 1998 Russian default and devaluation. The latter led to the *flight to quality* and widening of spreads that was such a problem for LTCM.

The old argument in favor of investing in bonds is that they provide current income and some degree of stability of capital. It is generally agreed that the shorter your investment horizon and the lower your risk tolerance, the higher the percentage of bonds you should have in your portfolio. But should the bond portion of a portfolio really be actively managed? Research suggests that professional forecasters find it difficult to beat a simple approach that always predicts that future interest rates are equal to current rates, and that after accounting for management fees, bond funds tend to underperform simple passive investment strategies.

Is the whole of active fixed-income management a fraud perpetuated by managers to increase fee income more than the gains, even if achieved, that could result? Certainly, bond markets are thought to be very efficient and fees should be examined carefully and, ideally, avoided entirely if possible. For example, it is hard to see how management can increase returns when the yield spread between thirty-year corporate bonds and thirty-year Treasuries is under 1%.

Then again, for individual investors, trading in the bond markets can be difficult since in many cases, the markets are not very transparent. While the bid-ask spread on US Treasuries is small because of the very liquid market, the spreads on corporate and foreign bonds can be as high as 5–6%. This is because bonds are usually traded *over the counter* with no real marketplace. Investors must rely on brokers who have a big incentive to give the bond seller and buyer the worst possible price in both directions as they make the difference.

## Guru response

Andy Carter comments:

> *I've always been amazed that people don't seem to realize that the US government is the biggest fraud in history. We generally did not pay our Revolutionary War soldiers at all, and what we did pay them with "wasn't worth a Continental." Another example: in the past thirty-five years, the US government has debased its currency by a factor of at least seven – but more probably ten-fold – thus defrauding all fixed-income investors of the vast bulk of their investment.*
>
> *It always amuses me that equities' long-term compound return is such a vastly high multiple of that from bonds in dollar terms, and yet the compound return stated as an annual percentage is only about twice as high. No one really gets to compound for very long. And the very fact that bonds are an inferior long-term holding argues that they probably should be given careful management. Someone does hold them, and that someone needs help all the more because bonds are a cheat.*
>
> *The idea that the less than 1% spread between thirty-year Treasuries and corporates means active management cannot*

*increase returns seems untrue. One could hire a manager for probably fifteen basis points and thus capture the spread. During most of my career, the spread has been under 1%, but I have captured a significant alpha for my clients. They have enjoyed an almost 7% real after-inflation rate of return since 1969, when I first decided to work with the bond market rather than against it because bonds for the first time ever contracted a future rate of return equivalent to the past nominal return from equities. There are a number of publicly offered bond funds that have rather consistently and handsomely outperformed the bond market. PIMCO, Standish, Ayer and Loomis, Sayles all have such public funds.*

*Finally, I believe you overemphasize the significance of LTCM, which is indicative of very little beyond itself. They are a hedge fund – and a highly leveraged one at that – and not a fixed-income management house.*

## Where next?

While it is true that fixed-income management is different from hedge funds, the issue of SEC registration is not really significant since it is more an issue of paperwork than a review of investment precepts. Hedge funds operating in bond markets have the same theories and practices as the most advanced fixed-income people, so there is a direct connection between the development of active bond management and LTCM. The latter is an extreme case but it comes with overconfidence in the models, and with a large segment of bond and derivative managers using the same models at the same time since they share the same education and same databases.

While historically stocks have provided substantially greater returns than bonds, there still may be good arguments for fixed-income investing. As the ads for investment products are all obliged to say, past performance is no guarantee of future performance, and many believe that bonds may outperform stocks over the next few years as stocks' recent strong performance makes them less attractive and as deflation becomes a more potent force than inflation.

Indeed, much of the recent interest on the plus side has been in the fixed-income market. While the stock market has been demonstrating volatility and generally crashing in emerging markets, the US bond market has been steadily strong. There have been two unusual circumstances: one is an inverted yield curve, where long-term rates are lower than short-term rates; the other is a flight to quality, with the quality preference spread widening dramatically. These previously occurred together in 1981, a highly inflationary period, and in 1990, when inflation was declining yet clearly positive. But to find a precedent for both happening for a sustained period, we need to look back to deflationary times almost a century ago.

It seems to be conventional wisdom that the US and European economies are in a healthy state of moderate inflation. But perhaps instead, they are mixed economies with some features still experiencing inflation, principally wages and salaries, and others experiencing deflation, principally those associated with materials and commodities. Today's forecasts are that there is likely to be even more competition from lower wages from the developing countries, which are experiencing extremely heavy deflationary pressures – and that these pressures may spread to the developed world. With the reality of deflation plus relatively high real interest rates, bonds become very attractive.

The bond markets may also be boosted by the expansion of the eurobond market in Europe in the wake of the single currency. All new government debt in the eleven *euroland* countries will be issued in euros, market practices will be harmonized giving incentives for more corporate bond issues in euros, and the market may become more transparent, liquid and efficient. It seems likely that the euro fixed-income market will come to resemble the US bond market.

Finally, it is often valuable to challenge unchallenged precepts. One of the most widely accepted assumptions is that US government short-term debt is the riskless base against which all other returns are measured. But is that always so? Not necessarily: since US debt is almost perpetual and refinanced, what happens when the debt holders, often non-US lenders today, have other uses for their funds? The largest holders of US Treasuries are Japanese and it is not difficult to imagine that they would have other uses for their funds than holding short-term US instruments. And if they and others withdraw from this market, the riskless security could become quite risky.

## Read on

### In print

- Michael Lewis, *Liar's Poker: Rising Through the Wreckage of Wall Street* (WW Norton, 1989)
- Steven Mintz, Dana Dakin, Thomas Willison and Andrew Tobias, *Beyond Wall Street: The Art of Investing* (John Wiley, 1998)
- Jeremy Siegel, *Stocks for the Long Run: The Definitive Guide to Financial Market Returns and Long-term Investment Strategies* (McGraw-Hill, 1998).

### Online

- *www.investinginbonds.com* – Bond Market Association website with useful introductory material on fixed-income investing.

# Foreign Exchange

oreign exchange (forex or FX) markets form the core of the global financial market, a seamless twenty-four hour structure dominated by sophisticated professional players – commercial banks, central banks, hedge funds and forex brokers – and often extremely volatile. Many investors, particularly American ones, tend to ignore currency movements, and few financial analysts are trained to analyze the details of forex markets. But this is a mistake. As the 1997 Asian crisis and its aftermath vividly reveal, foreign exchange these days tends to lead economic activity. And the foreign exchange markets are huge, growing and increasingly powerful.

According to the Bank for International Settlements, the central bank for central banks, average daily turnover on the world's foreign exchange markets reached almost $1,500 billion ($1.5 *trillion*) in April 1998, 26% higher than when it last measured forex flows in 43 different countries three years earlier. Transactions involving dollars on one side of the trade accounted for 87% of that forex business. Almost a third of all forex trading takes place in London, by far the world's largest center, with New York and Tokyo second and third. Although London forex trading grew more slowly than New York over the three years to 1998, its average daily turnover remains greater than New York and Tokyo combined, having risen from $464 billion to $637 billion.

To put these figures in perspective, daily trading volume on the New York Stock Exchange (NYSE) is only about $20 billion; activity in short-term US government securities is around ten times that at $200 billion; and so at $1,500 billion, foreign exchange trading is seven and a half times the volume of trading in short-term US government securities and seventy-five times NYSE trading. This volume is far greater than the size of foreign currency reserves held by any single country. The forex markets cannot be ignored: for their size and forecasting ability; and for the potential that developments in these markets have for the future of the dollar as the world's dominant currency.

In the past, trading in the real economy controlled relative currency relationships. Since most currency flows were to settle trading patterns, there was a balance as goods and capital moved at about the same speed. But now the leads and lags are the other way around. While in name, forex markets exist to facilitate international trade, in practice, the bulk of turnover in these markets is attributable to speculation. Because financial flows are many times the size of trade flows and because financial flows are nearly instantaneous, currency market levels now tend to set trade: if a country's currency becomes low relative to others, domestic producers find it easier to export. The market sets the economy.

## Foreign exchange guru: Richard Olsen

In the pre-radio and telephony days, information about markets moved by post, horses and even by carrier pigeons. Investors with information in one market would send their instructions to other markets and success was often an outcome of the speed of transferring the messages.

Today's global environment also puts a premium on speed, but it is not measured in days or hours but nanoseconds. Currency-trading departments are decentralized so that individuals, usually young, nimble and quick, can make massive decisions on their own. The trading rooms of major institutions trading currencies for their own accounts often contain no one over the age of 35, none with bonus possibilities less than multiple millions and all eager to take risks to achieve personal gain.

It is perhaps not surprising that currency markets trading in hundreds of billion dollars a day, open 24 hours and with information moving so fast that there is always the chance of an information advantage, would attract speculative attention. And not surprising either that the value of speed and ability to grasp all the markets' information at once would attract academics building new models. One of these, and one of the best, is Richard Olsen of Olsen and Associates (O&A), a high-frequency data processing firm in Zurich in which Dean LeBaron has personally invested.

A visit to O&A, in a refurbished flour mill alongside Zurichsee is like a visit to Silicon Valley. Attire is California casual, tee shirts and jeans, though Olsen does wear a tie to see clients. Dogs and bikes sit outside offices while their owners are huddled over computer keyboards. Conversation is usually in English though it is hardly the first language for the majority. Academic disciplines are mathematics, economics or almost anything else. The common characteristic of the people is smart, very smart.

Olsen and his colleagues are the best at acquiring and analyzing high-frequency data, using very advanced mathematical techniques to forecast currency movements. By high frequency, they mean second by second, and forecasting might be for an hour or so ahead, perhaps even a week if long-term – the value of high-frequency forecasts decay rapidly as the information that produced it is disseminated.

## Counterpoint

Smart as it is, there are times when the approach of Olsen and his colleagues has failed to work. Like other more simple *data mining* and historically based methods, it works in periods when currency movements are following a trend but gets *whipsawed* with penalizing transaction costs in trendless markets. And during a change in the trend, O&A might identify a turn but not know the difference between a minor and a major turn.

Yet this group comes closer to modeling how the foreign exchange world really works than others. When there are new academic insights, they are likely to note them early.

A broader social counterpoint to today's forex markets is that with this daily volume of electronic, invisible money flowing throughout the world, a single nimble trader can drive a monetary institution to the wall. A trader is often compensated by a share of the trading profit, which can put tens of millions into his or her pocket. The trading institution takes the risk and the trader takes the profit: a true asymmetrical payoff scheme operates to pyramid risks. A central bank seeking to dampen its currency swings may come forward with a few billion but this is typically something that a single trader could command. In these circumstances, a central bank attempting to influence a currency is like sending a bicycle onto a superhighway.

The size of forex trade has played its part in the series of currency crises in emerging nations during the 1990s. The capacity for massive daily foreign currency flows to take place made possible the almost overnight collapses of the currencies of Thailand, Indonesia and Russia in 1997-8. As confidence in the economies of these countries fell away, demand for their currencies dried up as investors took their capital out or stopped bringing it in. Governments had tried to buy their own currencies to underpin their value but could not keep up with the sellers. When they stopped their own forex activity, the forces of demand and supply saw the baht, rupiah and ruble in turn crash in value, deepening the crisis of confidence and economic slowdown.

Some commentators are now recommending a tax on forex dealings: for example, Nobel Laureate James Tobin has warned that free capital markets with flexible exchange rates encourage short-term speculation that can have a "devastating impact on specific industries and whole economies." To avoid this real economic havoc, he advocates a 0.5% tax on all foreign exchange transactions in order to deter speculators, a remedy dubbed the *Tobin tax*.

There are three rationales for the proposed Tobin tax: the first is that the volume of foreign exchange transactions is excessive – fifty to a hundred times greater than that required to finance international trade; the second is related to the first – reducing volatility offers more independence to national economic policy-makers; and the third is simply the tax-raising abilities of such a tax, which is linked with the view that the financial sector is relatively undertaxed.

## Guru response

Richard Olsen comments:

*Why have we focused on studying the forex markets? Researching these markets is like doing research in a nuclear reactor, where basic processes can be studied in states of high energy. In such an environment it is easier to identify the forces that drive financial markets and distinguish them from random market effects.*

*People fail to realize the importance of forex markets to support the globalization of the "investment business." Relative to trade flows, investments across borders have increased much more dramatically. The forex markets have to be able to accommodate the demands of these international investors, who want to sell their foreign holdings at a moment's notice. Even though the forex markets have grown, the growth has been insufficient to support the requirements of an international investment community.*

*The introduction of electronic transaction systems has speeded up transactions in forex dramatically during the past six years. There is a side effect that has been neglected by many of the commentators. Similar to the money multiplier, there is a* market liquidity multiplier. *If the efficiency of the transaction system increases, then transactions are settled much more quickly. This has the effect that liquidity dries up much more rapidly than in the past.*

*My inference is that today's forex markets are far too small to support our globalized financial community. The effect will be erratic price movements, as we saw on 7 October 1998 with the 20% shift in the dollar–yen exchange rate.*

*The introduction of the euro will make things worse. I think that we have to look at the euro as a merger of the European countries. Europe will thus become like one big football stadium with a strong US counterpart. The world will thus have two big football stadia. The stadia need wide roads, that is,*

*highly liquid forex markets. Unfortunately, the new dollar–*
*euro exchange rate will not be sufficiently liquid to absorb the*
*large shifts of capital that will occur between the dollar and the*
*euro.*

*Professor Amartya Sen, who received the 1998 Nobel Prize*
*for Economics, explained in great detail that starvation is not a*
*problem of a lack of food, but deficiencies in the distribution*
*system. We face a similar situation with the financial markets,*
*where the fundamental economy is in satisfactory shape, but*
*the* allocation system, *that is, the financial markets and in*
*particular the forex markets and the balance sheets of the banks,*
*are in deep trouble.*

## Where next?

Currency attacks are becoming a depressingly common feature of
the global economy. But the exact timing of the onset of an attack is
notoriously difficult to predict. Richard Olsen has developed a global financial early-warning system, which tries to do the same thing
as a gadget that tells someone when they are getting their next heart
attack.

Olsen comments:

*We have been looking at the data now for many years and we*
*have learned a lot about what really makes a market function*
*successfully. And, most importantly, how the components within*
*the market – that is, the market makers, the medium and long-*
*term investors – interact, and what is required to build a healthy*
*market or, in reverse, what leads to a negative market with*
*large-scale shocks.*

For obvious reasons, such a system would be of immense interest
to regulators and speculators.

The core determining factor of a currency's value is the health
of the real national economy, especially the balance-of-payments

current account. If there is a surplus in the current account, that is, a country sells more goods than it buys, then buyers have to acquire that currency to purchase goods. This adds to foreign reserves and bids up the price of that currency. Conversely, a current account deficit implies the need to sell the local currency in order to acquire foreign goods. Persistent current account deficits, particularly if allied with relatively low foreign reserves, indicate a problem.

A currency's value is also affected by levels of inflation and the domestic rate of interest. High rates of interest and low inflation make a currency attractive for those holding assets denominated in it. So typically one country raising interest rates while others remain the same will raise the value of its currency as money flows into the country. This will have a limited effect if the *fundamentals* are wrong.

Comparative inflation rates, interest rates and balances of payments will all give clues to likely medium-term movements of a currency. But a key factor determining short-term currency values is market sentiment. There can be a self-fueling process in which enthusiasm for a currency, or the lack of it, drives the exchange rate. Speculators might decide, as they did during the European Monetary System debacle of 1992–3 and the Asian and Russian crises of 1997–8, that a currency is overvalued or simply that there are speculative gains to be made by selling it.

Currency attacks are triggered when a small shock to the fundamentals of the economy is combined with systemic weaknesses in the corporate and banking sectors. One facet of such systemic weaknesses is the effect of belated hedging activity by some economic actors in the economy whose currency is under attack. The more these actors try to hedge, the greater is the incentive for others to follow suit. This unleashes a whiplash effect, which turns a potentially orderly depreciation into a collapse of the currency. In other words, if speculators believe a currency will come under attack, their actions will precipitate the crisis; while if they believe the currency is not in danger, their inaction will spare it from attack – attacks are self-fulfilling.

The magnitude of the shock necessary to trigger an attack need not be large, which makes predictions very difficult. Nevertheless, it is possible to draw some broad conclusions on the vulnerability of currencies to attack. In particular, there must be a pre-existing weakness, which will prevent the authorities from conducting a full-fledged defense of the currency by raising interest rates. The weakness may not be lethal in itself (though it can become lethal once the situation deteriorates) so it is a necessary condition but not a sufficient condition for a speculative attack.

Self-fulfilling attacks may affect any country – with a fixed exchange rate and high capital mobility – that is in the gray area between *fully safe* and *sure to be attacked*. Recent research suggests that countries with strong trade links with a country that has recently experienced a currency crisis is highly likely to face an attack itself – the growing phenomenon of contagion in foreign exchange markets.

## Read on

### Online

- *www.forex-cmc.co.uk* – a website called *Forex Watch*, which has a mass of charts and technical analysis of currency movements
- *www.olsen.ch* and *www.oanda.com* – the websites of O&A.

# Global Investing

*on't put all your eggs in one basket*, the principle of portfolio diversification, is widely accepted by investors. It is normally thought of in terms of the number of assets, industries or companies across which an investor is spread: a well-diversified portfolio contains equities (as well as bonds, cash, etc.) in industries whose returns do not move together. And the lower the correlation between the returns on the various equities or other assets, the less wildly the value of the whole portfolio should swing.

Less frequently is diversification considered in relation to owning equities and other assets from different countries. But with many national markets often highly uncorrelated, this form of diversification would seem to offer the strongest potential for reducing risk, while at the same time promising enhanced returns. Particularly for investors in one of the highly valued markets of the developed world, buying foreign equities uncorrelated with their domestic market should, in principle, make their overall equity portfolios less risky and more valuable.

So global investing is in the first instance about asset allocation between equities, bonds, cash and other instruments; and second, about investing in global markets. Asset allocators benefit by diversifying across asset classes; international investors benefit by diversifying their portfolio across assets in a range of different countries. The key factor for the latter is the degree of integration of the real economies of the countries concerned. It is important to understand co-movements among different markets: the more markets move together, the fewer the benefits of international diversification.

Global data for 1998 reveals significant performance differentials between regions. The MSCI World Index rose 19.7% but only two regions – Europe at 26.5% and North America at 27.1% – exceeded that. Across the emerging markets, performance ranged from a spectacular 137.5% gain in South Korea to an 83.2% decline for Russia (see *Emerging Markets*). Though somewhat narrower, differences in the developed world are just as striking: Finland gained 119.1% while Norway declined 31.2%. This large regional performance differential underscores the importance of a global portfolio strategy. An asset allocation strategy that on average correctly anticipated these differences would have added significant value.

Global investment provides a security hedge and a currency hedge. Frequently, investors do not separate the two (see *Foreign Exchange*). Nearly all academic studies suggest that the question of currency hedging should be dealt with explicitly and should not be treated as incorporated automatically within the overall global allocation. And it is important to recognize that currency hedging may be costly and can increase risk. The Asian meltdown in 1998, for example, led to the double whammy of currency devaluation and stock market collapse.

## Global investing guru: Gary Brinson

Gary Brinson is a staunch advocate of asset allocation techniques and a pioneer of global investing. In 1974, the firm now known as Brinson Partners (then a unit of First Chicago) was one of the first to invest overseas. Brinson led a management buyout of the unit in 1989 and the firm was later acquired by Swiss Bank Corporation. The latter has since merged with Union Bank of Switzerland and as a result, Brinson directs over $300 billion in institutional assets, making it one of the world's largest money managers. Brinson is also co-author with Yale finance professor Roger Ibbotson of a book about asset classes, investment theory and international investing.

The Swiss banks were interested in Brinson Partners for its money management business but perhaps even more for its ability to bring North American investment techniques to Europe and elsewhere in its network. Features that are taken for granted in the United States like performance measurement, incentive compensation, quantitative tools and hedging are less familiar in Europe (see *Performance Measurement, Quantitative Investing* and *Risk Management*). At first, the relationships were rather loose with interns coming to the Chicago headquarters for training and management coordination with the Swiss management largely by encrypted videoconferencing. More recently, the risk management and tighter controls at headquarters have dictated closer ties.

Brinson has promoted the professionalism of investment management by taking an active part in its industry association, the Association of Investment Management & Research (AIMR) and its Research Foundation. He is an advocate of small, steady incremental gains in improvement of standards. Similarly, he is an advocate for small changes in asset allocation. Consistent with the Swiss style of investing, major swings are generally unlikely to take place.

Brinson argues strongly that investment decisions should focus first and foremost on markets or asset classes since that explains roughly 90% of returns. The key is to consider overall portfolio risk rather than the risk of individual assets: a sound asset allocation combines diverse asset classes in ways that increase returns without an equal increase in risk – or reduce risk without sacrificing returns.

The world is getting smaller, so portfolios should be getting broader, Brinson contends:

> *For people to say just because I'm a resident of the United States that I'm going to restrict my investments to the United States is terribly myopic and numerous studies have shown that it really curtails investment opportunities. The more one thinks about global investment opportunities, the greater the chances of success.*

His global asset allocation strategy rests on four basic principles:

- Think global.
- The value of asset classes should not rise and fall together.
- Focus on the long term.

- Monitor and adjust allocations to accommodate changed investment climates.

Brinson believes that in a relatively short time, it will seem as odd to most investors to discuss a Europe fund's country allocations as it does now to discuss a US fund's relative exposure to each of the fifty states. In his mind, country concerns will be minimal in comparison with company concerns.

## Counterpoint

If global investing is superior to investing in only one market, why do so many investors hold disproportionate amounts of their portfolios in equities of their own domestic markets? Even sophisticated institutional investors, such as pension funds and insurance companies, tend to concentrate well over three-quarters of their equity funds in domestically quoted shares, a phenomenon known as *home bias*. Evidence of wide discrepancies between national market performances over certain periods of time suggests that these investors would maximize their returns and minimize their risks more effectively by diversifying more fully across stocks in different countries.

Various explanations for home bias have been advanced. These include IMF officials' arguments that it is, in large part, due to the substantial risks of adverse exchange rate changes, which cannot be guarded against with standard hedging techniques. Currency risks may be compounded by the different supervisory environments in particular markets, by fears that capital controls may be instituted, by taxes on international trading or simply by a wish to avoid the time and expense of maintaining and researching a more widely spread international portfolio.

Such reasoning is supported by arguments that the benefits of international diversification arise merely from the fact that different stock markets have their shares concentrated in different industries. For example, the UK privatization program of the 1980s means that utilities are a more important part of the London market than else-where (see *Initial Public Offerings*). Similarly, investment in the Swiss market implies a disproportionate bet on banking stocks, and investment in the Swedish market a commitment to basic industries. The implication is that global investing offers nothing more than exposure to additional industries.

Yet home bias on the part of institutional investors seems to be more a result of government restrictions on the amount of foreign assets pension funds and insurance companies in any given country are allowed to hold. It also may arise from the way in which fund managers' performance is assessed through reference to a local market index: even if passive indexing is not their dominant strategy, there is inevitably a strong incentive to own a good slice of the index's components (see *Indexing*). And industry analysts are often more prevalent than country analysts in fund managers' offices, suggesting a disposition to choose industrial over international diversification.

There is evidence that the covariances of global markets may be sliding closer, though Japan may be a special case. For the other members of the G-7, coordinated banking policies and facilitated information flows should tend to drive markets into a more steady alignment. On the surface, such an increase in stability could be seen as beneficial for business but would be a lessened benefit for portfolio investors attempting to diversify risk.

For example, closer links between European economies following the introduction of the euro will increase the incentive for US investors to diversify into European markets. At the same time, this may also strengthen the relationship between different European stock markets, reducing the incentive for diversification within Europe.

## *Where next?*

Recent research indicates that Americans are more likely to invest in their local regional Bell operating company than in any other.

Considering that everyone's local operator cannot be a better investment choice than any of the other six, this finding suggests the importance of investors' psychological need to feel comfortable with where they put their money. Perhaps it relates to the *endowment effect*, a phenomenon noted by behavioral finance, where people set a higher value on something they already own than they would be prepared to pay to acquire it (see *Investor Psychology*).

But if people still do have a predilection for investing in familiar stocks, they are likely to leave largely unexploited international investment opportunities and hold sub-optimally diversified portfolios. It is tempting to conjecture that such a psychological attitude might be even more pronounced in the highly diverse cultural contexts of European countries. Such an attitude could explain the lack of cross-country portfolio investments within Europe, and suggest that the internationalization of European individual portfolios will be a slow process even in the wake of the euro.

On the other hand, the potential development of a European identity and the increasing tendency to *think European* rather than *French* or *German* – a tendency that is likely to be enhanced by the advent of a shared currency – could make European investors less reluctant to hold equity stakes in companies residing in a European state different from their own. Perhaps European home bias will fade.

Of course, none of the reasons for home bias apply to the individual global investor with the funds, access to broking services and time to conduct research on the opportunities in the international equity market. It seems likely that home bias and low market correlation will diminish over time as the interconnections of the global economy become closer and the confidence of investors in overseas markets grows. But in the meantime, by leaving some lower risk and higher return possibilities relatively unexplored, they might help an investor to formulate an international investment strategy that can beat the market consistently.

There is also now a vast amount of information on global investment opportunities available on the internet. Any point on the globe is as accessible as next door. It is cheap and often free. It shifts control of time, depth of information and source to empower the user. And it is open: anyone can come in taking its knowledge and offering skills. Financial centers are described on a satellite connection, not geographic coordinates or proximity to other financial talent centers. Work takes a different form in time and space with email, videoconferencing and the internet, all of which are available at a price for the single user at his or her own site. Location becomes irrelevant.

A visit to South Africa from the United States, for example, requires probably a week of preparation, a week there, and a week of decompression on the other side – a total of three weeks, assuming we are efficient. Compare that with a day on the internet. How much information could one get on South Africa in the course of a few hours on the web? The information might be different, but it is going to be a large volume in a short period of time. You would understand the culture and the issues, and you could gain a lot of information that is hard to find out otherwise.

According to that well-known fan of investment management, Bill Gates: "Anyone who is not intimately involved with the internet and the web does so at extreme peril." This statement applies with particular force to investment analysts and private investors. For those of us who are dedicated to moving our craft forward, being ahead of others and using the best tools available, the internet is our mandate.

## Read on

### In print

- Stephen Eckett, *Investing Online: Dealing in Global Markets on the Internet* (Financial Times Pitman Publishing, 1997)
- Roger Ibbotson and Gary Brinson, *Global Investing: The Professional's Guide to the World Capital Markets* (McGraw-Hill, 1993).

## Online

- *www.global-investor.com* – Stephen Eckett's website with lots of useful links for the global investor.

# Growth Investing

G rowth investing is one of the two classical styles of investment. There are numerous different definitions of the style and some confusion about the precise relationship between growth companies and growth stocks. But a focus on growth is generally contrasted with value investing, which tends to rely more on quantitative methods of analysis (see *Value Investing*). Growth investing tends to be based more on qualitative judgments about the kind of companies that will offer remarkable growth rates and exceptional returns performance.

Growth stock investing arose as a definable concept in the United States of the 1930s – the counterpoint to the safe, secure income investing of the depression years. It was presumed that companies with a past record of growth in revenues and earnings had the momentum to carry them into the future. And they had to go farther into the future or at greater rates of growth than the market had already accorded in its discounting through current prices. T Rowe Price, who first set out the *principles of growth stock valuation* in the 1930s, wrote:

> *Growth stocks can be defined as shares in business enterprise that have demonstrated favorable underlying long-term growth in earnings and that, after careful research study, give indications of continued secular growth in the future.*

In order to turn a capital commitment into appreciation, the growth investor needs prescience about earnings or rate of growth or the market's willingness to pay for future events. At certain times in the market – for example, in the late 1960s and early 1970s and, more recently, in the late 1990s – the growth investor has been rewarded with handsome returns. Those returns have in part been the result of an increase in the number of growth investors rather than a change in the valuation systems used by an existing population of investors.

And the agreement runs backwards in that those equities that have appreciated are assumed to have growth characteristics. Almost any list of the best managed companies – a popular and recurring article in business publications – will be composed of those stocks that have had an unusually favorable price performance for some past period. Growth stocks may see the future through the rear view mirror.

## Growth investing guru: Peter Lynch

Peter Lynch is one of the best-known names in investing. He ran Fidelity's Magellan Fund for thirteen years from 1977 and in that period, Magellan was up over 2700%. Lynch managed a vast portfolio, containing over fourteen thousand stocks at any time, and turned over the whole portfolio on average once a year. Yet even in difficult markets, he was almost always opposed to assets sitting in bonds and cash. Instead, he advocated holding good quality stocks with low volatility when going defensive.

Lynch's basic message is that an individual investor can actually find great stocks before Wall Street does: using a combination of intelligence, reflection, perseverance and discipline, it is possible for the average person to uncover great investments. His central point is that products and services you use and enjoy are often provided by excellent companies. If you research these companies and find out whether or not the stock that corresponds to them is priced favorably, you have an outstanding chance at compounding market-beating returns (see *Market Efficiency*).

Critics call this simply a *buy what you like* or *invest in what you know* strategy of stock picking. Lynch counters:

*A good stock picker is good precisely because he or she loves the process: sifting through thousands of public companies; studying balance sheets; learning the workings, the real details, of industries and businesses; investigating how a company treats its customers and vice versa. This is the only way I know to find great companies, and nothing beats the feeling when it pays off.*

*While a fund manager is more or less forced into owning a long list of stocks, an individual has the luxury of owning just a few. That means you can afford to be choosy and invest only in outfits that you understand and that have a superior product or franchise with clear opportunities for expansion. You can wait until the company repeats its successful formula in several places or markets (same-store sales on the rise, earnings on the rise) before you buy the first share.*

*If you put together a portfolio of five to ten of these high achievers, there's a decent chance one of them will turn out to be a ten-, a twenty- or even a fifty-bagger, where you can make ten, twenty or fifty times your investment. With your stake divided among a handful of issues, all it takes is a couple of gains of this magnitude in a lifetime to produce superior returns.*

So what advice does Lynch give to the typical individual investor? Writing in his regular column in *Worth* magazine, he recommends:

*Find your edge and put it to work by adhering to the following rules:*

- *With every stock you own, keep track of its story in a logbook. Note any new developments and pay close attention to earnings. Is this a growth play, a cyclical play or a value play? Stocks do well for a reason and do poorly for a reason. Make sure you know the reasons.*
- *Pay attention to facts, not forecasts.*
- *Ask yourself: what will I make if I'm right, and what could I lose if I'm wrong? Look for a risk-reward ratio of three to one or better.*
- *Before you invest, check the balance sheet to see if the company is financially sound.*

- *Don't buy options, and don't invest on margin. With options, time works against you, and if you're on margin, a drop in the market can wipe you out.*
- *When several insiders are buying the company's stock at the same time, it's a positive.*
- *Average investors should be able to monitor five to ten companies at a time, but nobody is forcing you to own any of them. If you like seven, buy seven. If you like three, buy three. If you like zero, buy zero.*
- *Be patient. The stocks that have been most rewarding to me have made their greatest gains in the third or fourth year I owned them. A few took ten years.*
- *Enter early – but not too early. I often think of investing in growth companies in terms of baseball. Try to join the game in the third inning, because a company has proved itself by then. If you buy before the line-up is announced, you're taking an unnecessary risk. There's plenty of time (ten to fifteen years in some cases) between the third and the seventh innings, which is where the ten- to fifty-baggers are made. If you buy in the late innings, you may be too late.*
- *Don't buy* cheap *stocks just because they're cheap. Buy them because the fundamentals are improving.*
- *Buy small companies after they've had a chance to prove they can make a profit.*
- *Long-shots usually backfire or become* no shots.
- *If you buy a stock for the dividend, make sure the company can comfortably afford to pay the dividend out of its earnings, even in an economic slump.*
- *Investigate ten companies and you're likely to find one with bright prospects that aren't reflected in the price. Investigate fifty and you're likely to find five.*

## Counterpoint

Growth investing? Why not? Of course, the purpose of equity investing is growth, is it not? So the two words seem to be inseparably linked. But perhaps we confuse growth with appreciation. And perhaps we automatically associate past growth with future appreciation. They can differ.

As Marc Faber, our guru for *Manias, Panics and Crashes*, points out, there are two reasons why highly popular stocks, which have become viewed as growth stocks, usually end up as costly disappointments:

> *First, exciting new markets often fail to keep growing as rapidly and profitably as expected. Second, when a business achieves great success, competitors are attracted into the field, slowing growth and shrinking profit margins for the early leaders. Gotta-own stocks are very likely to be losers.*

Certainly, when growth stocks start to decelerate, when momentum ends, the price of failure is high. Once a growth stock starts to fall, it loses its momentum attractions, followers of the trend start to desert, forcing the price down further and creating a downward spiral. In such circumstances, there can be high penalties for earnings disappointments. Eventually, growth stocks fail to fulfill their original promise and disappoint investors. Then, as fallen angels they become potential seeds for future value stocks.

Some growth industries never produce any growth stocks: competition is so fierce that no one makes any money. And in a classic article published in the *Harvard Business Review* over 40 years ago, Peter Bernstein (see *Economic Forecasting*), makes the important distinction between growth stocks and growth companies:

> *Growth stocks are a happy and haphazard category of investments which, curiously enough, have little or nothing to do with growth companies. Indeed, the term* growth stock *is meaningless; a growth stock can only be identified with hindsight – it is simply a stock which went way up. But the concept of* growth company *can be used to identify the most creative, most imaginative management groups; and if, in addition, their stocks*

*are valued at a reasonable ratio to their increase in earnings power over time, the odds are favorable for appreciation in the future.*

While Peter Lynch likes growth companies, out of self-professed lack of understanding, he has tended to avoid the high-tech area, where many of the biggest individual growth stock gains of the 1990s have been made (see *Internet Investing*). His style is also limited to investing in US equities. Of course, it is true that the concept of investment in growth companies as a distinct style of equity investing seems to emerge only in maturing economies. Growth is assumed to be an integral element of any stock selection criteria in many other parts of the world (see *Emerging Markets* and *Global Investing*).

## Where next?

The epitome of growth investing was the one-decision stock era of the bull market of the early 1970s. The notion was that growth of earnings per share could be projected as a straight line on semi-log paper for the most durable, well managed companies. Predictable growth would be valued richly by investors, which would make equity capital cheaper and easier to raise. In turn, this equity could be invested at higher than average rates of return on capital, which cycled into more earnings per share. And so the money machine would turn. The proper investment strategy was to buy the right companies and hold them forever.

The index funds of the late 1990s get some of the same influence although not by overtly selecting highly regarded stocks (see *Indexing* and *Mutual Funds*). But the index tends to be more heavily weighted in those stocks. The one-decision phenomenon of the 1970s and the indexing craze of the 1990s may end up at the same place: ownership of a handful of richly valued companies whose history is not a precursor of their future. And the indexer, like the one-decision investor, is disciplined to stay invested no matter what.

Jeremy Grantham of Grantham, Mayo, Van Otterloo & Co. LLC comments:

> *Historically, at the stock levels in the United States, equity investors have over-paid for comfort (stability, information, size, consensus, market domination, brand names). Historically, equity investors have over-paid for excitement and sex appeal (growth, profitability, management skills, technological change, cyclicality, volatility, and most of all, acceleration in the above).*
>
> *Paying-up for comfort and excitement as growth managers do for example, is not necessarily foolish, for clients also like these characteristics. Conversely, when a value manager is very wrong – as he will be sooner or later – he will be fired more quickly than a growth manager. To add insult to injury, the data indicates that the best growth managers add more to growth than the best value managers can add to value, probably because the fundamentals and the prices are more dynamic for growth stocks.*

Finally, beyond the financial details of potential growth companies and growth stocks, what are the broad requirements of a successful business? And conversely, what are the features of business failure? We suggest three characteristics which, if found together, will guarantee success for failure. If a business has a combination of passion, authenticity and integrity, it will succeed. In contrast, whenever you find together the three ingredients of mediocrity, arrogance and isolation, the business or indeed the country concerned will fail.

## *Read on*

### In print

- Peter Bernstein, "Growth Companies versus Growth Stocks," *Harvard Business Review*, 1956

- Peter Lynch with John Rothchild, *Beating the Street*
- Peter Lynch with John Rothchild, *Learn to Earn: A Beginner's Guide to the Basics of Investing and Business*
- Peter Lynch with John Rothchild, *One Up on Wall Street: How to Use What You Already Know to Make Money in the Market.*

## Online

- *www.worth.com* – website of *Worth* magazine, including an archive of Peter Lynch's regular column.

# Hedge Funds

*ighwaymen of the global economy* was Malaysian prime minister Mahathir Mohamad's description of hedge funds after the devastation of his country's currency and stock market in 1997–8, which he blamed on them, particularly the fund led by George Soros. The near-collapse and $3.6 billion bailout of John Meriwether's Long Term Capital Management (LTCM) by fourteen Wall Street banks and brokerage houses in the late summer of 1998 did little to restore the reputation of these shadowy investment vehicles. What are they all about?

Hedge funds typically pool the capital of no more than a hundred high net worth individuals or institutions under the direction of a single manager or small team. Their name originally comes from the fact that unlike most institutional investors, they were able to deal in derivatives and short selling – in theory to protect or "hedge" their positions. But having begun as a way of minimizing risk, the conservative activity of hedging has become the least important of their pursuits.

Usually based in offshore tax havens like the Cayman Islands to escape the regulators and the standard reporting requirements of mutual funds, hedge funds use their freedom to borrow aggressively, to sell short, to leverage up to 20 times their paid-in capital (though LTCM had somehow borrowed over 50 times its capital base) and generally to make big but highly risky bets. They tend to focus on absolute rather than relative returns, aiming simply to make money rather than to beat an index.

But the only real difference between hedge funds and other funds are their compensation strategies. Hedge fund managers tend to be paid for performance, with a modest management fee but a substantial share of the profits the fund makes – typically 15–20% though LTCM charged 25%.

Otherwise, hedge funds are a diverse grouping of independent asset managers pursuing a variety of investment strategies, usually with minimal disclosure to investors and regulators, and most operating in a niche where they feel they understand the "rules of the game" better than anyone else. Consultancy Financial Risk Management categorizes them into four main groups in a comprehensive overview of the hedge fund market produced with investment bank Goldman Sachs.

First, there are the *macro-funds* of which Soros's fund is a leading example. These indulge in *tactical trading*, one-way speculation on the future direction of currencies, commodities, equities, bonds, derivatives or other assets. Their most-publicized activities involve speculation on exchange rate movements, usually shorting the currencies of countries whose economic policies look questionable and whose ability to maintain an exchange rate peg is weak (see *Short Selling*). Macro-funds constitute the most volatile hedge fund sector in performance terms and their correlation with traditional benchmarks is low.

Second, there are the *market-neutral* or *relative value* funds, the kind of fund LTCM described itself as. These funds are supposedly low risk because they do not depend on the direction of market movements. Instead, they try to exploit transitory pricing anomalies, regardless of whether markets rise or fall, through an arbitrage technique called *convergence trading*: spotting apparently unjustified differences in prices of assets with similar risks and betting that the prices will revert to their normal relationship. For example, LTCM was betting that historically wide spreads between emerging market and US assets and between corporate bonds and US Treasuries would narrow. Of course, as it turned out, history proved no guide to the future as spreads widened and everything moved in the wrong direction at once.

Third, there are *event-driven* funds, which invest in the arbitrage opportunities created by actual or anticipated corporate events, such as mergers, reorganizations, share buybacks and bankruptcies. Merger arbitrage, for example, involves trading in the stocks of both bidder and target on the assumption that their prices will converge if the deal goes ahead.

Lastly, there are *long-short strategy* funds, which combine equities and/or bonds in long and short positions to reduce market exposure and isolate the performance of the fund from the asset class as a whole.

Given the lack of a strict definition of hedge funds and the fact that they file no reports, it is difficult to estimate the extent of their activity. Figures for 1998 from the Hedge Fund Association suggest there are between 4000 and 5000 funds with total assets in excess of $250 billion; while according to TASS, a performance measurement firm, there are only 3000 funds but with over $300 billion in assets. But as the experience of LTCM shows, the total assets may not be a true representation of the amount of money dedicated to short-term trading activity since the funds frequently borrow substantially in order to make leveraged bets.

## Hedge fund guru: George Soros

A number of energetic people fled from behind the Iron Curtain in the years after World War II. One, George Soros, carried with him a European's sense of philosophy that he applied to understanding markets. Although not trained as an economist or accountant – perhaps because of this gap – Soros took a psychological and cultural approach to predicting markets. Through his flagship fund, the Quantum Fund, registered outside the United States for flexibility, he would take major positions for or against foreign exchange, derivatives, emerging markets, bonds, private markets or almost anything. Any market was fair game for his group. And he would use leverage to amplify his wagers when called for. Results were outstanding although the volatility was not for the faint.

More recently, he has been writing about his investment style. Coverage in news reverses his trading desk mentality never to discuss his trading positions. And his model book on reflexivity, *The Alchemy of Finance*, explains his investment approach, which factors investment expectation into structure to make things that seem obvious actually occur. Indeed, the Quantum Fund's name is a reference to Heisenberg's *Uncertainty Principle*, which describes our inability to predict the behavior of sub-atomic particles.

But Soros's main skill is as a guerrilla investor willing to explore any market, study it more than others, strike with style and quietly withdraw, most often with a profit. In 1992, he became known as "the man who broke the Bank of England" after his attack on sterling forced its exit from the European Union's fixed exchange rate system and reputedly netted the Quantum Fund $1 billion in a day.

George Soros is a complete person and public figure, described variously as hard-nosed financier, philosopher-king, and latter-day Robin Hood. The activities of his charities are well-covered and substantial, especially in the former Soviet sphere, where his Soros Foundation has been more generous than all but two other entities, both of which are big countries. He claims that over half his time now is spent giving money away. So his life is making the transition to that which could be called a *private statesman*.

Nevertheless, in 1998, Soros suffered some serious setbacks. Not only was his new book on global capitalism poorly received and the Quantum Fund forced into restructuring, but his August letter to the *Financial Times* on the economic chaos in Russia seemed to trigger the country's debt default and currency devaluation. As the *Moscow Times* noted, Soros issued what was perhaps the most humiliating statement of his career: "The turmoil in Russian financial markets is not due to anything I said or did. We have no intention of shorting the currency. In fact our portfolio would be hurt by any devaluation." But it was too late: the theory of reflexivity played a cruel joke on its creator – and on the ruble.

## Counterpoint

Hedge funds deal in a paradoxical private language worthy of the worlds of Lewis Carroll or George Orwell. Words seem to be able to mean whatever managers want them to mean: *market-neutral* positions can bankrupt a fund; *long-term capital* means a small amount of short-term capital leveraged to the hilt; and to *hedge* means to take wildly risky positions. Sometimes, even the investors do not know what strategies their funds are using. The rules of LTCM, for example, forbade investors asking what it was that gave the fund its promised edge, ostensibly because of fears of secret investment strategies leaking to competitors.

What is more, it is often not clear if, when hedge funds perform spectacularly well, their high returns owe more to investment judgment, to leverage or to the chance outcomes of purely speculative bets. After all, when a bet is risky, it will make a lot of money if the outcome is as hoped; but when it is relatively safe, the profit is meager unless the bet is big.

Hedge funds claim to be arbitrageurs rather than speculators. But it is generally agreed that there are relatively few real arbitrage opportunities – even LTCM returned money to investors in early 1998 claiming lack of opportunities – so when you find them, you have to bet big. And when the bets go wrong, you need enough capital or credit lines to stay at the table. Of course, the richer and more powerful a fund becomes, the greater its ability to influence the market in which it deals, often leading to self-fulfilling prophecies. As has been pointed out about Soros, it is not that difficult to move markets when you back your bet with $2 billion and can ride roughshod over markets and governments.

Indeed, hedge funds offer potentially high returns for the lucky few but considerable dangers when their heavy borrowing can damage a whole financial system, and their trading strategies can destabilize whole countries and markets that are not equipped to cope with mass selling of their currencies and equity markets. There is some dispute about the real impact of hedge funds but it seems indisputable that they are powerful and dominant in many markets, including emerging markets, high-yielding debt and mortgage derivatives. And the LTCM bailout suggests that there were real fears that its collapse and the fire sale of its positions would send the global markets into a tailspin.

Soros himself provides this counterpoint to some degree in his 1998 book, where he argues that markets have grown so large and powerful they can destroy countries; and markets have become so frightened that they will withdraw capital from most countries in the world. He calls for more international regulation of markets, perhaps through an international central bank or an agency to guarantee loans – a cry from the heart that MIT economics professor Paul Krugman has amusingly if harshly translated as "stop me before I speculate again."

In a different article, this one carried by *Slate* magazine, Krugman discusses LTCM and the possibility that hedge fund compensation arrangements create the incentives to take inordinate risks since managers share in the upside but not the downside. He points out that if someone lends you a trillion, they have effectively given you a put option on whatever you buy: since you can always declare bankruptcy and walk away, it is as if you owned the right to sell those assets at a fixed price whatever happens to the market. He argues that the rational way to maximize the value of the options is to invest in the riskiest, most volatile assets since if you win, you win massively, and if you lose, you merely get some bad press and lose the money you yourself put in.

## Where next?

Hedge funds and their appetite for risk continue to appeal to investors, perhaps reflecting the late stages of a bull market, where attitudes to risk shift in two complementary ways: the future appears less risky; and, at the same time, investors' appetite for risk rises. But their bad experiences in 1998, the possibility of worse in the future, and the potential regulatory backlash suggest that their fashionable status as high-end mutual funds may wane.

But one hedge fund manager definitely worth continuing to be aware of is James Cramer of Cramer, Berkowitz & Co., who is also co-founder, co-chairman and contributing editor of *TheStreet.com*, an online financial publication self-described as "dedicated to providing investors with timely, insightful, and irreverent reporting and bringing accountability to the markets and the media that cover them." This is one of the most entertaining investment sites on the internet.

## Read on

### In print

- George Soros, *The Alchemy of Finance: Reading the Mind of the Market* (John Wiley, 1994)
- George Soros, *The Crisis of Global Capitalism: Open Society Endangered* (Public Affairs, 1998)
- George Soros, *Opening the Soviet System / Underwriting Democracy*
- George Soros, *Soros on Soros: Staying Ahead of the Curve* (John Wiley, 1995).

### Online

- *web.mit.edu/krugman/www* – Paul Krugman's website (related articles are in *Slate* magazine at *www.slate.com*)
- *www.soros.org* – website of the Soros Foundation
- *www.thestreet.com* – James Cramer's online financial publication.

# *Indexing*

ndexing is an investment practice that aims to match the returns of a specified market benchmark. An indexing manager or tracker attempts to replicate the target index by holding all – or, with very large indexes, a representative sample – of the securities in the index. Traditional active management is avoided with no investments made in individual stocks or industry sectors in an effort to beat the index. The indexing approach is often described as passive, emphasizing broad diversification, low trading activity and low costs.

Indexing as an investment practice has won acceptability in the last two decades as the mechanical outgrowth of a body of academic insights about markets and managers. Indeed, it was one of the first ideas to be propounded by finance academics from their empirical studies. These pointed out that the average manager would produce sub-average results due to expenses – and above average managers would be identified and given more assets until they too became less than average. The system was the trap. After all, index accounts have prices set by all managers. In a sense, these accounts are the most managed of portfolios.

Indexing seems dull. Stock selection is done by a nameless committee at Standard & Poor's (S&P) or elsewhere for other indexes. Proportions are set by market prices, which are the aggregate wisdom of all participants. And administration is relatively simple because transactions are bunched together at the very instant at month end when the index composition may be rearranged.

In the late stages of the one-decision bull market of the 1960s, the idea of mechanically investing in the average just because it was the average would have failed. But in the mid-1970s, when a sharp market correction slayed the old gods and raised up new ones, it was just the thing. Nothing could challenge a roster of active, aggressive managers better than to have a mechanical bunny running the performance race with them – and the bunny did not require dog food.

## Indexing gurus

Early proponents of indexing were Wells Fargo, American National Bank and Batterymarch. Each had a slight variation that was designed to be superior; each had a booster or two from academia and each garnered a small percentage of some of the large pension funds in the United States. Curiously, university endowment funds, run by successful alumni, not faculty, were not among the early entrants.

Timing of the acceptance of indexing was critical. Following the nearly 50% US market decline in 1973–4, new ideas which might have been rejected just a few years earlier were sought. Ideas that challenged convention were readily accepted since conventional ideas had just demonstrated they could be costly in a decline. Each market phase brings forth its selection of new strategies to support hope and expectations. Indexing was right for the time and the time was right for indexing.

Wells Fargo endorsed investment in the full S&P 500 stock index with only a handful of de-selectees for prudence (reputedly, these handily outperformed even a risk-adjusted measure). American National had a sophisticated sampling technique to reduce transaction costs, a likely source of underperformance. And Batterymarch, thinking that index investors would ignore month to month wiggles of sampling error that would cancel in time, just bought the largest 250 stocks, which were 90% of the total. Batterymarch also tried, and failed, to promote the notion that low cost mechanical replication of any index, not just the S&P, was the goal.

Early clients were happy with the results, which kept pace with active managers even when small stocks pulled ahead in the new, quantitatively-driven market then just beginning. And more money came into the strategy in the billions. Meanwhile, the debates between passive managers, as the indexers were called in error (they were quite active promoters), and the active ones continued. Hardly an analyst meeting could be held without a debate on the program. Since there were few indexers and many active managers, the indexers' voices were strained. But they made their case with evangelistic fervor. More converts came to their side.

Investor meetings are always popular: they are usually held at attractive resorts, the topics are the most controversial, informal conversation often focuses on what to buy and sell – and they are often job markets. There are so many meetings that organizers have difficulty filling the speaker slots – so it is readily apparent how indexing could easily become the hot topic on the circuit.

Each of the major index firms did their time in the investment-meeting wrestling arena. The most common format was a challenge debate between an indexer and an active manager. One set of debaters was the late Roger Murray, formerly of Columbia University and CREEF, matched with Dean LeBaron, one of the co-authors of this book. These two appeared together so many times that they would delight each other with a *new* point. And once, in boredom with their repetitious roles, they reversed sides.

Murray's key point was that of course you could beat the averages and he had some former students who were doing just that. Besides, it was thwarting the capitalist system if everyone became a pricing parasite. LeBaron took an easily defended side – it seemed easy at the time – to do a little of both. And he had diversification charts, history, transaction prices, the lot. While to most people, indexing just did not seem right, why not try a little?

The indexers' cause was aided by negotiated brokerage transaction fees instead of fixed fees going into effect in May 1975. Since indexers were not paying for research with so-called soft dollars (to the investment manager, soft dollars are someone else's money and hard dollars are your own), they could drive down commissions immediately. And they did, often to 25% of the original levels. Later, commission rates for indexers would be zero and even less than zero when the indexer was providing merchandise for a broker to buy/sell at higher rates to other clients.

Eventually indexing, at the institutional level, became a performance tracking game. Monthly tracking with the index was the way in which managers' quality was established. Even if the index committees did something silly like add a moderately thinly-traded stock at a single moment, indexing managers would have to add one too or face the risk that waiting would prove *active* and expensive – one must behave slavishly to track.

As many expenses would be put outside the funds as possible to keep the real outcome close to the theoretical one, and since all indexers large and small were acting in concert anyway, there was no disadvantage in large size. So the big managers got bigger.

## Counterpoint

Indexing derives originally from the concept of market efficiency (see *Market Efficiency*). But markets are efficient only if investors study all available information and move prices to reflect the published data. This implies that as the market share of indexers rises, institutions will employ fewer and fewer analysts, the market will become less efficient, and this will give active managers the chance to outperform the index and index managers.

Of course, there will always be actively managed funds that outpace index funds over long periods. But is it luck or skill? Probability indicates that some investment managers may provide exceptional returns over lengthy winning streaks. But there may also be some investment managers with truly outstanding abilities who can earn superior returns over time. The problem in selecting actively managed funds is how to identify in advance those that will be consistently superior over time.

On the surface, all stock index funds should have identical total returns. But they do not because their expenses vary. Expense ratios (the percentage of costs to assets) generally range from 0.2–0.6%. The average for actively managed funds is 1.3%. Since many index funds began only in the past few years, the high-cost ones usually justify themselves by saying there was a significant start-up expense. And some index managers admit privately that high expenses exist because the funds feel they can get away with it.

Another potential problem with indexing relates to corporate governance. As indexing took off, proxy voting slowly became an issue when the normal tool for expressing dissatisfaction with corporate behavior – liquidation of a stock position – was unavailable.

Part of the index fund advantage has resulted from being 100% invested in stocks at all times in a bull market – buying stocks going up and selling those going down because of companies going in and out of the index. Indeed, this drives up the market as trackers are fully invested and do not allocate assets between equities, bonds and cash. Since most equity funds maintain cash reserves of 5–10% of net assets, they lost ground to index funds in the bull market in stocks during the 1980s and 1990s.

Of course, in periods of market declines, index funds can be expected to have somewhat larger declines than funds maintaining cash reserves. Yet they may convey the illusion of *safety*. Stock picking may work better in a flat or bear market – another justification for active managers.

Lastly, as John Kay, Director of Oxford University's Said Business School, points out, some indexes are by no means representative of their local economies:

> *When you buy the index you buy a very particular selection of companies and industries. Half the market capitalization of the FT-SE 100 today is made up of financial services, pharmaceutical and telecommunications companies. And yet these activities account for less than 10% of economic activity in Britain today.*

Kay continues:

> *Investing passively is not the same as minimizing risk – unless the risk you minimize is the risk of not matching the index, which may be true for many fund managers and trustees. But while this may be the objective of the money manager, the ob-*

*jectives of those whose money they manage are and should be different. They are concerned with absolute, not relative, risk and return. Minimizing risk, or obtaining the most efficient trade-off of risk and reward, is about diversification. And a portfolio of the stocks of large, quoted British companies has ceased to be in any way diversified, as a result of the herd instinct of capital markets and business leaders. Today it consists of a group of similar companies, with similar management styles, aspirations and strategies, increasingly concentrated in three or four global industries.*

## Where next?

Today, indexing might be 20% of total US institutional equity. And now indexing is done on a number of indices like emerging markets, industry groups and other security classes. It is rather surprising that it is not greater. One feature that may have been restraining growth is the *agency cover* of indexing, which is not as great as with an active manager: more of the responsibility of investment selection may, under some interpretations, reside with the index client than with active managers. Furthermore, if equity markets have an extended decline, indexing may be arrested in its growth.

Indexing lends itself well to being packaged with other services like performance measurement, custody and administration and corporate governance monitoring (see *Performance Measurement* and *Corporate Governance*). Thus, the management cost of indexing is often bundled with services customarily offered by large integrated banks.

Indexing is a strategy that has been applied to many different categories of investing. It provides an efficient way for investors to participate in broadly diversified portfolios. Nevertheless, many investors will continue to be attracted to the distinctive investment philosophies and strategies offered by the wide range of actively managed funds (see *Active Portfolio Management*). A suitable compromise may be to build equity and bond portfolios (or even combine them through a balanced approach) with a core holding in an appropriate index fund. Around that core investment, an investor may select specific actively managed funds that appear likely, in the investor's judgment, to add incremental investment performance over the long run.

## Read on

### In print

- Peter L Bernstein, *Capital Ideas: The Improbable Origins of Modern Wall Street* (Free Press, 1992) – contains more on the academic development and practitioner adoption of indexing.

### Online

- *www.stanford.edu/~wfsharpe* – the website of Nobel Laureate Bill Sharpe, a critic of active management
- *www.vanguard.com* – website of the Vanguard Group, which has pioneered index funds for individual investors.

# Initial Public Offerings

O ne of the most seemingly attractive areas of investment is that of initial public offerings (IPOs). Buying shares the first time they are offered to the public has considerable natural appeal, especially in a bull market, tempting investors with potentially phenomenal short-term returns as well as exposure to exciting new companies and industries. And since the early 1980s, privatizations of state-owned enterprises around the world have become an additional source of new issues, providing investors with the opportunity to get low-priced stakes in big, stable businesses, often the dominant incumbents in core sectors of the global economy.

The objective of any new issue is to achieve the highest value for the issuer, while ensuring a buoyant start to secondary trading. Shares are generally offered at a fixed price, set by the sponsors of the issue, and based on multiples, forecasts of likely future profits, or a combination of multiples and forecasts. Alternatively, in countries outside the United States, like the UK, there might be a tender offer, where no price is set in advance, leaving it to the market forces of demand and supply.

Fixed-price IPOs are frequently underpriced, providing opportunities for *stags*, investors who buy in anticipation of an immediate price rise. Big instant profits may often be made if shares can be purchased at the offer price and sold soon after dealing begins – returns in the order of 5–15% in one day, but with high variance across offerings. Understandably, such offers are often oversubscribed, leaving the sponsors to decide on the appropriate equity allocation: by ballot, by scaling-down large applications, or by giving preferential treatment to certain investors, typically their favored clients though in some cases the private investor. The method varies by country: in some countries, like the United States, it is discretionary; in others, it is mandated equal for equal submissions.

The UK privatization issues of the 1980s and 1990s tended to be markedly underpriced, sometimes coming with incentives for the private investor, and positively discriminating against the institutions in terms of allocation and even price. They have generally been regarded as a success in terms of investor returns, government revenues and improvement in corporate performance. Certainly, the UK program has inspired numerous other governments around the world to begin turning their public-sector companies into publicly quoted ones, though perhaps this is more inspired by the real performance of companies post-IPO than the amount raised at the IPO.

Like privatizations, private sector new issues are often viewed as a route to quick and easy profits, but for every ten or so successes, there is usually one that goes wrong or seriously fails to perform. Indeed, one study of the US market reveals that of nearly 5000 IPOs initiated between May 1988 and July 1998, nearly a third no longer trade their stock and 44% sell at a market price below their original offering price.

So private investors must always show great caution, being careful to study the prospectus, balance sheet and profit and loss account of any potential investment. Investing in IPOs is intrinsically risky and not for the faint of heart. Companies that have recently reported very good results or which are in fashionable industries with their best results at an indeterminate point in the future should be scrutinized especially diligently.

Investors should also note that conflicts of interest and potential abuses are rife in the distribution of new issues. IPOs are inevitably timed to benefit the seller not the buyer, aiming to extract the maximum value from the market. Indeed, several studies indicate that IPOs are usually not good investments, underperforming the market over the longer term. This may be a reflection of companies *preparing* the numbers for a couple of years, and underwriters over-hyping and sales people overselling the shares. Such activities may be particularly prevalent in the late stages of a bull market.

## Guru of IPO analysis: Ivo Welch

Finance professor Ivo Welch has an excellent "resource page" of IPO data, literature and links on his website. One feature is an assessment of the twin phenomena of short-run underpricing and long-run underperformance of new issues. On the first point, Welch notes that the typical IPO underpricing – the return from the offer price to the price when the market starts trading – is about 10%, an astonishing figure for an average daily return. He asks why issuers "leave so much money on the table" and suggests a number of reasons:

- When applying for shares in an IPO, you will typically get all the shares you requested if it is overpriced – you are a victim of the *winner's curse*. But when an IPO is underpriced, you will only get shares on rare occasions, especially if you are not a favored client of the underwriters. As a result, you come out down on average and are unlikely to apply for shares in a *fair-priced* offering. So to get you to participate at all, issuers set a lower price, and while it appears that the average IPO leaves money on the table, the typical investor cannot profit from it.
- Issuers like to donate some money to investors since they may want to return later for further funds. Investors will remember how good a deal they got with the IPO.
- Underpricing solicits information from investors about their potential interest. Why would investors tell underwriters they like an offering unless they know that by doing so, the underwriter will give them more shares for a better price?
- If one important investor defects, maybe all investors will follow. Hence, to ensure the first investor does not defect, it is better to play it safe and underprice.
- There is an agency problem for the issuer: because underwriters naturally prefer easier to harder work (especially when the price is high, which makes selling difficult), it is best to make selling a little easier for them and underprice.

While IPOs can be very profitable for institutions with relatively short investment horizons and which have access to them at their offer price, this is rather like a quick payback for early support. For in the longer term, new issues are not attractive investments. A significant body of evidence indicates that on aggregate, they have underperformed the market, typically 30–50% below comparable companies over three- to five-year periods. A study by Tim Loughran and Jay Ritter discusses some of that research and presents their own findings, which confirm IPOs' poor performance.

How can this long-run underperformance be explained? Welch explores the two most prominent explanations, the first of which is that corporate managers are smarter than the market and thus good at timing, taking advantage of *overpriced* stock. The second is that managers manipulate earnings, past and forecast, dressing IPOs up for sale. While analysts advising investors should spot these exaggerated figures, they are paid by firms in the business of selling IPOs.

## Counterpoint

In *The Intelligent Investor*, Benjamin Graham describes new issues as having a special kind of salesmanship behind them, which calls for a special degree of sales resistance. Brokers are typically rewarded with double and triple commissions for pushing new issues, and their firms earn handsome fees for advice, structure, pricing and support of the aftermarket.

Brokerage firms almost always push their own IPOs, and usually rather aggressively. In the aftermarket support function, advice to customers who have bought the stock is often one-sided. There is little evidence that issuing houses will make sale recommendations to customers who have bought the new issue even if such recommendations are warranted. And if an analyst forgets and does recommend an action counter to the distribution, that analyst will have new opportunities to explore the job market.

Studies have shown that expense control can be an important determinant of long-term investment return. But expenses tend to be ignored during exuberant markets, despite their importance, only attracting attention when markets are declining. And expenses are especially high for IPOs. By the time all underwriting and service expenses are accumulated, charges of 5–10% of an offering price are the norm. High sales charges are one of the incentives for sales people to push new issues and there are all the legal, accounting and corporate expenses that must be covered.

While privatizations around the world might seem attractive following investors' positive experiences with the UK, there are numerous complications with overseas IPOs on top of the regular difficulties of global investing. These include international differences in accounting practices and settlement arrangements; the identity and reputation of the sponsor; the language in which the prospectus is written; whether some issues are not available to non-residents; and the procedures for scaling down an application in the event of oversubscription. For example, if a German stock is oversubscribed, a non-*euroland* investor may suffer considerable exchange losses converting in and out of euros. In a great many countries, investors will have difficulty in getting the information needed, and a good broker heavily involved in this kind of business will often be hard to find.

New issues and privatizations in developing markets can cause additional conflicts. Brokering and banking may be combined so that an investment banking manager may have to offer interim financing to win the IPO business. Sometimes this link can bring down a top-notch firm like Peregrine in Hong Kong, which failed because it tied a $250 million loan guarantee to an Indonesian taxi company to tide it over until a share offer could be arranged. In between the loan guarantee and the planned share offer, Indonesia had a currency crisis and Peregrine had a balance sheet crisis.

It is conceivable that similar problems may arise as US banks get back into the new issues market. After the Depression, banking and securities were separated, but now they have come back together to meet international competition. It is possible that Goldman Sachs was close to going bankrupt in the British Telecom IPO because of a guarantee similar to that provided by Peregrine in Indonesia.

## Guru response

Ivo Welch comments:

> *Unless you are a professional like Fidelity, investing in IPOs is dangerous to your wealth. Retail investors without an especially close relationship with their broker are better off staying away from IPO offerings (or firms that have had an IPO within the last three to five years) altogether – and when it comes to money,* relationship *is a rather fleeting concept.*
>
> *The deck is stacked against retail investors. Unlike other firms, IPO issuers are explicitly permitted to restate their pre-IPO financial statements, which many IPO issuers use to show accelerating growth. In addition, like many other firms, IPO issuers can be generous in their management of reported earnings. (Manipulation is a less friendly term, but because manipulation implies an illegal activity, I have chosen to call it management.) In fact, 25–50% of all IPO issuers are so aggressive in their reported IPO earnings that investors are disappointed to the tune of 40–50% underperformance (relative to the market) in the three to five years post-IPO. An ordinary retail investor has little chance to determine this.*
>
> *You would be hard-pressed to find an investment opportunity in the public equity markets that performed as poorly as investing in IPOs. So, why do retail investors continue to pour money into IPOs? Two reasons:*
>
> - *First, some investors saliently remember such firms as Microsoft and believe that they can separate future companies like the (now bankrupt) Digital Research from the Microsofts of the world. Unfortunately, for every Microsoft and Dell, there are dozens of firms that never make it. (As*

*noted, on average, investing in all IPOs indiscriminately is a bad strategy.) My advice: don't be jealous of the neighbor who boasts about her investment in Microsoft at the time of the IPO. She probably does not tell you about her many losses.*

- *Second, many of the worst performing IPOs are pushed onto the weakest investors: widows, orphans and trust funds. They will buy and hold whatever their broker recommends. My advice: don't be one of them.*

*Most finance professors that I know – and I know hundreds – would agree that unsophisticated retail investors should put their money into some combination of bond index and stock index funds. In fact, most finance professors do this themselves, even though they spend a lot of time trying to understand which firms are good investments and which are not.*

*As I am writing this, we are witnessing the most unusual IPO market and post-IPO market that I have ever seen. Internet-related firms' public valuations have climbed through the roof. Most of these internet firms have gone public within the last two years, so they have dodged my predictions above. It seems that right now there are many more companies like Microsoft than companies like Digital Research in the internet sector.*

*But I am still sitting on the sidelines, waiting to see if internet investors are playing a game of musical chairs, with the last investors being ruined. Even though I admit that I wish I had followed my friends who have made millions speculating on the internet, the last laugh is still the best laugh.*

## Where next?

Research shows that IPOs are far more likely when valuations are high than when they are average or low. They seem to be fixtures of a bull market – an offensive strategy, often cynical – though some would say that IPOs follow up markets more than they forecast down markets.

But why, for example, did Goldman Sachs decide to cancel its planned IPO as the market turned down in the late summer of 1998? Because the market no longer supported a valuation above what the insiders considered the investment bank to be worth. But as with any IPO, that implies that they were previously planning to sell it for more than they thought it was really worth – and that potential buyers were getting carried away on a wave of overconfidence and overselling.

So IPOs should be treated as suspect. A simple trading rule is that if they start selling below the offer price on the first day of settlement, you should stop buying them. And if you are unable to acquire them at the offer price, the deck is stacked against you.

Otherwise, *flip* to your heart's – and wallet's – content. But buying new issues should be no different from investing in existing quoted companies, with decisions made on the basis of as much knowledge as you can accumulate on company and price. Supply is always likely to outweigh demand, so you can be highly selective.

Will IPOs be launched over the internet in future, and might that make them more accessible at a reasonable price to the private investor? Certainly, electronic trading is growing many times faster than conventional trading. But the potential for electronic IPOs will be greater when electronic brokers can overcome the traditional resistance of blending conventional selling groups with electronic commerce specialists. At the moment, there are regulatory impediments in the United States that presume new issues will be offered state by state to meet *blue sky* regulations rather than globally; and paper prospectuses have to be issued, which contain outmoded information compared to what a machine could do in real time.

Electronic IPOs today look more like regular issues with machines rather than telephones. They present only a modest adaptation of the old-fashioned system and maintain the normal agency price structure. However, when there is a combination of market pressure for lower costs, a regulatory framework designed for the advantages of computers and high quality issuers who demand the best technology for their issues, we shall see global electronic IPOs with an open market book, fully disclosed interests and real-time corporate information at issue costs at tiny fractions of money raised.

## Read on

### In print

- Benjamin Graham, *The Intelligent Investor: A Book of Practical Counsel* (Reprinted by HarperCollins, 1985)
- Tim Loughran and Jay Ritter, "The New Issues Puzzle," *Journal of Finance*, March 1995.

### Online

- *linux.agsm.ucla.edu/ipo* – Ivo Welch's "IPO resource page" with useful links to other relevant sites
- *www.sec.gov* – the SEC's website, which includes details of recent and forthcoming offerings through its EDGAR database
- *www.ipocentral.com* – another IPO information website.

# International Money

nvestment decisions must increasingly be made with an eye on what is happening throughout the world economy. As barriers to trade and financial flows between countries have come down, the global movement of goods, services and capital has made national economies more and more interdependent. Daily currency flows approximate four months of world trade. A single country's long-term financial plans can be swamped in a few days by ravenous traders sensing weakness. And watertight doors of credit agreements and domestic central banks collapse under the weight of collective monetary movements.

In these circumstances, it is no longer possible for governments and central banks to conduct monetary policy at the national level: policy cooperation through international bodies like the IMF and the G-7 has become essential. And it seems certain that a crisis in one part of the world will ultimately affect everyone else. One senses that the private view of government officials and bankers is that something has to be done. But what? Disagreements that were previously guarded now flare in public. Yet all that can be agreed is to form a new committee or meeting group.

The forces of globalization and liberalization have led to major changes in the way central banks go about their principal tasks. Markets have become much more powerful: they discipline unsustainable policies; and they give participants ways to get round administrative restrictions on their freedom of action. This means that central banks have to work with rather than against market forces. Maintaining low inflation requires the credibility to harness market expectations in its support. And effective prudential supervision involves *incentive-compatible* regulation.

In monetary policy, attempts to exploit a supposed trade-off between inflation and unemployment have given way to a focus on achieving price stability as the best environment in which to pursue sustainable growth. The intermediate goals of monetary policy have also changed. Monetary targets and exchange-rate pegs have proved difficult to use in practice, and an increasing number of countries have adopted inflation targets, backed up by transparency in the policy-making process and independence of action for central banks.

The objective of financial stability has acquired much more prominence in recent years, following various high-profile mishaps at individual institutions and severe problems in some financial systems. It has become harder to segment different types of financial activity or to apply restrictions to the activities of individual institutions. Systemic stability requires ensuring that financial institutions properly understand and manage the risks they acquire, and hold an appropriate level of capital against them.

The international monetary system has been through a major transformation in the past 25 years. The Bretton Woods system developed at the end of World War II was *government-led*: official bodies decided on exchange rates and the provision of liquidity, and oversaw the international adjustment process. Now, the system is *market-led*: major exchange rates are floating; liquidity is determined by the market; and the adjustment mechanism operates through market forces. The job of central banks is to see that market forces work efficiently and that any instability is counteracted. This seems to mean stable and sustainable macroeconomic policies, and, where possible, action to ensure that inevitable changes in the direction and intensity of capital flows do not destabilize financial systems.

Changes in interest rates, inflation rates and exchange rates across the international monetary system are likely to have a significant impact on investments of all kinds. But of overriding importance at this turn of the century is what has become known as the global crisis. What started in the summer of 1997 as a regional economic and financial crisis in Asia had developed into global financial turmoil by the summer of 1998. The troubles spread to Russia with its debt default and currency devaluation; and they have since threatened Latin America. Meanwhile, Japan, the number two economy in the world, has sunk into a depression from which it seems powerless to recover.

Despite the respite seemingly provided by coordinated interest rate cuts led by the US Federal Reserve, the global crisis is still with us. It seems unlikely that the United States can continue for long to be "an island of prosperity in a sea of depression." In a new and increasingly unstable system, the benefits gained by quickly grasping the dynamics are huge. A scholarly and instinctive approach is needed.

## Guru of international money: Martin Barnes

Martin Barnes has a tough job. He took over the editorship of the *Bank Credit Analyst*, the leading newsletter of international monetary commentary, from Tony Boeckh, who put the publication on the map. Following Boeckh, who in turn had succeeded the newsletter's founder, Hamilton Bolton, was no simple task. Barnes had to be balanced but appeal to the generally conservative, absolute return clientele that he served. And he did it in a masterly way so that now the BCA, as the monthly publication is informally called, carries his stamp.

Barnes is the serious Scot of literature. But talking about finance and global figures brings forth a twinkle. He finds global finance a world of amazement and wonder. And his charge is to survey it all, to sort and make something of the pieces he likes. He brings a classicist's range of intellect to the task. And numbers are the language of his choice. Give him a set of data, and he is likely to produce a chart, perhaps going back fifty years, illustrating a parallel to the conditions he sees today.

Barnes is a real long-termer in a market where the long term typically means a week or a little longer over holidays. Thus he has trouble with the market demands of hour-by-hour trading insights. His tools are not that fine but rather suited to cycles: one of his favorites, for example, is long-wave dynamics, which have a periodicity of about 60 years. But Barnes balances the demand for *nowism* with perspective. And he, Boeckh and their colleagues have broadened the geographic coverage of the BCA and its stablemate publications in the BCA group to cover with equal intensity every developed market, most major developing ones and all instruments. If you had to choose between a daily chart book or the BCA, you would be better off taking Barnes' work. It not only tells you where you are on the investment map but, more importantly, which map you have.

Barnes' research and writing cover a broad spectrum of subjects of relevance to investors. In the past few years, he has written extensively about new technologies and long-wave cycles, the financial market implications of low inflation and trends in corporate profitability. For example, in the BCA's outlook for 1999, he outlines his perspective on the changing nature of international economics:

> *The key problem facing the global economy is excess supply, not financial fragility. The key symptoms of excess supply are falling returns on capital and downward pressure on traded goods prices. This creates a deflationary environment that is very bearish for corporate earnings. There are several other imbalances in the world economy. The United States has a negative personal savings rate, a large current account deficit and massive household exposure to an extremely overvalued stock market. In Japan, there is the opposite problem of excess savings and a current account surplus.*

Barnes detects the possible end of a financial era as the millennium looms. In the October 1998 issue of the BCA, he writes:

> *The combined real returns from US bonds and equities were at an all-time record during the bull market since 1982, spawning a massive expansion in the economy's financial infrastructure. This extraordinary financial era, largely driven by declining inflation and falling interest rates, is drawing to a close. A decline in financial returns to more normal levels will probably*

*trigger a major consolidation in the financial services sector.
This could be a volatile adjustment as hedge funds and other
money managers strive to sustain double digit returns in a single
digit world.*

## Counterpoint

"Money makes the world go round," went the song from *The
Threepenny Opera* – and it does. But the theory of money is often
misunderstood. Many of us think of money as a thing, as a constant, as capital, as something that can be preserved. We forget that
money is not a thing. It is a promise – a promise amid a chain of
other promises. And if any part of that chain breaks and cannot be
replaced by some stronger action or force, or replaced within the
chain itself, then all the promises are broken. Money is now shrinking on a global basis, and shrinking very drastically because we are
doubtful that the promises can be kept.

Old ideas are abandoned only when they have proven faulty,
and surely many of the premises of the international monetary system have given a resounding signal that they are no good. Despite
the work and the money spent in studying global economics, we
know very little. Largely, we are studying old, outmoded precepts.
We can do no harm by accepting the challenge to use complexity to
find new ones. When we incorporate the principles of complexity,
we have a chance, just a chance, to understand this adaptive world
better.

For example, the conventional IMF view of development says
that sound policies – tight money, balanced budgets, flexible labor
markets – will attract capital, boost exports and help promote non-
inflationary economic growth. Indeed, much of the work of the
IMF is offering macroeconomic policy advice that politicians can
sell as their own, and promoting microeconomic reforms that might
otherwise be politically unacceptable. A complexity view, in contrast, suggests that economies are not necessarily homogeneous and
that growth can come in many forms: through internal demand as

in China as well as through exports as in the Asian tigers prior to the crisis.

There is an idea on the part of developing countries that pre-scribed behavior – democracy, human rights, environmental con-cerns – will lead to cheap, long-term money. It is quite possible that the advice of the post-war period for development of war-ravaged areas was good for the early days of developing markets, coupled with large amounts of money when none other was available. But it may be that growth, at whatever cost, is more necessary. And post-war Japan under General MacArthur and Chile under Pinochet were hardly paragons of democratic virtue. The advice prescription from complexity is to adapt to the times.

The financial collapse in Russia has further lessons. The IMF has come to be viewed as global lender of last resort during a liquid-ity crunch, though this role was not spelled out at Bretton Woods. And the crisis has shown the institution to be no longer effective on the global scene. It is out of money, with the US Congress, among others, refusing to give it more, and it is unable to stop the flow of crisis from Asia to Japan to Russia, potentially back to China, East-ern Europe, and maybe even back to the United States. The system is broken and it seems unlikely that we can fix it at the same time as we are putting out fires. Building a new "international financial archi-tecture" is a global issue and it will take a global solution.

## Guru response

Martin Barnes comments:

> As far as the global picture is concerned, I suppose one question is whether the crisis that started in Asia represents a failure of the free-market system, as some have contended. I do not be-lieve so and I would argue that the move to more open markets simply exposed the fault lines created in economies where mar-ket forces were being suppressed or distorted by government in-tervention, crony capitalism and a lack of financial transpar-

*ency. One could further argue that the growth of information technology will force governments to be more open to the benefit of long-run economic prospects. Perhaps there is no room for the middle ground. Governments will have to decide to either fully embrace a free-market model or impose a closed siege economy, with all that entails. The latter will be increasingly hard to do, however, in an* information age *of e-cash, the internet etc.*

*Perhaps it is not so much a new global financial architecture that is needed as a more open endorsement of free-trade principles. Of course, there will always be lots of volatility in capital flows and often these can be destabilizing to individual economies. I would have thought that such problems could be dealt with by micro-policies aimed at controlling certain types of short-term capital flows.*

*I continue to be struck by the growing divergence between the US and overseas economies. It has long struck me that Europeans have always misunderstood and underestimated the strength of America. They find the US political system chaotic compared with a parliamentary system, but fail to take account of the checks and balances. They mistakenly think that many of the new jobs are* hamburger flippers, *they are obsessed with the US crime rate and income inequalities. Yet look at the record: who has fast growth, low unemployment, a budget surplus, a lead in high-tech innovation, etc., etc.? Certainly not Europe!*

*Yes, the United States cannot remain an island of prosperity in a global sea of depression, but the benefits of having a flexible and dynamic economic structure will become increasingly important in the new global economy and the United States has a big advantage on that score. Could the United States remain in a long-wave upturn while the rest of the world flounders? It would not seem possible yet we cannot rule it out. Most likely, I suppose that building global deflationary forces would eventually crush the US stock market and that could unleash a very bearish cycle of negative feedback loops.*

## *Where next?*

The world economy seems to be at a rare inflection point with sharply declining commodity prices; the impotence of institutions set up to correct long-outmoded problems; an increase in local control and a turn away from globalization; financial breakdowns with sharply reduced money velocity; an absence of political leadership; and an evaporation of wealth in many parts of the world.

Perhaps we can learn where we are in the economic cycle by studying culture rather than economics. Culture generally precedes economics rather than the other way round. Culturally, fifty years ago, we had the development of very strong western institutions. Governments were strong; multinational organizations were strong. The system developed at Bretton Woods created interlocking currencies, which were held strong by the agreements of central banks.

Twenty-five years ago, we began seeing the rise of independence of some institutions, the development of tribes and clans and coordinating activities among these tribes and clans. Individuals were beginning to feel confident about their futures, and they developed a need for teamwork and coaching, rather than hierarchies and autocracies.

Now, we are even further along in the cycle. Individuals want to be pre-eminent. Instead of being interlocked by communications, we are empowering individuals with technology. And individuals themselves want to be measured and judged based on their own entrepreneurial, economic returns rather than on their membership in a team or group. This is a normal stage of a sixty-year upwards economic cycle. But the important thing is, what comes next: do we want a safety net or do we want an open roof?

One major economic and cultural shift looks likely to be a transition from inflation to deflation. In an inflationary environment, where money steadily loses its purchasing power, the public holds as little money as is convenient for transaction purposes, and the store-of-value property of money is of secondary importance for monetary policy. In contrast, money can become a relatively desirable asset in a deflationary world in which its purchasing power is expected to rise steadily.

Once the possibility of deflation is in the public's mind, central banks should begin to take steps to reduce the likelihood of deflation scares. Such scares are potentially dangerous because they can lead people to behave in a way that actually creates deflation. If people begin to believe that the purchasing power of money will rise significantly over time, then it has an incentive to hoard cash. By hoarding cash and deferring spending, the public creates a deficiency of aggregate demand and unemployment – the very conditions that can bring on deflation.

Protracted inflation is a monetary phenomenon that can be controlled by a determined central bank. Similarly, a central bank has the power to guard against deflation by pursuing sufficiently expansionary monetary policy. To begin the fight against deflation, central banks might consider explaining the mechanics of deflation fighting to the public. It would also be helpful to announce a lower bound on a tolerance range for inflation. They might even announce their contingency plans for fighting deflation in order to increase further their anti-deflation credibility.

Martin Barnes comments:

> *Interestingly, at their December 1998 meeting, one member of the Bank of Japan's Policy Board proposed a directive aimed at boosting the inflation rate to 1% in the medium term. This proposal was defeated by eight votes to one, even though many members were concerned about the risks of deflation. It is perhaps not surprising that the Bank of Japan is unwilling to support debt monetization as this is the kind of action that central bankers around the world have spent the past 20 years discrediting.*

Finally, there is the central issue of creating a new global lender of last resort, whose role is formally recognized by national governments and financial markets. Bretton Woods almost launched a worldwide central bank but the project was abandoned at the last moment because the United States did not want it. Now, the need has arisen again, recognized even by Stanley Fischer, first deputy director at the IMF, who has nominated his institution for such a role. But the IMF has no money and cannot create it: it must get money from its major members on a case-by-case basis. The IMF is far from a global central bank although perhaps the Bank for International Settlements might be reconstructed to be one. Whatever institution is developed for the role, it will not happen fast enough, but it is a vital way of fixing the international monetary system.

## Read on

### In print

- *The Bank Credit Analyst* – a monthly forecast and analysis of trends in business conditions and major investment markets based on a continuous appraisal of money and credit flows.

### Online

- *www.bcapub.com* – website of the *Bank Credit Analyst* and its companion newsletters
- *www.stern.nyu.edu/~nroubini/asia/asiahomepage.html* – Nouriel Roubini's website collects key articles on the global economic crisis
- *www.1-888.com/longwave* – website with background information on long waves.

# Internet Investing

I nvesting in the internet and investing via the internet have become the new investment frontier. The potential impact of this new communications medium on business and society has been reflected in a frenzy of speculation in internet stocks, driving prices to extraordinary levels. Much of the speculation has come through online trading: the internet has enabled the emergence of the "electronic day traders," who take advantage of the wealth of online data available and the low transactions costs of online brokers to place very short-term bets on stock price movements.

Wilshire Associates, who manage the Wilshire 5000 index, a yardstick that includes all of the seventy-four thousand publicly traded companies based in the United States, calculate that internet stocks were responsible for a fifth of 1998's market gain. The big-name internet companies like Yahoo, Amazon.com and Netscape made three or four digit percentage gains that year. And NASDAQ, home of the market's hottest technology stocks, made its third biggest annual gain since being launched in 1971.

Since most internet companies are yet to show a profit, the boom in their stocks has sparked an entertaining debate about how they can be valued. Traditional tools are hardly suitable so there is instead talk of such practices as "monetizing the top line growth." Jim Seymour in *TheStreet.com* offers a tongue-in-cheek formula: "There is a very profound, if wildly inexact, kind of algebra at work here: M(omentum) + F(uture, the) = L(ooks cheap today)."

Normally, companies in an early and rapid stage of their growth have difficulties financing it. Requirements for working capital, expense *burn rates* and the discipline of optimistic forecasts used to attract financing all put pressures on the financial side of rapid-growth companies. But not with the internet: growth of customers, not necessarily revenues, seems to bring opportunities for early public issuance of stock (see *Initial Public Offerings*). Thus companies have the opportunity to *monetize* the prospect for revenue growth – monetize the top line – even before the growth can be tested as a revenue generator and before profit margins can be estimated.

By early 1999, investors seemed willing to pay virtually any price for internet stocks, causing Federal Reserve chairman Alan Greenspan to warn of a "lottery mentality." At the same time, he conceded that investors' enthusiasm for the internet made some sense:

> *The size of that potential market is so huge that you have these pie-in-the-sky type of potentials for a lot of different vehicles. And undoubtedly some of these small companies are going to succeed. The vast majority are almost sure to fail.*

For the securities industry itself, the internet has helped to democratize the investment process by providing widespread access to even the most specialized data and thus leveling the playing field for individual investors. Many freely available websites display real-time stock quotes and chat rooms provide forums for stocks not widely followed on Wall Street. There are now ways of getting information on companies, countries, regions, peoples and cultures that were, until only very recently, totally inaccessible.

## *High-tech investing guru: Geoffrey Moore*

The Technology Adoption Life Cycle, a model developed in the 1950s by Everett Rogers, describes how a new technology gets taken up by consumers. It explains how high-tech markets go through five phases as a new technology is adopted in turn by innovators, early adopters, the early majority of users, the late majority of users and the laggards. Geoffrey Moore, president of the Chasm Group, a high-tech market strategy consulting practice based in San Mateo, California, has extended this concept into marketing in the era of the personal computer and the internet. He adds the key insight that there is no smooth progression between the different stages. He has also applied the idea to the business of investing in high-tech companies.

Moore's first book, *Crossing the Chasm*, introduces the idea of a gap or *chasm* that innovative companies and their products must cross in order to reach the lucrative mainstream market. He provides guidelines for adjusting market development and marketing communications strategies to ensure that products are positioned to break into that market. The sequel, *Inside the Tornado*, explores how to capitalize on the potential for hypergrowth beyond the chasm, an ambition that demands radical shifts in market strategy.

*The Gorilla Game*, Moore's third book, co-authored with Paul Johnson and Tom Kippola, combines the market analysis methodology of the earlier books with stock valuation models to suggest how to build a solid investment strategy around purchasing and holding the stocks in what the authors call *gorilla* companies. It is distinguished from more general growth investment books (see *Growth Investing*) because it focuses exclusively on high-tech, specifically on product-oriented companies that sell into mass markets undergoing hypergrowth. Moore claims that above-average returns can be made by investing in high-tech companies that *own* their markets and are therefore worth more than traditional Wall Street accounting allows.

Moore's basic story is that the way markets adopt certain kinds of technologies ends up catapulting a single company into an extraordinarily powerful and enduring position. These companies are called gorillas, and the key for successful investors is to learn the difference between gorillas, chimps and monkeys. Gorillas are the companies that come up with the standard architecture, such as operating systems, whereas monkeys offer compatible products. Chimps are companies that tried to be gorillas but their architecture was not selected by the market.

The essence of the game is to buy a basket of stocks in all potential gorilla companies; as the gorilla emerges, sell off the rest of the basket; and hold the gorilla stock for the long term, selling it only when a new technology threatens to eradicate its power. Moore argues that the significant appreciation in gorilla stocks is directly linked to the periods of competitive advantage they enjoy and which far outreach their competitors.

## *Counterpoint*

In 1958, fiberglass boat stocks were the hot thing on the stock market and Dean LeBaron, one of the co-authors of this book, was the world's greatest expert on them. At that time, fiberglass was going to wipe out wooden boats completely: it was indestructible, light and leak-proof, and it had very low maintenance. Furthermore, from the standpoint of the builder, you could pay about $300,000 for a mold, $50 for what you put in it, and stamp out as many boats as you liked. Fiberglass fitted with the leisure-time theme of the late 1950s; it fit the manufacturing notion of high fixed costs and low variable costs; everything was right. And of course, there were not very many fiberglass boat stocks: Glaspar, Glastron and American Molded Fiberglass were the big names.

Today, internet stocks may be the equivalent of fiberglass boat stocks. Yes, the arguments are strong. Yes, there are high fixed costs and very low variable costs, and the technology does some wonderful things and fits into some major themes. But who remembers the fiberglass boat stocks now, forty years later? And who may remember the internet stocks of today, forty years or even four years from now?

Another more recent analogy for the internet industry might be the experience of the emerging markets in the early to mid-1990s: there is the same excitement of discovery, with the glamour of seemingly unbridled growth and almost infinite demand. Investors were attracted to emerging markets because little was known about the risks or any of the eventual outcomes. This is not so now: we are going through a period of increasing maturity and sobriety (see *Emerging Markets*).

The internet, on the other hand, is at the stage of emerging markets a couple of years before the Asian crisis, with enthusiasm that seems completely unchecked. Portal websites, for example, seem to be important, but it is hard to imagine that this will continue to be the case when consumers are able to comparison shop easily. The internet seems to be emerging markets all over again and it may follow exactly the same path. We are on the upside now.

As Marc Faber, our guru for *Manias, Panics and Crashes*, has pointed out, the most dangerous moment in any market boom is when fund suppliers stop paying attention and take on trust the value of the assets they are funding just because everyone else is doing it. Whenever it is expensive to monitor the value of assets but the opportunity costs of missing out on an investment appear too high to resist, a switchback effect occurs: investors stop monitoring the underlying value of the assets and look for reassurance in momentum and herd behavior.

Getting a real understanding of how internet technology will develop is very difficult, and many investors seem not to be looking very hard at the revenues of companies whose stocks they are bidding up. Indeed, many seem to believe that picking a few winners in a bull market, especially risky high-tech stocks, is a certificate of brilliance in investing. What will happen if and when markets turn down? Will online brokers be able to trade large volumes of stock in what are thin markets?

Ed Yardeni, our guru for *Politics and Investing*, also has a skeptical view of internet stocks. He writes:

> The New Economy is now the Yahoo Economy, where even the sky is no longer the limit. The outer limits are somewhere out there in cyberspace. GM and IBM were once market leaders. Now the internet stocks provide the leadership. The new theory of relativity posits that website accessors, not earnings, matter. As the custodian of yardeni.com, I should be a big supporter of this theory. Maybe I should even consider an IPO. However, while I am cyber-savvy, I'm also old-fashioned. I

*was taught that stock prices should equal the present discounted value of future earnings. In my opinion, the internet is fundamentally deflationary, which is fundamentally bad for earnings.*

## Where next?

The internet is becoming increasingly deeply embedded in our daily lives. Some of its fastest-growing uses are the commercial, wholesale and retail transactions of e-commerce. These are empowering consumers in a number of ways: advertising can be customized and directed at people who will actually find the products interesting; the purchasing convenience is tremendous; and comparison shopping becomes easy.

Intelligent mobile agents or *bots*, a new form of computing ideally suited to the heterogeneous nature of the internet, will become increasingly important. These are programs that act independently on our behalf. For example, a bot searching for airline tickets from virtual travel agencies on the internet can match preferred dates, price-range, class of travel and other features of the journey, without having to come back to us for approval. Bots equipped with some negotiating skills can be used to schedule meetings, participate in online auctions and trade in financial markets.

Library research used to depend on proximity to a well stocked set of library shelves. And then it was dependent on your research resource skills – how good you were at retrieval, sorting, copying and summarizing. Not now. It is possible to assign a bot a research task, which it will tirelessly pursue one hundred and sixty-eight hours a week, no fringe benefits required. And in theory, you could have many, many bots – and perhaps a bot to manage the bots.

Once someone becomes moderately adept at research and commerce on the web, a web addict is created. At that point, it is difficult to imagine going back to the conventional practice of looking for something through the Dewey decimal system or actually to walk – or drive in the case of the United States – to a store. Bots may also diminish the importance of branding, which we are accustomed to thinking about in a world where information is scarce. With the internet, information is not scarce – overwhelming perhaps, but not scarce – and the power of brands and portal websites may be reduced.

What is more, with new technology like agents, it may be increasingly difficult for companies to get the *lock-in* competitive advantages that the gorilla game strategy demands unless they are builders of the net or their customers are other businesses. And the empowering nature of the internet may well threaten the margins of even those companies with large market share. This explains why it is possible to be very enthusiastic about the potential of the internet but skeptical about the high valuations of internet stocks.

So is the internet primarily a spoiler of profits in industries or a net builder of profit for its industry and a breeder of new industrial applications? We can see some of the areas that it will spoil: brokers are being replaced by online financial services; e-shopping is taking over though curiously, it is not producing any more profits for the vendors; and mail is being threatened. We do know that some new industries will come, but we cannot really see what they are. It may well be that the ease of entry into the internet is so great that none of the companies will make any money by it. After all, we compare the internet with the printing press and we know that the printing press put an awful lot of monks and scribes out of business.

It seems likely that investing online will continue to expand enormously and go far beyond the speculative world of the day traders. But what impact will it have on traditional financial services? Wall Street's brokers, for example, are facing a considerable challenge as they try to deal with online discount brokers.

Bill Miller, our guru for *Active Portfolio Management*, comments:

*I think the online market is like the discount business – it just further segments the market; it doesn't replace traditional trading or brokerage. Sort of like TV to the movies, then VCRs, etc. Online traders are most like traditional discount customers, which is why Schwab is so successful at it. The do-it-yourself market is big and growing in a lot of industries, but it rarely if ever totally displaces those who want to pay for service and advice. This is different from, say, book retailing, where the best customers of Borders are the best potential customers of Amazon. The best brokerage customers, equity-oriented wealthy families who use margin are not the profile of the E-trade customer, whose demographics are entirely different. They may merge in a generation or so, but by then only the most dimwitted brokers will not have been able to adapt.*

Paul Farrell, mutual funds editor of *CBS MarketWatch*, takes a different view:

*The Wall Street Establishment is like a medieval priest caste, believing that they have some kind of divine right, some superior insight, some special access to the God of The Markets. No wonder the online investing revolution scares the devil out of Wall Street, why they hate do-it-yourself investors, the new breed of investors has no loyalty, isn't dependent on Wall Street, and does not believe in the Myth of Wall Street's Special Wisdom.*

Farrell continues:

*Bottom line: Wall Street's brokers are about to become the monks of the new millennium, thanks to the online investing technologies, especially the new fund supermarkets. By the year 2000, over 25% of all 65 million mutual fund investors will have online investing accounts. They are emerging as a critical mass that will control the market, transferring power from Wall Street to Main Street where the allegiance is solely to the computer, the internet and their own inner spirit.*

In June 1998, the self-styled "magazine of the digerati," *Wired*, launched what it called an index of the new blue chips:

*... in the spirit of the intrepid Mr Dow, we are launching the Wired Index. Our aim is to do for the information age what the Dow did for its predecessor: track the growth of the companies that are building the new economy – not just the usual high-tech suspects, but a broad range of enterprises that are using technology, networks and information to reshape the world.*

The magazine continued:

*Traditional financial tools are less and less effective in an economy defined more and more by intangibles. In creating the Wired Index, we looked instead for fast learners – companies already exploiting the new realities of a digital, networked world. Their fundamental qualities are: globalism (exploiting world-wide markets and open systems); communication (building brands and mindshare; networking); innovation (creating and utilizing new ideas; speed and agility); technology (using new tools to maximum effect; adaptation); and strategic vision (understanding how to be in the right place, and stay there).*

Governments try mightily to regulate the internet. Some pornographic material gets into the hands of minors and some to the citizens of countries like Singapore where it is offensive. Some governments try to tax e-commerce. And others, like the US government, seem to think the internet superhighway should be regulated on general principles. The early days of internet growth seemed driven by non-monetary goals of accomplishment. Now that money is such a component of net company planning and with shareholder expectations high and government rule-making seemingly ready to grab hold, will the internet be more useful than we have seen? It hardly seems likely, yet to date, every forecast has been broken – on the upside.

# *Read on*

## In print

- Stephen Eckett, *Investing Online: Dealing in Global Markets on the Internet* (Financial Times Pitman Publishing, 1997)
- Geoffrey Moore, *Crossing the Chasm: Marketing and Selling Technology Products to Mainstream Customers* (HarperBusiness/ Capstone Publishing, 1995)
- Geoffrey Moore, *Inside the Tornado: Marketing Strategies from Silicon Valley's Cutting Edge* (HarperBusiness/Capstone Publishing, 1995)
- Geoffrey Moore, Paul Johnson and Tom Kippola, *The Gorilla Game: An Investor's Guide to Picking Winners in High Technology* (HarperBusiness/Capstone Publishing, 1998).

## Online

- *fisher.ecn.bris.ac.uk/staff/ecnv* – website of Nir Vulkan with research on the economic implications of agent technology and e-commerce
- *stocks.wired.com* – website of the Wired Index, run in real time
- *www.gorillagame.com* – the website of the book
- *www.imagination-engines.com* – a website that illustrates what a bot will do
- *www.thestreet.com* – a good source of information and entertaining writing about the stock market
- *www.yardeni.com* – Ed Yardeni's website.

# Investment Consultants

**F**ew individual investors have the time, skills or technology to assess the value of large publicly traded corporations and other assets. Yet all are obliged to make far-reaching personal investment decisions. As a consequence, many rely on outside counsel to try and avoid costly mistakes and improve the performance of their portfolios. They seek help from a variety of brokers, financial advisers, mutual fund managers and the like.

Similarly, institutional investors such as pension funds draw on outside advice, primarily in the form of investment management firms. But in addition, the executives of these funds increasingly make use of another level of counsel: how to select the managers of their money. The need for objective information about investment managers – their people, products, processes, performance and principles – has led to the development of the institutional investment consulting industry.

Today, institutional consulting involves much more than picking good managers. The better consultants are expert on all aspects of large fund management, including asset allocation, governance and asset class strategy and structure.

## Investment consultant guru: George Russell

Some individuals in this book started companies. Some started investment styles. But few started industries. George Russell started the institutional investment consulting industry.

Pension funds began entering the equity markets in the United States during the 1960s. Following World War II, most institutions invested only in bonds to reinvest the income and protect assets in the event that the widely expected depression put the funds in danger. When confidence began to return in the 1950s and 1960s, pension funds began to look to equities for return. But their experience was limited to bonds from the previous 30 years.

George Russell saw the need for investment counsel on the research and selection of investment managers, expected demand to be huge and he met it. Using his grandfather's small mutual fund distribution company in Tacoma, Washington as a base, he went to the largest pension funds in the United States – by definition, those most in need. He brought market information gleaned from his marketing visits packaged as research and applied it to extensive work at each fund. He had a keen sense of quality, was comfortable in the corporate setting and gave conviction to the newly responsible corporate officials who hired him.

And the Russell organization, coming from what was then an improbable northwestern base, grew in stature and importance. With Russell providing sales guidance and doing the high-level contact work, and a research organization that had the first manager database, he became a necessity for pension funds and later endowment funds.

Russell could speed-dial almost anyone. He could even enter the money management field in competition with the money managers on whose performance he advised Russell consulting clients. Indeed, he formed a large and very successful investment management business based on the multi-asset class, multi-style, multi-manager strategy he used with his consulting clients. The firm's growth charged forward as Russell initiated a major international effort, with non-US firms wanting to emulate the returns in the United States.

Other consultants went into the business. Some offered more personalized services but none grew to the same scale as the Russell organization under George Russell's leadership. Every project he undertook was pursued with zeal. When raising money for a glass museum, he had a list of targets everywhere in the world. No one was safe from his aim. When he supervised the building of a large boat for himself and his wife Jane, he carried the plans with him everywhere. They would often come out between meetings and be penciled on with improvements to the builder. Mountain climbing memorabilia abound in his office. You can tell he likes to attack and win the summit.

In the early 1990s, George Russell founded Russell 20:20, a group composed of twenty money managers and twenty institutional investors interested in studying opportunities in the emerging market world. The representatives in these groups were generally chief executives or chief investment officers. High-level group visits would be planned each year to some promising command economy undergoing economic transition.

The stated purpose of studying investment possibilities was a desirable one during the emerging market boom of the early to mid-1990s. But other functions took place as well. Despite admonitions not to engage in selling, you could not put a group of twenty vendors and twenty high-level buyers together without selling taking place, albeit with subtlety. And George Russell would deny he was one of the aggressive violators of the group norm: "I am not going to push this outstanding private placement on you although there is only one place left."

The combination of a high energy level, a keen sense of needs and how to meet them, and an ability to be personal with a large number of important people produced someone who could start an industry. And someone who has wide interests in public service and support of the arts.

## Counterpoint

Conflicts of interest and business experience are often two sides of the same issue. Consultants are challenged to defend how they can preserve confidence when they consult for clients in competitive markets. They also enter into competition with money managers whom they may have as customers for services, including strategy services.

And some consultants are paid in "soft dollars" – a dubious but common practice of leaving an excess of transactions fees in commissions for easy payments for research, consulting and a wide range of other items that otherwise would be "hard dollars" – directly on the agent's account or dollars deposited directly into the fund's account, effectively reducing brokerage costs. This compensation practice is accepted as an accommodation to almost every part of the investment business but, by its inherent nature, it is a violation of the quest for lowest execution costs.

At the same time, by being in the middle of these questionable practices, consultants do get to expand their information base. In this way, they become more useful to clients, although perhaps they do so after their own needs have been met.

Increasingly, consultants have tried to shift their business from hourly fees for services to products like funds. The Russell organization has been most aggressive in competing in the consulting arena and with managed funds. And the managed funds often use the same managers as the consulting arm recommends, but at a lower fee than is accepted by the manager for clients without such influence. (The rationale for a lower fee charged to a consultant-based fund is that there is no marketing expense.)

However it may be, consultants are in the middle of almost everything that happens. The consulting firms are accused of failing to use their information for better decision recommendations to clients. Instead, the consultants may be hired to support decisions made by the client's staff people. The consultant might just be needed to give credibility, especially to bodies like pension committees of boards of directors, where the staff people need more "cover".

Charles Ellis (our guru for *Investment Policy*) writes:

> *Investment consultants – I call them selection advisers – have made a great difference in one dimension of the business and no difference at all in another. They have made a difference in terms of increasing the speed at which some investment managers accumulate or lose assets. They have had a large influence on the redistribution of assets from larger organizations to smaller ones. They have not made a difference in terms of adding value for the clients. They are not able to prove that they choose better money managers. They've gotten a lot of investors to pay*

*attention to more data, but I think they have a pretty short time horizon.*

Ellis adds:

> *There's a wonderful sign in Vail, Colorado, that all investors and clients of investors should contemplate. It's near the children's ski slope. It says: "Leave your kids for the day – $15. You watch – $20. You help – $30." The same sound interest in benign neglect should apply to investment management.*

The use of investment consultants by institutional investors outside the United States has been growing significantly in recent years. As many parts of the world have tried to recreate the financial structure developed in the United States, it is thought that a quick and easy way of doing this is to hire a consultant. Marketing advice, performance measurement and general corporate strategy have all been popular areas for which non-US managers hire consultants. The products these customers expect to receive are the techniques developed by US managers serviced by the consultant.

Consultants can provide a useful service, often if pushed to go beyond mere support for ideas already grasped. But they do so at large cost and at the risk to investment managers, who share information with them, of reducing the time a proprietary investment function may be profitable for its inventor.

## Guru response

George Russell comments:

> *It is tough to make broad generalizations about consultants. Like investment managers, they should be analyzed individually, giving credit and blame where due. Some add much more value than others. Russell has actually measured the perfor-*

mance of our buy ranked managers, and our ranks have added value. The clients who have followed our advice have shared in that outperformance; Russell's own funds certainly have.

But why do some clients not benefit from the value of our buy list? Manager research is only one element of the success. Effective implementation is equally important, and this sometimes gets neglected. Our experience has taught us that effective and timely decision-making, along with an emphasis on portfolio construction, is critical to capturing added value in a multimanager context. Plan sponsors often do not have the skills and resources required to implement as effectively as a manager of managers.

We currently advise clients with total assets in excess of $1 trillion and can document the value added in relationships that now exceed twenty-five years. With less than a 2% turnover in our client list, their long-range evaluation of the value added speaks for us. The firm, since its original goal of forty US large pension consulting clients was met in 1974, has grown at an annual compound growth rate of 24% per year since then – minor evidence of the market's opinion of at least one consultant.

The consulting business has evolved since its beginnings and things will continue to change. Our view is that going forward, companies and foundations must either build expertise internally to oversee effectively asset class strategy, implementation and selecting managers; or hire someone who can do it for them. We believe more funds will outsource the investment management function to fund-of-fund providers who do this as a core business.

## Where next?

Investment firms have a choice on how to guide their activities. They can strive to be first in some or several fields. In this case, they may be first and foolish, but they will gain a pioneering reputation for themselves and often win high rewards for clients. Or they can decide to be best. This usually means copying others, improving on their methods, taking small incremental steps to be better and marketing intensively. Both approaches are suitable to the institutional marketplace. The selection of one or the other is often due to personality, but each requires vastly different resources.

But how should institutions select their investment managers? Essentially, there are three kinds of managers. The first – the easiest to recognize – are the mediocre and arrogant ones, the ones most likely to damage you. Fortunately, there are few of these since the really bad ones are deselected quite quickly, and business takes them out of the universe. Picking the bottom 20% to ignore – assuming 20% of managers have a skill set one standard deviation below the mean – is rather easy. Most investment people can recognize the qualities to avoid in almost any profession. The middle is where it is toughest to discriminate: everyone looks alike under their marketing blankets and the differences will be minor. But it is the top group – the 20% of managers one standard deviation above the mean – that you want to look at most carefully.

Investment consultants advise looking for the three Ps: people, performance and process. Of course, people count and minds count: the investment business is a thinking one. Performance measurement too seems necessary since managers rarely get hired if they are in the bottom half of the performance spectrum. And process or *housekeeping* is obviously important. But today it is a given with the off-the-shelf tools common to most institutional managers.

Armed with these three Ps, search teams form and make decisions, usually with disappointing results. Half the managers with durable past records stumble, people come and go, process gets tighter (usually to the benchmark) and time flies. Every manager will be retained until their results are poor and they are absolutely sure to be in that position sometime. Can you look at managers and say you want them when their results are bad?

What's missing to improve the winner ratio? Two more Ps, taking the number up to five, the last of which is the most important of all and the least considered:

- Product must be examined: what is it and do you want it? Can you understand it? Most importantly, is it an asset class that will gain in usefulness and popularity? Is it sound and is it adaptable? Product tends to be forgotten except to define the niches to be filled in an asset array. But product means more than a niche or a benchmark. It means the rationale behind it: how is it adaptive and what will it become? Investment is not static and the changes are more important than the positions.
- And the last is principles: what are the manager's fundamental guides – intellectual challenge, money, selflessness or selfishness, ego, collegiality? In the clutch, when the manager has to move on instinct – and this will happen at critical positions – what will the manager do? This question depends on judgment that it is not possible to make based on facts. In naval leadership training, officers are taught that any decision that comes to the captain will not be made on facts; otherwise, it would already have been made at lower levels. So the captain's job is to make the decision on the basis of principles and to be decisive.

So in selecting an investment manager, examine the principles. If you find they do not exist, flee. If you find they do exist but you do not like them, walk away slowly. But if you find them consistent with your belief system, and if enough of the other Ps are present to satisfy you, stop searching: you are home.

## Read on

### Online

- *www.russell.com* – website of the Russell organization.

# Investment Policy

Investment policy is an all-encompassing term to describe an institutional or individual investor's overall approach to management of their portfolio: goals, asset mix, stock selection and investment strategy. As our investment policy guru Charles Ellis describes it in his classic book on the subject:

*Investment policy, wisely formulated by realistic and well-informed clients with a long-term perspective and clearly defined objectives, is the foundation upon which portfolios should be constructed and managed over time and through market cycles.*

The central point of investment policy is that different investors are in very different situations and have very different objectives. So whether acting for themselves or employing an agent, they should carefully think through the implications of their situation and objectives for the way their portfolio is to be managed. And once they have formulated the appropriate investment policy, taking account of what potential achievements are realistic, they should stick with it.

## Guru of investment policy: Charles Ellis

Charles Ellis is one of the world's most prodigious workers. He never stops. His attaché case is always with him. And he writes. And he writes. And he writes.

Ellis has written more than a dozen investment books, sends countless notes daily to people exhorting them to do something, and runs an investment consulting firm he founded. On the last point, he is at pains to remind friends and colleagues that he does not run this firm and never has. It has such great people: it does not need running. But he is the role model at least and more than that involves himself in everything.

The idea of Greenwich Associates was to survey users of financial services to find out what they wanted, what they thought of what they were getting and from whom, and to distill the data into information that could be prescriptive for vendors of services. Not very unusual although there were important differences from the norm. Senior people did the interviews, which were highly structured, and the emphasis was not on the data but on the action plans that followed. And Ellis never let any one of his clients forget that action was the important part. His notes goaded people to move.

Ellis's intensity is a way of life. He writes about the parallel between defensive tennis as a winning strategy to winning portfolios. But his tennis is anything but defensive. It is hard, determined and "exploitative of the opponent" tennis. And it wins not by flash but by never letting up for one minute. He never displays a weakness that the opponent could charge.

He is the model of the goal-oriented person. His short book on investment policy proclaims boldly that here is all you need to know in about ninety pages. And then he proceeds to demonstrate that he is correct: it is all you need to know. He sets targets for each day, each month, each year and pulls himself up to it or beyond. If he overshoots, it is because, in his opinion, he was not tough enough on himself at the beginning.

Dean LeBaron, one of this book's co-authors, says:

*I can call Charley one of a tiny group of my most treasured friends. We have worked together (I was one of his clients for a long time), vacationed together on river rafts and other challenging pursuits, helped students, been fund directors and shared mutual inspirational times when we both started companies about the same time. He never ever flagged.*

Ellis's classic book *Investment Policy*, first issued in 1985, sums up certain fundamental truths for institutional investors. His central

point is that investment has become a loser's game rather like amateur tennis, where you win by putting the ball into the net less often
than your opponent. So simply by avoiding mistakes, you will come
out ahead. His basic advice: make a long-term commitment to equities and stay invested.

In 1998, Ellis repackaged his book for the individual investor
as *Winning the Loser's Game,* which debunks any idea of investment
wizardry among the professionals. He is especially hard on market
timing, the idea that you can hope to buy the market when it is
cheap and sell near the top later on. While this sounds simple, it
does not work: markets move too fast, and even stock selection is
very hard. The key to long-term success is understanding investment risks: general market risk and specific stock risk. Indexing
carries only market risk while trying to beat the market carries extra
risks (see *Active Portfolio Management* and *Indexing*).

Ellis writes:

> *The best way to achieve long-term success is not in stock-pick-
> ing and not in market timing and not even in changing portfo-
> lio strategy. Sure, these approaches all have their current he-
> roes and "war stories," but few hero investors last for long and
> not all war stories are entirely true. The great pathway to long-
> term success comes via sound, sustained investment policy: set-
> ting the right asset mix and holding onto it.*
>
> *There are three levels of decision for the investor to make
> and whereas most investors take investment services as a blended
> package, services can be unbundled into three separate compo-
> nents or levels:*
>
> - *Level One – the optimal proportion of equities as the "policy
>   normal" for the investor's portfolio.*
> - *Level Two – equity mix, policy normal proportions in vari-
>   ous types of stocks (growth versus value, large capitalization
>   versus small capitalization, domestic versus international).*
> - *Level Three – active versus passive management.*

*Investment counseling on asset mix and on equity mix is inexpensive and needed only once every few years. (An individual investor with $1 million can buy this service from an expert for less than $5,000 once every five or ten years. An institution with $10 billion might pay $250,000.) Active management can cost – for the management and the transactions – about 1% of the $1 million investor's assets.*

*The irony is that the most value-adding service available to investors – that is, investment counseling – although demonstrably valuable and cheap, is in very little demand. Active management, though usually not successful at adding value, comes at a high cost.*

## Counterpoint

Investment managers *run* money. They *achieve* results. They *identify* errors and *correct* them. All these macho steps should produce superior, controlled investment results. But is that really how the investment world works? The physical world does not.

Instead, we may be in an iterative game of chance during which we can assess the odds used by other participants in this game and, when we find variance with *reality*, attempt to exploit the hypocrisy or stupidity of our opponents. All in real time. No wonder investment management was once described as "an exercise where you make major decisions on the basis of flimsy information in a system largely governed by chance, when you may be wrong slightly more than 50% of the time, publicly, and ... you have to go back and do it again." Most sensible people do not expose their careers to such a capricious system.

So investment policy may not be the enduring truth Charles Ellis supposes it to be. Rather it is a function of a stable, growing system where past successes can be replicated for more success to come. It does not deal with turbulence, outliers of statistical events and major changes. Policy is sluggish by its nature. Since policy is most often formulated by committees, it is hardly flexible in response to new conditions, suffers from group norm patterns, which predetermine a less than outstanding outcome, and holds its merit in preventing unconventional failure.

And policy can be discussed over and over safely with sage agreement supporting its assertions. Sturdy investment policy will triumph when conditions are more stationary than anticipated, when conventional wisdom triumphs and when group norms are respected.

The Harvard Business School had an investment case called "Vassar College," which was taught in the 1960s when Charles Ellis and Dean LeBaron were students. Vassar had an investment policy rooted in history with the support of some of the best minds of Wall Street to buy bonds in the period following World War II when yields were just a few percent. And when yields rose, and the value of the bond portfolios went down, the policy dictated, as it would, buy more bonds – until bonds yielded in the teens and Vassar's portfolio was a fraction of its original value. Policy had its costs.

In the climate of the late 1990s, investment policy, founded as it is on a long-term commitment to equities, looks fine after a long bull market. But the conventional wisdom that equities always outperform other investments eventually drives prices up to a level from which, finally, they will fail to do so. At what point does it make sense to pull back on the equity commitment?

And does investment policy as formulated by Ellis fail to take adequate account of the new opportunities of the 1990s and the next millennium, previously undreamed of? Global investing, emerging markets, internet investing – all discussed elsewhere in this book – were only a relatively short time ago never conceived of as investment ideas.

## Guru response

Charles Ellis comments:

*Death* is *every individual's ultimate reality. But as an* inves-tor, *you just may be making too much of it. If, for example, you plan to leave most of your capital in bequests to your children, the appropriate time horizon for your* family *investment policy – even if you are well into your seventies or eighties – may well be so long term that you'd be correct to ignore such investment conventions as that canard, "Older people should invest in bonds for higher income and greater safety."*

*This may* sound *okay, but the more efficacious decision for you and your family is probably to invest 100% in equities, because your* investing *horizon is far, far longer than your* liv-ing *horizon. If the people you love (your family and heirs) or even the organizations you love (your favorite charities) are likely to outlive you – as they almost certainly will – then you should extend your investment horizon to cover not just your own life span but theirs as well.*

*Don't change your investments just because you have come to a different age – or have retired. If you can afford fine paint-ings, you wouldn't change the ones you love most simply be-cause you had reached retirement or had celebrated your sev-entieth or eightieth birthday. It's the same with investments: maintain the strategy you have set for yourself if you can afford to do so.*

*Investors can – and certainly should – substantially in-crease their lifetime success by giving appropriate attention to what chess players know is important: the* endgame.

*Deciding what will be done with your capital to maximize its real value in use can be just as important as deciding how to save, accumulate and invest it. Providing for your retirement is one of three important challenges. Bequests and gifts to those you love is another. The third – "giving back" to our society – can be exciting and fulfilling.*

*Since money is such an effective way to store or transfer value, the investor with a surplus beyond his or her own lifetime's wants and needs will have the opportunity to make a difference*

*to others. Blessed is the investor whose assets do* good*; cursed*
*are those who, despite all their best intentions, cause* harm.

## Where next?

Charles Ellis defines three approaches to the pursuit of superior
investment results. They provide a useful way of thinking about
how you invest. One is intellectually difficult, one physically difficult and one emotionally difficult, as he describes:

> *Intellectually difficult investing is pursued by those who have a*
> *deep and profound understanding of the true nature of invest-*
> *ing, see the future more clearly and take long-term positions*
> *that turn out to be remarkably successful.*
>
> *Most of the crowd is deeply involved in the physically dif-*
> *ficult way of beating the market. In every way they can, they*
> *put enormous energy into trying to beat the market by outwork-*
> *ing the competition. What they don't seem to recognize is that*
> *so is almost everyone else.*
>
> *Being incapable of doing the intellectually difficult, and*
> *reluctant about the physically difficult, I have set about the*
> *emotionally difficult approach to investing. This straightforward,*
> *untiring approach is simply to work out the long-term invest-*
> *ment policy that's truly right for you and your particular cir-*
> *cumstances and is realistic given the history of the capital mar-*
> *kets, commit to it, and – here is the emotionally difficult part –*
> *hold on.*

A high-tech alternative to Ellis's vision might be tailored investment
management portfolios, where individuals could express their preferences, their psychological makeup, look at portfolios, their characteristics – and implement them all by machine. This idea got
started with indexing; then into automated trading; then stock
screening and portfolio optimization; then understanding something about mechanical asset allocation and strategic analysis of

investment options with a dose of risk management. And finally you are down to the final nub of a personality preference.

Could this all be put together into one seamless stream to build customized, personal portfolios for individuals, on-the-fly, continuously, at virtually zero implementation cost? Fifteen years or so ago, there was a project to do this. Yes, there were legal barriers, but they could have been overcome. And yes, there were barriers of feeling that you needed to have a personal contact, the "know your client" aspect, but they could have probably been overcome. In any event, for better or worse, this project did not continue through to fruition.

But others are taking it up now. For example, two firms – Financial Engines, founded by Nobel Laureate Bill Sharpe; and Rational Investors of Peabody, Massachusetts in association with Standard and Poor's – are working on applications of automated plans for employees' 401(k) retirement accounts, although they will claim it is not investment management. Perhaps the model to look at is the tailoring of clothes by machine. Landsend.com takes your measurements, puts you in an avatar on the screen so you can select your clothes, perfectly tailored, made to order for you – no inventory at Land's End. It is a tailored portfolio of clothes. Why has it taken us so long to do it for investments?

## Read on

### In print

- *The Future of Investment Management* – the presentations from four 1998 AIMR seminars, including one by Charles Ellis entitled "Lessons from the Warwick and Chateau Chambord"
- Charles Ellis, *Investment Policy: How to Win the Loser's Game* (Second edition, Irwin Professional Publishing, 1992)
- Charles Ellis, *Winning the Loser's Game: Timeless Strategies for Successful Investing* (McGraw-Hill, 1998)

- Charles Ellis with James Vertin, *The Investor's Anthology: Original Ideas from the Industry's Greatest Minds* (John Wiley, 1997).

## Online

- *www.financialengines.com* – Bill Sharpe's website for Financial Engines
- *www.landsend.com* – for the experience of "mass customized" tailored clothes, perhaps a precursor of tailored portfolios
- *www.rationalinvestors.com* – Rational Investors' website.

# Investor Psychology

W hat drives investor behavior? We would all like to think we always behave rationally while at the same time assuming that others often do not. But as investment manager Arnold Wood of Martingale Asset Management says, "if you sit down at a poker table and can't spot the sucker who will be taken that night, get up – it's you."

Most financial theory is based on the idea that everyone takes careful account of all available information before making investment decisions. But there is much evidence that this is not the case. Behavioral finance, a study of the markets that draws on psychology, is throwing more light on why people buy or sell the stocks they do – and even why they do not buy stocks at all. This research on investor behavior helps to explain the various *market anomalies* that challenge standard theory. It is emerging from the academic world and beginning to be used in money management.

An article by Yale finance professor Robert Shiller, which is available on his website, surveys some of the key ideas in behavioral finance, including:

- prospect theory
- regret theory
- anchoring
- over- and under-reaction.

Prospect theory suggests that people respond differently to equivalent situations depending on whether it is presented in the context of a loss or a gain. Typically, they become considerably more distressed at the prospect of losses than they are made happy by equivalent gains. This *loss aversion* means that people are willing to take more risks to avoid losses than to realize gains: even faced with sure gain, most investors are risk-averse; but faced with sure loss, they become risk-takers. According to the related *endowment effect*, people set a higher price on something they own than they would be prepared to pay to acquire it.

Regret theory is about people's emotional reaction to having made an error of judgment, whether buying a stock that has gone down or not buying one they considered and which has subsequently gone up. Investors may avoid selling stocks that have gone down in order to avoid the regret of having made a bad investment and the embarrassment of reporting the loss. They may also find it easier to follow the crowd and buy a popular stock: if it subsequently goes down, it can be rationalized as everyone else owned it. Going against conventional wisdom is harder since it raises the possibility of feeling regret if decisions prove incorrect (see *Contrarian Investing*).

Anchoring is a phenomenon in which, in the absence of better information, investors assume current prices are about right. In a bull market, for example, each new high is *anchored* by its closeness to the last record, and more distant history increasingly becomes an irrelevance. People tend to give too much weight to recent experience, extrapolating recent trends that are often at odds with long-run averages and probabilities.

The consequence of investors putting too much weight on recent news at the expense of other data is market over- or underreaction. People show overconfidence. They tend to become more optimistic when the market goes up and more pessimistic when the market goes down. Hence, prices fall too much on bad news and rise too much on good news. And in certain circumstances, this can lead to extreme events (see *Manias, Panics and Crashes*).

Two psychological theories underpin these views of investor behavior. The first is what Daniel Kahneman and the late Amos Tversky (co-authors of prospect theory) call the *representativeness heuristic* – where people tend to see patterns in random sequences, for example, in financial data. The second, *conservatism*, is where people chase what they see as a trend but remain slow to change their opinions in the face of new evidence that runs counter to their current view of the world.

The ideas of behavioral finance apply as much to financial analysts as they do to individual investors. For example, research indicates that professional analysts are remarkably bad at forecasting the earnings growth of individual companies. Indeed, it seems that forecasts for a particular company can be made more accurately by ignoring analysts' forecasts and forecasting earnings growth at the same rate as the average company. The underlying reasons for the abject failure of the professionals are classic behavioral finance: they like to stay close to the crowd; and their forecasts tend to extrapolate from recent past performance, which is very often a poor guide to the future (see *Economic Forecasting*).

There is evidence that institutional investors behave differently from individuals, in part because they are agents acting on behalf of the *ultimate* investors. Compensation devices like profit-splitting schemes seek to align the interests of principals with their agents – portfolio managers and other advisers – but still differences persist. For example, agents may be reluctant to take risks – even when probabilities strongly suggest they should for their clients' interests – when the risks are small but real that they might be fired.

Similarly, agents tend to favor well-known and popular companies because they are less likely to be fired if they underperform. Stock analysts as a group engage in herd behavior in part because they are constantly evaluated against their peers (see *Performance Measurement*), though research does suggest that when forecasting earnings, young analysts try to fit in with the crowd – even if the crowd is wrong – more than older ones. This is probably because a few notable failures can destroy reputations. When analysts are older and more established, it is possible that they face less risk in pursuing an independent line of thought.

Santa Clara finance professor Meir Statman makes the case for behavioral finance when he writes:

*Standard finance is so weighted down with anomalies that it makes much sense to continue the reconstruction of financial theory on behavioral lines. Proponents of standard finance often concede that their financial theory does poorly as a descrip-*

*tive or positive theory of the behavior of individuals. They re-
treat to a second line of defense: that standard finance does well
as a descriptive theory of the equilibrium that results from the
interaction of individuals in the markets. But even the second
line of defense does not hold. Evidence is mounting that even
the* capital asset pricing model *(CAPM), the market equilibrium theory by which risk and expected returns are determined
in standard finance, is not a good description of reality.*

## Gurus of behavioral finance: Richard Thaler and Robert Vishny

Considering the widespread popular acceptance of the ideas thrown
up by behavioral finance, it is unusual to observe the relatively small
amount of academic research, though what has been done is of good
quality. Experts in the field besides Kahneman and Tversky, Shiller
and Statman include Richard Thaler and Robert Vishny. Practitioners include David Dreman, who describes his investment strategies as being "totally based on behavioral finance," Bill Miller at
Legg, Mason (see *Active Portfolio Management*) and Russell Fuller.

Behavioral finance still remains at the fringes of portfolio management and modern financial theory, perhaps because there is still
no behavioral equivalent of the CAPM, a technique developed in
academia but widely used in practice. Yet many believe that the
human flaws pointed out by the analysis of investor psychology are
consistent and predictable, and that they offer investment opportunities. In his satirical novel *A Tenured Professor*, John Kenneth
Galbraith describes a Harvard academic who pursues just such a
scheme, developing a technique called the "index of irrational expectations" based on the idea that investors have a tendency to get
carried away by optimism. Can such a concept work in reality?

In a sense, Chicago finance professor Robert Vishny believes
so. His firm LSV Asset Management, which he set up with fellow
scholars Josef Lakonishok and Andre Shleifer, aims to exploit behavioral inconsistencies through the value investing approach of

buying *losers* and selling *winners* (see *Value Investing*). Vishny believes that market anomalies and investor behavior are uniform around the world – in both developed and emerging countries – and that value is a behavioral phenomenon of under-reaction. What happens is that investors underprice out-of-favor stocks while at the same time being irrationally overconfident about exciting growth companies. Not only do they like to follow the crowd, but they also get pleasure and pride from owning growth stocks (see *Growth Investing*).

Vishny believes that investors can also exploit under-reaction in momentum investing. For example, his research suggests that stocks with high past six- or twelve-month returns tend to have high future six- to twelve-month returns. This may be because of an under-reaction to information, such as dividend changes or stock splits. *Conservatism* suggests that in response to objective information, people usually recognize it, but move slowly.

Richard Thaler, professor of behavioral science and economics at the University of Chicago's business school and a pioneer of research on *quasi-rational economics*, is another scholar trying to apply his ideas in investment practice. In 1998, he co-founded with Russell Fuller, Fuller and Thaler Asset Management, a firm offering a broad line of behavioral-based investment strategies to pension funds and other institutions. Thaler intends to have a major role in strategy and marketing the firm's investment products, doing "everything but picking stocks."

Thaler describes his firm's investment approach thus:

*We capitalize on systematic mental mistakes that are caused by behavioral biases. These mental mistakes by investors result in the market developing biased expectations of future profitability and earnings of companies which, in turn, cause the securities of these companies to be mispriced. Because human behavior changes slowly, past market inefficiencies due to behavioral biases are likely to persist.*

## Counterpoint

The primary critics of behavioral finance and its use of psychology for investment management are the progenitors of the *efficient market hypothesis* (EMH). For example, Chicago finance professor Eugene Fama, one of our gurus for *Market Efficiency*, argues that:

> ... the empirical evidence is weak, they don't have a coherent theory and without that, there is no behavioral finance. Until you find something that can replace the theory of efficient markets with a systematic alternative theory, you don't have anything.

Peter Bernstein who devotes two chapters of his best-selling book on risk to the gurus of behavioral finance – whom he calls the *theory police* – is less dismissive though still critical:

> While it is important to understand that the market doesn't work the way classical models think – there is a lot of evidence of herding, the behavioral finance concept of investors irrationally following the same course of action – but I don't know what you can do with that information to manage money. I remain unconvinced anyone is consistently making money out of it.

MIT finance professor Andrew Lo concurs:

> ... taking advantage of individual irrationality cannot be a recipe for long-term success.

Certainly, it is true that there is no behavioral equivalent of the CAPM, and while markets obviously do not work as the strong versions of the EMH suggest, it can be difficult to see how a behavioral approach can be used to manage money. Perhaps behavioral finance is more of an attitude than an investment system: a helpful check at potential turning points but not an everyday guide.

## Guru response

Richard Thaler comments:

> *Regarding the absence of a behavioral CAPM, I think the two camps are equally at a loss. We know from the work of Fama and his colleague Kenneth French that the rational CAPM is false, so neither side has a complete theory. Several recent papers have tried to develop behaviorally based theories of asset pricing and while they are not the final word, they are better than nothing.*
>
> *As to whether one can make money using investor irrationality, I would ask a similar question: what else can you do? The only investment strategy consistent with rational efficient markets is indexing, and we know that if everyone indexes, the markets are no longer efficient. To me, any active management strategy that has a chance of being successful must rely either on better information or on an understanding of why other investors are producing mispriced securities. The one strategy that everyone seems to agree has worked well for a very long period of time is value – buying low price-to-earnings (p/e) or price-to-book (p/b) stocks. As Fama and French have shown, this strategy does well all around the world. I view this as a classic behavioral strategy, first advocated by Benjamin Graham in the 1930s. Time will tell as to whether other behaviorally motivated strategies yield superior long-term returns.*

Thaler goes on to explain the practical application of his ideas:

> *Behavioral biases that affect security pricing can be divided into two classes: non-economic behavior, for example, when agents do not maximize the expected value of their portfolio because they are maximizing other behavioral factors; and heuristic biases. Heuristics are mental shortcuts or rules-of-thumb, which people use to solve complex problems. But in some instances, reliance on heuristics can result in biased or mistaken*

*judgments. Such biases can cause investors to make systematic mental mistakes in evaluating new information and forming expectations about the future prospects of firms.*

*By focusing on behavioral factors that cause the market's expectations to be biased, we have successfully identified mispriced securities and generated above normal returns for our clients. We have developed strategies for exploiting the heuristic biases that cause over- and under-reaction to information. Because the heuristics are different, these strategies identify different types of stocks and, as a result, different portfolio characteristics. But both strategies tend to focus on small to mid-cap size companies.*

*For example, our growth portfolios capitalize on anchoring bias that, under certain circumstances, causes investors to under-react to new, positive information. As a result, the market's expectations are biased concerning the future profitability of these companies and their stocks tend to be underpriced. This strategy typically selects stocks that have growth characteristics. For example, these stocks generally have above average betas, p/e ratios and p/b ratios. Portfolio turnover for this strategy tends to be higher than average.*

*Our value portfolios capitalize on heuristic biases associated with representativeness and saliency. Reliance on these heuristics causes investors to over-react to bad, but temporary, information concerning the profitability of companies. In such cases, the market naively extrapolates the recent temporary negative news concerning a company, resulting in biased expectations of the company's future prospects and these stocks tend to be underpriced. This strategy typically selects stocks with value characteristics. For example, these stocks generally have below average betas, p/e ratios and p/b ratios. Portfolio turnover for this strategy tends to be below average.*

## *Where next?*

The analysis of investor psychology is having a growing impact on both investment research and practice as it seeks to expose and explain the shortcomings of modern financial theory: problems in the models used to price stocks and the difficulties of making sense of market anomalies like calendar effects. It is an important dimension of investment and almost all investors consciously or unconsciously take it into account though they call it different things. George Soros' concept of reflexivity (see *Hedge Funds*), momentum investing and agency theory all point to the *ultimate* insufficiency of traditional tools of analysis in economics and investment.

The new directions of behavioral finance are being pushed toward biological metaphors by researchers like Andrew Lo, our guru for *Financial Engineering*. If purely mechanical number computation fails to give us useful models, perhaps the complex biological functions will. Early evidence is strongly suggestive of success.

## *Read on*

### In print

- Peter L Bernstein, *Against the Gods: The Remarkable Story of Risk* (John Wiley, 1996)
- John Kenneth Galbraith, *A Tenured Professor* (Houghton Mifflin, 1991)
- Robert Shiller, *Market Volatility* (MIT Press, 1990)
- Richard Thaler (ed.), *Advances in Behavioral Finance* (Russell Sage Foundation, 1993)
- Richard Thaler, *Quasi-Rational Economics* (Russell Sage Foundation, 1992)
- Richard Thaler, *The Winner's Curse: Paradoxes and Anomalies of Economic Life* (Princeton University Press, 1994).

## Online

- *www.econ.yale.edu/~shiller/* – Robert Shiller's website
- *www.fullerthaler.com* – website of Fuller and Thaler Asset Management
- *www.undiscoveredmanagers.com* – website of a mutual fund manager featuring a useful *behavioral finance* library.

# Manias, Panics and Crashes

F inancial markets are particularly susceptible to manias, panics and crashes, where asset prices rise to extraordinary heights only for confidence and greed to turn to fear and despair, sending the market into freefall. One of the first analysts of these phenomena was Walter Bagehot, nineteenth-century editor of *The Economist*. His 1873 book, *Lombard Street*, is a powerful account of the psychology of financial markets: how investors overdose on hope and then despair, and how central banking may, to some degree, restrain self-destructive cycles of elation and panic.

Many of the classic stories of market mayhem are told in Charles Mackay's *Extraordinary Popular Delusions and the Madness of Crowds*, written in the 1840s. This study of crowd psychology and mass mania through the ages includes accounts of numerous market scams, madnesses and deceptions, notably the Mississippi Scheme that swept France in 1720; the South Sea Bubble that ruined thousands in England at the same time; and the Dutch tulipmania, when fortunes were made and lost on single tulip bulbs.

More recent histories of these extraordinary events include Martin Fridson's *It Was a Very Good Year* and *Manias, Panics and Crashes* by economist Charles Kindleberger. Kindleberger argues that there is a consistent pattern to financial manias and panics – quite apart from the ebb and flow of the business cycle – which can be controlled or moderated. He spells out the stages of the credit cycle of boom and bust:

- The upswing usually starts with an opportunity – new markets, new technologies or some dramatic political change – and investors looking for good returns.
- It proceeds through the euphoria of rising prices, particularly of assets, while an expansion of credit inflates the bubble.

- In the manic phase, investors scramble to get out of money and into illiquid things such as stocks, commodities, real estate or tulip bulbs: "a larger and larger group of people seeks to become rich without a real understanding of the processes involved."
- Ultimately, the markets stop rising and people who have borrowed heavily find themselves overstretched. This is *distress*, which generates unexpected failures, followed by *revulsion* or *discredit*.
- The final phase is a self-feeding panic, where the bubble bursts. People of wealth and credit scramble to unload whatever they have bought at greater and greater losses, and cash becomes king.

## *Guru of manias, panics and crashes: Marc Faber*

It is a German rickshaw, this white "fully dressed" BMW K1000 motorcycle weaving in and out of Hong Kong traffic. From under the helmet, the driver's ponytail bobs in the wind. No, the costume is not worn by the local constabulary but might well be a Chinese meditation gown. Where could the driver be going through the financial canyons on the Hong Kong side of the island? Surely not to the Stock Exchange building towards which he is heading, but most likely to the Bank of China building to bless some new function in its China Club.

The driver parks in a tiny space and races to an investment lunch where, of all things, he is the prestigious speaker. He is Marc Faber, Swiss by birth, oriental by self-selection, revolutionary art collector, economic historian and contrary investor to his core. Faber can expound on price indices in the first millennium after Christ, the latest technical patterns in the Malaysian market and the inner workings of China from his perch in Hong Kong. His clientele read his volumes and are devoted to his admonitions that one must flee the crowd to succeed. After turning his back on emerging markets, his forte, when they became popular, he went into Africa in a quest for the unexploited.

When cultural, economic and technical tools are blended in an inquisitive mind, one can learn some powerful market insights. For some, the wrappings of Faber's views are jarring, but to others they are an invitation to come on in to see some different facet of the world investment scene.

Faber really knows and, as his sometime label as *Doctor Doom* suggests, enjoys the extreme events of manias, panics and crashes. His monthly publication, *The Gloom, Boom & Doom Report*, is full of insights into market psychology as the following extracts on the characteristics of a speculative mania illustrate:

> *In a buying frenzy, there is, through the effect of contagion, a universal urge to participate in the whirlwind of speculation. No one wants to miss out: the public because it sees only profits and no risks and argues "what else can I invest in – there are no alternatives"; the corporate sector because it overestimates the demand for its products or is overly optimistic about future prospects; and the professional investors because they cannot afford to be out of a rapidly appreciating market.*
>
> *Near-term performance orientation, indexation, and money flows into the best performing funds force them to be in sectors which have the strongest upward moves. In a mania, therefore, the expression one hears again and again is "we cannot afford not to be in the market" or "we cannot afford not to be in this sector."*
>
> *Characteristic of every investment mania is the formation of investment pools and a rising number of new issues flooding the market. During every manic phase, cash is always regarded as a totally unattractive investment alternative.*
>
> *At the end of an investment mania, corporate insiders step up the selling of their company's shares, recognizing their overvaluations, or in anticipation of less favorable business conditions. Also symptomatic are pros who turn bearish too early, sell short and get very badly squeezed.*

## *Counterpoint*

The common theme of investment manias is that investors' enthusiasm for the market – whether it is for stakes in emerging economies, internet stocks or whatever – rapidly loses touch with the reality of what it is they are buying, even when the concept they are buying has some validity (see *Emerging Markets* and *Internet Investing*). But does that mean that they are behaving irrationally, bucking the central notions of economics, or are there sane reasons for insane markets?

Many of the behavioral finance ideas discussed in our *Investor Psychology* chapter, such as overconfidence and anchoring, can help explain the phenomena of manias and panics. For example, up or down, the market may have the right reaction to news but wildly over-react, or it may get the basic reaction wrong and/or ignore crucial bits of information. There might also be gambling on the upside, with some investors doubling their bets in a rising market, attracted by the thrill of winning and the whiff of danger.

In effect, bubbles and crashes are the *tails* of investor psychology, where herd behavior leads to extreme outcomes, first on the upside and then on the downside as confidence turns to panic. Economists use the term *multiple equilibria*, where small jolts can knock the economy from a high profit equilibrium to a low profit equilibrium, and where the fear of jolts causes market gyrations.

But what is the relationship between *rational* individuals and the irrational whole? First, people change, starting off rational but then losing contact with reality. Second, rationality can differ among different groups. And third, everyone succumbs to the *fallacy of composition*: each individual decision can be rationalized but not the whole.

The Asian crisis of 1997–8 and its fallout in Russia, Latin America and even in the United States, with the near-collapse of Long Term Capital Management, suggest that the credit cycle of mania and panic continues today on a global scale. But is it a traditional credit cycle? There are a number of reasons for thinking not:

- The period of expansion has been very long – perhaps fifty years by the post-war measure or twenty-three years, since the early 1970s, by another. Managers have not been trained by previous credit cycle experience.
- Interconnections are stronger, quicker and tighter than formerly with new institutions in the loop.
- With more instruments in the financial system, each can *create* money of an unknown amount. There are no data nor estimates of velocity, amounts or leverage, and we do not know about correlations under *stress*, the tails of the distribution.
- In the United States at least, the public is *in*. Equities are a key part of savings, which makes a crisis vulnerable to political solution, possibly compounding the problem.
- The global central bank, the IMF, is not powerful enough against the speculators to give confidence to the markets.

## Guru response

Marc Faber comments:

*A tidal wave of speculation raised the Japanese stock market in the late 1980s, then moved on to the emerging markets in 1993, and seems to have now reached the shores of the United States.*

*Today, a wave of optimism and new era thinking is sweeping through the investment community. The breakdown of communism, the opening of a large number of new markets, promising new technology, corporate downsizing and layoffs, the lack of any military threat, low inflation, falling interest rates, globalization, free trade, etc., are expected to bring about endless profit opportunities. Thus, Wall Street, led by the more speculative NASDAQ index, has displayed a stunning performance since 1990. But could we, today, be caught in a financial bubble which occurs once a generation and which will end the way previous new era-based bull markets have ended?*

*I really have no idea how many more investment books have to make the bestseller list and by how much more the shelf space they occupy in bookstores has to expand, or how many more times successful investment managers, technology companies and the internet will have to appear on front covers or make headlines, or how much more crowded high-tech conferences will become before it all ends, but clearly, the symptoms are awesome.*

## Where next?

Are there investment strategies that can take advantage of manias and panics? For contrarians like Marc Faber, who was bearish about the Asian markets for some while before the crisis began in July 1997, there are certainly opportunities. But as with all contrarian investing, it takes an unusual mindset to take positions against the views of the majority (see *Contrarian Investing*).

And there is some dispute about whether events like the Asian crisis really constitute market manias and panics. There are essentially two views: first, that it was just like a nineteenth-century British bank panic, calling for prompt action by a global "lender of last resort;" and second, that it was much worse – nothing less than the bursting of a new South Sea Bubble, a latter day long-wave cycle of liquidity evaporation, not reallocation.

Jeffrey Sachs is associated with the first analysis. He stresses the liquidity crisis facing the emerging Asian economies as foreign short-term credit was withdrawn in what he calls a creditor panic. Such *coordination failure* on the part of creditors can be appropriately handled by injecting liquidity – or by forcing creditors to roll over their loans – as Bagehot pointed out. But if the panic is triggered by fundamentals, then structural change – not just liquidity – is needed.

What if, for example, global capital had been lured by tales of miraculous growth to pouring money into a spectacular but unsustainable Asian bubble? When this bubble ended, then – just as in

Japan in 1989-90 – financial institutions would face more than a liquidity problem: they would collectively be bankrupt. And even institutions that are not bankrupt might face incentives to gamble. This account, championed by Paul Krugman, helps to explain why the IMF was unwilling or unable to throw money at the problem.

The Asian crisis points out two emerging features of the global financial landscape: deflation and nationalism. Asian countries, and almost all developing economies, sell a deflating commodity: low wage labor. They also sell commodities, which, along with the labor, have entered a long, steady decline in realizable prices. Faced with having to beg for money to stabilize, not just to grow, these countries increasingly fall back on their own resources.

As much to avoid IMF lectures as for economic purposes, countries like Malaysia are pulling back from the global community and the global idea of free and open markets. For example, Malaysian Prime Minister Mahathir Mohamad has imposed currency controls to protect his country's foreign reserves. Others may be considering the same move, which may be an end to the world's goal of a freely floating world monetary system.

The Asian crisis also indicates the dangers of financial market bubbles and crashes to the rest of the global economy. Faber argues that "major manias are usually once-a-generation affairs and lead to some serious economic damage once they come to an end." And John Kenneth Galbraith's classic account of the Great Crash notes the five weaknesses of the 1929 US economy, which led from the Crash to the Depression of the 1930s: an unequal distribution of income; bad corporate governance; a weak banking structure; a "dubious" balance of trade position; and bad economic advice.

## Read on

### In print

- Frederick Lewis Allen, *Only Yesterday: An Informal History of the 1920s* (John Wiley, 1997) – an informal history of the 1920s that includes what Walter Deemer (see *Technical Analysis*) calls the most readable and most gripping account of the events of 1929 in print

- Walter Bagehot, *Lombard Street: A Description of the Money Market* (John Wiley, 1999)
- Marc Faber, *The Great Money Illusion*
- Marc Faber's monthly newsletter, *The Gloom, Boom & Doom Report*
- Martin Fridson, *It Was a Very Good Year: Extraordinary Moments in Stock Market History* (John Wiley, 1998)
- John Kenneth Galbraith, *The Great Crash 1929* (Reprinted by Houghton Mifflin, 1997)
- Charles Kindleberger, *Manias, Panics and Crashes: A History of Financial Crises* (Third edition, John Wiley, 1996)
- Charles Mackay, *Extraordinary Popular Delusions and the Madness of Crowds* (Reprinted by John Wiley, 1995)
- Nury Vittachi, *Riding the Millennial Storm: Marc Faber's Path to Profit in the Financial Crisis* (John Wiley, 1998)
- Barnie Winkleman, *Ten Years of Wall Street* (Fraser Publishing, 1987) – contemporary account of the 1929 era first published in 1932.

## Online

- *www.marcfaber.com* – Marc Faber's website
- *web.mit.edu/krugman/www* – Paul Krugman's website
- *www.stern.nyu.edu/~nroubini/asia/asiahomepage.html* – Nouriel Roubini's website, which brings together key writings on the Asian crisis and its aftermath.

# Market Efficiency

T he efficient market hypothesis (EMH) says that at any given time, asset prices fully reflect all available information. That seemingly straightforward proposition is one of the most controversial ideas in all of social science research, and its implications continue to reverberate through investment practice. As MIT finance professor Andrew Lo writes in the introduction to two volumes that collect the key articles on the EMH:

> *... it is disarmingly simple to state, has far-reaching consequences for academic pursuits and business practice and yet it is surprisingly resilient to empirical proof or refutation.*

The simple statement implies but does not limit information to be strictly financial in nature. It may incorporate investor perceptions whether correct or otherwise. This richer interpretation of the EMH provides for variations from its stronger forms, which suggest that further data study, unless perhaps insider-based, is unlikely to be fruitful. The second derivative of an investor perception overlay on financial information allows for intuition, judgment and the quest for new tools that markets may discover in the pursuit of profits above the average.

The chief corollary of the idea that markets are efficient – that prices fully reflect all information – is that price movements do not follow any patterns or trends. This means that past price movements cannot be used to predict future price movements. Rather, prices follow what is known as a *random walk*, an intrinsically unpredictable pattern. The random walk is often compared to the path a sailor might follow out of a bar after a long, hard night of drinking.

In the world of the strong form EMH, trying to beat the market becomes a game of chance not skill. There will be superior performers generating better investment returns but only because statistically there are always some people above the average and others below. Hence, debate about the EMH becomes a question of whether active portfolio management works: is it possible to beat the market or are you better off avoiding the transactions costs and simply buying an index fund? And, as an active manager, the issue is whether it works for me, a sample size of one (see *Active Portfolio Management*)?

The answer to these questions depends not only on whether you accept the EMH but, if so, in what form. There are essentially three:

- The weak form of the EMH asserts that all past market prices and data are fully reflected in asset prices. The implication of this is that technical analysis cannot be used to beat the market (see *Technical Analysis*).
- The semi-strong form of the EMH asserts that all publicly available information is fully reflected in asset prices. The implication of this is that neither technical nor fundamental analysis can be used to beat the market.
- The strong form of the EMH asserts that all information – public and private – is fully reflected in asset prices. The implication of this is that not even insider information can be used to beat the market.

## Gurus of efficient markets: Eugene Fama and Burton Malkiel

Although the concept of the random walk can be traced back to French mathematician Louis Bachelier's doctoral thesis *The Theory of Speculation* in 1900, the EMH really starts with Nobel Laureate Paul Samuelson and his 1965 article, *Proof that Properly Anticipated Prices Fluctuate Randomly*. But it was Chicago finance professor Eugene Fama with his 1970 paper *Efficient Capital Markets* who coined the term EMH and made it operational with the foundational epithet that in efficient markets, "prices fully reflect all available information."

Fama argued that in an active market of large numbers of well-informed and intelligent investors, stocks will be appropriately priced and reflect all available information. In these circumstances, no information or analysis can be expected to result in outperformance of an appropriate benchmark. Because of the wide availability of public information, it is nearly impossible for an individual to beat the market consistently.

Another professor, Burton Malkiel of Princeton, popularized the notion of the random walk implication in his bestseller *A Random Walk Down Wall Street*. He suggested that throwing darts (or, more realistically, a towel) at the newspaper stock listings is as good a way as any to pick stocks and is likely to beat most professional investment managers. Malkiel does suggest in the later part of his work how those who insist on trying to beat the market might attempt to do so, but he indicates that they are unlikely to be successful.

Since the EMH was formulated, countless empirical studies have tried to determine whether specific markets are really efficient and, if so, to what degree. Andrew Lo's volumes bring together some of the most significant contributions, including a paper called simply *Noise* by the late Fischer Black. It says:

> *Noise in the sense of a large number of small events makes trading in financial markets possible. Noise causes markets to be somewhat inefficient, but often prevents us from taking advantage of inefficiencies. Most generally, noise makes it very difficult to test either practical or academic theories about the way that financial or economic markets work. We are forced to act largely in the dark.*

## Counterpoint

A central challenge to the EMH is the existence of stock market anomalies: reliable, widely known and inexplicable patterns in returns. Commonly discussed anomalies include size effects, where small firms may offer higher stock returns than large ones; and calendar effects, such as the *January effect* – which seems to indicate that higher returns can be earned in the first month compared with the rest of the year – and the *weekend effect* or *blue Monday on Wall Street* – which suggests that you should not buy stocks on Friday afternoon or Monday morning since they tend to be selling at slightly higher prices. There are also the supposed indicators of undervalued stocks used by value investors, such as low price-to-earnings ratios and high dividend yields (see *Value Investing*).

But while there is no doubt that anomalies occur in even the most liquid and densely populated markets, whether they can be exploited to earn superior returns in the future remains open to question. If anomalies do persist, transactions and hidden costs may prevent them being used to produce outperformance, as well as the rush of other investors trying to exploit the same anomalies. It may be possible that opportunities arise in quanta bursts and then disappear rather like the track in a cloud chamber. If so, by the time we wish to measure the recurrence of an event, it has occurred and passed by, unlikely to be repeated in the same form.

Further challenges to the EMH come from the study of behavioral finance, which examines the psychology underlying investors' decisions and uses it to explain such phenomena as stock price over-reaction to past price changes and stock price under-reaction to new information (see *Investor Psychology*). Many studies seem to confirm the implication of over- and under-reaction that there are "pockets of predictability" in the markets: contrarian strategies of buying "losers" and selling "winners" can generate superior returns; and prices do tend to regress to the mean.

A light-hearted yet cutting angle on the impact of psychology on market efficiency turns up in a 1997 article on the website of MIT economics professor Paul Krugman. Attending a big conference of money managers, Krugman detects *The Seven Habits of Highly Defective Investors*, the behavioral traits that he says make the markets anything but efficient: think short-term; be greedy; believe in the greater fool; run with the herd; overgeneralize; be trendy; and play with other people's money. "What I saw," Krugman recounts, "was not a predatory pack of speculative wolves: it was an extremely dangerous flock of financial sheep."

Of course, the vast majority of successful professional investors claim they have disproved the EMH. (The unsuccessful are engaged in other pursuits giving this sample technique hindsight bias.) And any active manager, no matter what his record, will be eager to argue that the markets are not efficient in order to justify his work as an agent for hire by others. Even the financial media has a powerful interest in decrying the EMH: if all information is fully reflected in prices, what value is there in the information they supply?

But are the investors who really beat the market consistently over, say, a five-year period simply the inevitable result of a standard distribution? After all, if a hundred people toss coins five times in a row, the probability is that two or three of them will have called correctly five times straight. In the same way, probability indicates that there will be someone occupying the Warren Buffett investment performance slot and it will be someone who has done the right things – but is it skill or luck? And by the time we might have statistical verification, such a long period – 50 years or so – will have passed to make the study useless.

And, of course, just as the challenge of stock picking is to identify a superior performer before the fact rather than in hindsight, so it is with investment managers. In many cases, strong performers in one period frequently turn around and underperform the next, and, as statistics would predict, a number of studies show that there is little or no correlation between strong performers from one period to the next.

Nevertheless, as Peter Bernstein points out in a 1998 address to European financial analysts: "even though beating the market is increasingly difficult, more and more people undertake the effort." He suggests that "the enormous volume of trading in today's markets is an important indication that market efficiency in the pure sense has no relevance to the real world of investing," and that "equilibrium prices are impossible in a dynamic and restless world of noise traders in the market."

Andrew Lo adds:

> *As with any other industry, innovation and creativity are the keys to success, so why should we find it surprising that those who are capable of such feats outperform the rest of the pack? If the EMH in its classical form seems to be violated so often, maybe we economists ought to re-examine our theory instead of arguing that the world is crazy.*

(See *Financial Engineering*.)


## Guru response

Burton Malkiel responds with extracts from the latest edition of his classic book. In a new chapter entitled "The Assault on the Random-Walk Theory: Is the Market Predictable After All?" he writes:

> *I have reviewed all the recent research proclaiming the demise of the efficient-market theory and purporting to show that market prices are, in fact, predictable. My conclusion is that such obituaries are greatly exaggerated and the extent to which the stock market is usefully predictable has been vastly overstated.*
>
> > *First, there are considerable questions regarding the long-run dependability of these effects. Many could be the result of* data snooping, *letting the computer search through the data sets of past securities prices in the hopes of finding some relationships. With the availability of fast computers and easily accessible stock market data, it is not surprising that some statistically significant correlations have been found, especially because published work is probably biased in favor of reporting anomalous results rather than boring confirmations of randomness. Thus, many of the predictable patterns that have been discovered may simply be the result of data mining – the result*

*of beating the data set in every conceivable way until it finally confesses. There may be little confidence that these relationships will continue in the future.*

*Second, even if there is a dependable predictable relationship, it may not be exploitable by investors. For example, the transaction costs involved in trying to capitalize on the January effect are sufficiently large that the predictable pattern is not economically meaningful. Third, the predictable pattern that has been found, such as the dividend-yield effect, may simply reflect general economic fluctuations in interest rates or, in the case of the small-firm effect, an appropriate premium for risk. Finally, if the pattern is a true anomaly, it is likely to self-destruct as profit maximizing investors seek to exploit it. Indeed, the more profitable any return predictability appears to be, the less likely it is to survive.*

*It is abundantly clear that techniques that work on paper do not necessarily work when investing real money and incurring the large transactions costs that are involved in the real world of investing. As a successful portfolio manager (ranked in the top 10% of all money managers) once sheepishly told me, "I have never met a back test I didn't like." But let's never forget that academic back tests are not the same thing as managing real money.*

*In summary, pricing irregularities and predictable patterns in stock returns may well exist and even persist for periods of time, and markets can be influenced by fads and fashions. Eventually, however, any excesses in market valuations will be corrected. Undoubtedly, with the passage of time and with the increasing sophistication of our databases and empirical techniques, we will document further apparent departures from efficiency and further patterns in the development of stock returns. Moreover, we may be able to understand their causes more fully. But I suspect that the end result will not be an abandonment of the belief of many in the profession that the stock market is remarkably efficient in its utilization of information.*

## Where next?

There is what Andrew Lo calls "a wonderfully counter-intuitive and seemingly contradictory flavor" to the idea of informationally efficient markets: the greater the number of participants, the better their training and knowledge and the faster the dissemination of information, the more efficient a market should be; and the more efficient the market, the more random the sequence of price changes it generates, until in the most efficient market, prices are completely random and unpredictable. That is to say that the more lemmings there are, the less likely they all are to fall over the cliff. Similarly, if everyone believes the market is efficient, then it will no longer be efficient since no one will invest actively. In effect, efficient markets depend on investors believing the market is inefficient and trying to beat it.

In reality, markets are neither perfectly efficient nor completely inefficient. All are efficient to a certain degree – and new technology probably serves to make them more efficient. But some markets are more efficient than others. And in markets with substantial pockets of predictability, active investors can strive for outperformance. Peter Bernstein concludes that there is hope for active management:

> ... the efficient market is a state of nature dreamed up by theoreticians. Neat, elegant, even majestic, it has nothing to do with the real world of uncertainty in which you and I must make decisions every day we are alive.

## Read on

### In print

- Andrew Lo, *Market Efficiency: Stock Market Behavior in Theory and Practice* (Edward Elgar, 1997), two volumes of the most important articles on the subject, including Eugene Fama's seminal 1970 review, Paul Samuelson's 1965 article and Fischer Black's 1986 article

- Andrew Lo and Craig Mackinlay, *A Non-Random Walk Down Wall Street* (Princeton University Press, 1999)
- Burton Malkiel, *A Random Walk Down Wall Street: Including a Life-Cycle Guide to Personal Investing* (Seventh edition, WW Norton, 1999), a long-time bestseller, first published in 1973 and now in its seventh edition.

## Online

- *web.mit.edu/krugman/www* – Paul Krugman's website
- *www.ssrn.com* – website of the Social Science Research Network, which features many important papers in investment, including Eugene Fama's *Market Efficiency, Long-term Returns and Behavioral Finance.*

# Mutual Funds

M utual funds have been one of the great success stories of the bull market that started in the early 1980s. Their professional management of large pools of capital appears to offer small individual investors some of the key advantages enjoyed by large institutional investors: a spread of investments to reduce risk; and reduced dealing costs. Certainly, small investors who buy stocks directly have historically faced much higher trading costs because they could not match pooled funds' ability to negotiate lower commissions from brokers. Nor do such investors typically have the size of assets to achieve effective diversification.

There are a number of ways of categorizing funds, for example, open-end versus closed-end and load versus no-load. Open-end funds (or unit trusts, as they are known in the UK) will sell as many shares as investors want but the shares cannot be traded on a secondary market; closed-end funds (investment trusts in the UK) issue only a limited number of shares but they can be traded. Load funds charge a commission when they are bought and sold; while no-load funds only charge a management fee. Funds can also be distinguished by their investing style – notably active versus passive; and value versus growth – and by the asset class in which they invest – bonds versus stocks versus money markets versus everything else; and within stocks, large cap versus small cap.

The wide selection of mutual funds now available allows individual investors to get exposure to many more asset classes, geographical markets and investment styles than was possible in the past (see, for example, *Emerging Markets*, *Fixed Income*, *Global Investing*, *Growth Investing* and *Value Investing*). But at the same time, because there are so many funds, it has become very difficult to choose among them. (Indeed, in some countries, there are more funds than there are listed stocks.) An entire industry has grown up to support the mutual fund business, providing information and apparently helping investors to evaluate funds. Fund consumers in the United States – and increasingly elsewhere – now have access to enormous amounts of data about their investments.

Fund rating is usually done on the basis of past performance, past volatility and expenses (though some rating agencies try to be more forward-looking and offer explicit recommendations). Morningstar, for example, which rates all mutual funds, awards between one and five stars based on a mechanical formula. These stars are not recommendations, but they are naturally used as marketing tools, and floods of money go into funds that have five stars on the assumption that those that have done well in the past will continue to do so in the future.

## Mutual funds guru: John C Bogle

Jack Bogle has a heart ... for investors. He has earned the reputation, almost unique among heads of mutual fund complexes, for unstinting dedication to the interests of fund investors. He promotes low costs and skepticism about investment management skills, regularly taking public positions on such traditional unmentionables as financial services compensation. And he takes his own medicine with the lowest cost structure in the industry, comparatively modest salaries and a reputation for being his own harshest critic.

Jack Bogle has a heart ... a new one. After years with a severely damaged heart, he continued active work while awaiting news of a transplant. Right beside the defibrilator in his office, required for the periodic heart failures, he kept a squash racket as a reminder of the tough, competitive life he longed to lead. Finally, a new heart was put in – and in what must have been the shortest recuperation on record, he was back again. This time, his board of directors insisted he take the title of senior chairman. He agreed on the condition that he would come to the office every day and remain active in Vanguard, his company ... although nominally it is a mutual owned by the fund shareholders.

The history of Vanguard and Jack Bogle's role in founding it may have formed the basis for many of his ideas. In the 1960s, he was the likely young successor to the head of Wellington Funds in Philadelphia, becoming Chief Executive in 1967. But then he decided to merge the company with a fledgling Boston firm run by four equally young Turks, who wanted to move the entire company to one location – theirs. A compromise was reached, perhaps grudgingly, to move the sales and investment operations to Boston, with the new owners thinking that they were about the only thing that counted. The operations side of the business stayed in Philadelphia as a mutual structure since, according to the understanding of the day, there was nothing of value there.

But there was. Wellington in Philadelphia under Jack Bogle's direction was closest to the mutual fund shareholder. Bringing out an index fund got the company into the investment management business, and going no-load eliminated the need for a distributor. Wellington in Boston, combined with Thorndike, Doran, Paine and Lewis, emphasized the then more attractive institutional business. There was an uneasy truce between the two places, and today the split is almost complete. Jack Bogle's single-minded endorsement of mutual fund shareholder concerns and an unresolved beginning partnership planted the seeds for the need for a truce.

Bogle has been a great advocate of mutual funds but he is skeptical about the ability of mutual fund managers to "beat the market." In a speech to the *Money Show* in early 1999, he argued:

> *The one great secret of investment success is that there is no secret. My judgment and my long experience have persuaded me that complex investment strategies are, finally, doomed to failure. Investment success, it turns out, lies in simplicity as basic as the virtues of thrift, independence of thought, financial discipline, realistic expectations and common sense.*
>
> *What does the past tell us about the complex investment strategies that entail selecting winning mutual funds? Over and over again, it sends the same message: don't go there. (Why? Because using Gertrude Stein's inspired phrase, "there is no*

*there there.") No matter where we look, the message of history is clear. Selecting funds that will significantly exceed market returns, a search in which hope springs eternal and in which past performance has proven of virtually no predictive value, is a loser's game.*

Bogle urges mutual fund investors to rely on simplicity and encourages them to set a simple standard as their objective:

*The realistic epitome of investment success is to realize the highest possible portion of the market returns earned in the financial asset class in which you invest – the stock market, the bond market or the money market – recognizing and accepting that that portion will be less than 100%.*

To accomplish this objective, Bogle recommends an index fund investing in the entire stock market, which is:

*... diversified across almost every publicly held corporation in America; essentially untouched by human hands; nearly bereft of costly portfolio turnover; remarkably cost-efficient; and extraordinarily tax-effective. Such a fund will provide you with – indeed, virtually guarantee you – 98–99% of the market's annual return over time, a vast improvement over the 85% or so that the typical mutual fund has provided.*

## Counterpoint

There are studies suggesting that some mutual fund managers may have a *hot hand* and that past mutual fund returns can dependably predict future returns. Princeton finance professor Burton Malkiel, who is also a director of Vanguard, is not persuaded by this work, which seems to indicate that you can pick mutual funds on the basis of their past performance (see *Market Efficiency*). In the seventh edition of his classic book *A Random Walk Down Wall Street,* he points out the problems and some of the questionable practices of mutual fund complexes and fund rating agencies:

*I am convinced that many studies have been flawed by the phenomenon of "survivorship bias," that is, including in their studies only the successful funds that survived over a long period of time, while excluding from the analysis all the unsuccessful funds that fell by the wayside. Commonly used data sets of mutual fund returns, such as those available from the Morningstar service, typically show the past records of all funds currently in existence. Clearly, today's investors are not interested in the records of funds that no longer exist. This creates the possibility of significant biases in the returns figures calculated from most of the available data sets.*

*Mutual funds that are unsuccessful with big risky bets usually do not survive. You are not alone in being reluctant to buy a mutual fund with a poor record. Mutual fund complexes typically allow such a fund to suffer a painless death by merging it into a more successful fund in the complex, thereby burying the bad fund's record. Thus, there will be a tendency for only the more successful funds to survive, and measures of the returns of such funds will tend to overstate the success of mutual fund management. Moreover, it may appear that high returns will tend to persist because funds whose bets were unsuccessful will tend to drop out of the sample.*

*Another little known factor in the behavior of mutual fund management companies also leads to the conclusion that survivorship bias may be quite severe. A number of mutual fund management complexes employ the practice of starting incubator funds. A complex may start ten small new equity funds with different in-house managers and wait to see which ones are successful. Suppose after a few years only three funds produce total returns better than the broad market averages. The complex begins to market those successful funds aggressively, dropping the other seven and burying their records. The full records from inception of the successful funds will be the only ones to appear in the usual publications of mutual fund returns.*

Malkiel has examined more than twenty years of data on the records of all mutual funds that were available to the public each year, whether or not they survived into the 1990s. His analysis of these mutual funds returns confirms his view that securities markets are remarkably efficient, and that, as Bogle suggests, most investors would be considerably better off purchasing a low expense index fund than trying to select an active fund manager who appears to have a *hot hand*.

The practice of launching many funds and subsequently dropping the losers explains the common question of company treasurers: why is it that everyone who comes to call on me has better than market performance but my managers are just scattered around average? But the real answer is that it is only worthwhile selling what the market will buy. A clever strategy for a fund complex might be to have widely diversified portfolios with extremely low correlations to the market averages but quite different from one another. This *dumb-bell* strategy almost guarantees that some will be performance disasters but a few will be big enough winners to attract attention. No one seems to follow the strategy but it would work.

One reason you can be far from confident that a stellar performer will continue to outperform the market is that outperformance naturally attracts a lot more cash to be invested in the funds. As funds become larger with success, it becomes more difficult to sustain excellent performance: the universe of securities that are realistically available shrinks. Another reason is that transactions costs increase with size: although big institutions can trade at relatively low commissions, shifting substantial blocks of securities tends to move market prices.

Jason Zweig, mutual funds columnist of *Money Magazine*, describes the problem of outperformance and excessive size well in a contribution to Peter Bernstein's newsletter *Economics and Portfolio Strategy*:

*Here, then, is one of the harshest truths of the information age: cash flow from clients now rivals the investment process itself as the main determinant of total return. Thousands of retail investors, each wielding only a few thousand dollars, can smother a fund manager with cash as soon as they detect what appears to be outperformance. Alpha has always been perishable, but in today's world of instantaneous information it is likely to have the shelf life of unrefrigerated fish. When a fund manager goes from absorbing a trickle of cash flow to drinking from a fire hose to surfing a tsunami, his past performance loses all relevance.*

But despite the problems Bogle and Malkiel identify with actively managed mutual funds, is indexing an appropriate response? Funds that follow a strategy of hugging the benchmark almost guarantee that they will neither lose nor win on performance, but they will require major sales efforts to distinguish themselves from the pack. And funds in the United States must be at least 90% committed to securities, limiting the asset allocation objective of diversification between assets and cash, and hence making themselves vulnerable to falling markets.

What is more, the funds must typically be in easily priced assets, and primarily in national rather than international assets, objectives that may be fine in a bull market but not so desirable when things turn bearish (see *Indexing*). Particularly for closed-end funds, there could be a severe liquidity problem if a large number of investors decide to liquidate their holdings: to whom will they sell? And might there be more interest in *guarantees* when the market goes down? In the United States at least, a substantial percentage of investors think their funds are like savings accounts, guaranteed by the US government.

Finally, there is a peculiarity of fund accounting that open-end funds are bought and sold at net asset value plus a commission. Net asset value is the sum of all the market or appraised value of assets held by the fund, unadjusted for capital appreciation or depreciation. Thus an investor purchasing a fund with large unrealized capital appreciation may find when these issues are sold by the fund that he or she has a large tax bill for appreciation that occurred during another investor's holding period. There is a good suggestion that GAAP (generally accepted accounting principles) should apply a reserve for taxes to be paid for funds as it would for a corporation, but the fund industry is against it.

## Where next?

In the past 40 years or so, investment products have gone from being bought by investors, usually on the basis of word-of-mouth, to being sold by intensive and expensive marketing programs. Is this necessarily the best development? Today, information on investment products can be disseminated effectively through the internet but, at the moment, we are barraged by rather simplistic publicity campaigns, often just a repeat of regular published paper information. We have not yet started using the informed comparison capability of the internet and perhaps this will not happen until after the next bear market. Investment marketing needs to be shaken up a great deal.

Discussing marketing of mutual funds in relation to their investments in internet stocks, James Cramer of *TheStreet.com* comments:

> *Mutual funds have about the worst truth-in-labeling problem I have come across in any industry. I think there should be a rule: the term* value *should not get applied to firms that own such high-multiple stocks. Value in this world has simply become a masquerade, a mean-spirited marketing tactic that lures people in the door who would otherwise have no desire to own such nosebleed stocks. You will never get the SEC to bring a case against a growth manager who has hidden behind the* value *nameplate. That would be too broad. But these big mutual fund families have a responsibility to market their products responsibly.*

Cramer's comment might be referring, among others, to Bill Miller's Legg Mason Value Trust questioning the appropriateness of a *value trust* that owns 25 hot technology stocks out of a portfolio of 30. Miller would defend such a position by saying it is "value tomorrow" (see *Active Portfolio Management*).

And what about the cost of financial services? Abby Joseph Cohen of Goldman Sachs points out that the only form of compensation that is going up is for financial services, and it is going straight up. We might have expected exactly the reverse – that the use of machines would drive costs down, and that performance measurement would make buyers realize that you could operate at lower cost and actually have better results. But this has not happened, and in the midst of a bull market, costs are going up. There is this huge system eating away at returns with costs that are at least 0.5% of assets a year and probably more. And of the proportion of assets that are actively managed, it may be as much as 10% by the time you take away the closet indexing.

Finally, some possible future developments for the mutual fund business:

- Customized portfolios: investors might be able to build their own *fund of funds* with tools provided by the fund complex.
- Easier switching from fund to fund within the same complex: rather like Fidelity sector funds with low or no switching costs except for the double taxation – an investor selling a fund at a gain pays taxes on the gain but another investor also pays when the fund makes a capital gain distribution on the gain that accrued to the selling investor.
- Funds could maintain live bulletin boards of information, a live FAQ (frequently asked questions) facility for marketing purposes. Currently, these answers have to be cleared legally, which slows the process.
- Fund regulation around the world could be made standard through IOSCO, the International Organization of Securities Commissioners and Officers.

# *Read on*

## In print

- John Bogle, *Bogle on Mutual Funds: New Perspectives for the Intelligent Investor* (Irwin Professional Publishing, 1993)
- John Bogle, *Common Sense on Mutual Funds: New Imperatives for the Intelligent Investor* (John Wiley, 1999)
- Paul Farrell, *Mutual Funds on the Net: Making Money Online* (John Wiley, 1997)
- Bill Griffeth, *The Mutual Fund Masters: A Revealing Look into the Minds and Strategies of Wall Street's Best and Brightest* (Probus Publishing, 1994)
- Burton Malkiel, *A Random Walk Down Wall Street: Including a Life-Cycle Guide to Personal Investing* (Seventh edition, WW Norton, 1999).

## Online

- *www.brill.com* – website with extensive information on mutual funds
- *www.iii.co.uk/performance* – website with investment performance details for UK funds
- *www.morningstar.com* – the Morningstar website
- *www.thestreet.com* – James Cramer's online financial publication
- *www.vanguard.com* – website of the Vanguard Group.

# Performance Measurement

We live in an age of measurement. We want to measure everything: how high, how heavy, how much, how many? Nowhere is this impulse more powerful than in the world of investment. The constant stream of data on financial markets now available at the touch of a computer keyboard is all measurement of one sort or another. And it keeps us continually up-to-date with the performance of our assets, our funds and the people managing them on our behalf.

Measures are essential if we are to try to make forecasts. For what can we say about how much or how many in the future unless we know the base from which we set off – the initial conditions. And in investment as elsewhere, most people implicitly accept that the past is as good a guide to the future as anything else. A whole industry of performance measurers has emerged in recent years, offering historical track records of money managers. Morningstar, for example, summarizes their past performance in the form of star ratings as if they were hotels or restaurants.

Of course, there should be performance measurement. But strangely enough, it was rare only a generation ago in investment management. Results then were described in vague qualitative terms and, with institutional investors' portfolios largely in bonds, the variations were not consequential. But a bull market in equities changed things. Demands began to be heard: "How well are we doing? And more importantly, how well are we doing compared with an index or our competition?"

## Performance measurement guru: Peter Dietz

At first, performance measurement crept into mutual fund merchandising under very strict SEC rules on advertising. The goal was less to inform shareholders and more to increase fund sales. But the standards of strict time and size weightings were developed at this time.

Institutions started getting concerned about performance during the bull market in equities in the 1960s. Peter Dietz of the Frank Russell Company wrote the initial book on the subject, *Pension Funds: Measuring Investment Performance*. Essentially, his work was an extension of mutual fund accounting except he discussed a range of alternatives. In particular, he pointed out the principal measurement aberration that could be introduced: the influence of initial size on the calculations.

In fund accounting, the same percentage changes are treated as equally meaningful on small amounts in a fund as on large ones. So a fund could demonstrate exciting performance on its starting investment amounts, attract new investors and find that such results became more difficult to achieve. Yet the numbers would give no indication of diminution in performance due to size. Similarly, the calculations suffered, at least originally, from changes in management and market cycles.

Dietz raised a number of other important statistical issues like the need for carefully ensuring that the database remained intact. There was a natural tendency for accounts to leave a management organization after poor results and hence to be dropped, since inception, from the calculations. Clearly, this distortion gave an upward bias to the results. Dietz gave a precise description of the appropriate measurement rules to follow and they were largely implemented by the institutional community.

Not surprisingly, the Russell organization was one of the first to develop techniques for its clients to help understand their results. As for Dietz, he opened the Russell office in Tokyo, introducing performance measurement to Japanese institutions who took it to ever more precise specificity. Japanese institutions became as performance hungry in their bull market that ended in the 1980s as American managers demonstrated in the 1990s. Sadly, Dietz died while his invention was flourishing.

Since the 1960s, a substantial number of academic studies have been done on the continuity of investment results. These suggest great caution with the predictability of returns – what is known as low auto-correlation – and mean that the results of one period cannot be predicted by another.

The use of performance measurement had become so widespread in the early 1980s that the Association of Investment Management & Research (AIMR), the industry association, determined that standards must be mandated for all investment firms presenting performance numbers. Dean LeBaron, one of the co-authors of this book, was one of the handful of brave souls to face the wrath of their peers by propounding standards that at first should, and later must, be followed. With hindsight, to have a broad representation of the membership of AIMR, some on this committee should have come from a group with poor results. But as it happened, and it may be a natural coincidence about those perceived to be leaders then, each member had results that could be widely publicized with pride.

The committee met and produced reform recommendations that were accepted, including the standards that commingled results had to include all accounts with no convenient dropping of those that left, and they had to follow, in general, mutual fund accounting. Another committee on implementation met and encouraged independent audits and clarified some interpretation issues. And an entire industry of performance measurement was born, encompassing software, practitioners and performance attribution specialists.

## Counterpoint

Teachers of science typically urge students not to record measurements to a greater degree of precision than their crude instruments allow. Although interpolation between the marks on a scale is possible, error rather than greater precision emerges by writing down numbers that are unsubstantiated. While this may seem counterintuitive, it is an observation worth noting when dealing with investment numbers, especially in these days of computers with their appetite for numbers to the right of the decimal point.

There are two levels of significance for investment numbers. The first is: do the numbers imply greater merit than is warranted by the underlying limitations of the measurement technique? The second is: are the numbers produced significant and/or predictive? Performance numbers are particularly subject to this scrutiny.

On the surface, performance measurement promises more than it is able to deliver, at least at our present level of statistical sophistication. Results can be calculated with honesty on the universe of accounts and funds and with some interpretation required on the type of fund, out to many decimal places. They look very precise and scientific. But they almost always fail standard statistical tests of significance and can hardly ever be projected forward. In all probability, they are subject to initial conditions that are unrepeatable and, in any case, such numbers are inherently non-predictive for the timeframes with which they are customarily used – three years or what used to be called a market cycle.

No matter how well the data is cleaned up and standards maintained, the tool of performance measurement is faulty unless used with caution as a guide to qualitative judgment. More harm has probably been done by the misleading information in performance figures than any other statistical evil. Improving the quality of the numbers does not necessarily improve the quality of the results; rather, the results should be of historic interest only, forming a basis for discussion.

But in practice, past performance is used as a predictive tool, especially by those investment managers whose case for superiority is supported by using the numbers. Fund managers with a five Morningstar rating, for example, are not slow to use it in their marketing campaigns just as hotels and restaurants often publicize their star ratings to attract business. And while, logically, half the managers in any performance comparison are below the mean, the only managers who solicit business on that basis are the ones with above-the-mean results.

Little work has been done to make performance measurement more predictive nor to help practitioners understand its limitations. Until then, performance standards may be likened to improving the cleanliness of cigarette factories, a worthy pursuit that provides a "clean factory" stamp to give the consumer more confidence in the product. In reality, the stamp of approval does not alter the likelihood that the proper stamp on investment performance numbers is "use of these numbers may be injurious to your wealth."

## Where next?

We are trying desperately to improve our ability to have accurate measures. And yet as we improve our data – which we do – but do not improve anything to do with the measures, the models in which they are used, in the end we come out with nothing that is any better.

The AIMR standards improved the data substantially by making it honest. But they did not improve anything about how the data was to be used. So as a result, the data is no more forecastable than it was then, although it looks better, and can be used, seemingly, with higher degrees of confidence. Similarly, with all other forms of data. We want to measure, but we are still using the same old linear, Newtonian, archaic tools rather than tools that are adaptive, dynamic and which allow for multiple outcomes and options.

Perhaps organizational and portfolio performance is better at the edge of chaos. Consider, for example, a personnel performance system that tells people there is a system for measurement – and there is – but that they will not know in advance what it is and how it changes. The system will be revealed at the end of the period. To do otherwise is like setting up a test-gaming exercise. The system must be as ambiguous as is the world.

In terms of selecting investment managers on the basis of short-term performance indicators, despite all the marketing money thrown at trumpeting past successes, they are no indication of future achievements. Indeed, it may be better to pick a solid long-term performer that has underperformed in the last couple of years on the assumption of regression to the mean. And perhaps managers should be rewarded, as hedge funds typically are, on the basis of actual performance rather than selected on the basis of past performance.

Performance measurement needs to be rethought to merit scientific recognition as a meaningful measure:

- As a start, we might remove the emphasis on precise point calculations, noting how often we see performance numbers shown with two or even four decimal places – a practice that ignores the science student's lesson not to write down data beyond the capability of the measuring instruments. Such specificity implies relevance.
- Next, we can adapt to results that always show a range, perhaps in terms of standard deviations that can be expected. Numerical results are equivalent in a cluster where each value, whether above or below another, is of equal merit.
- And finally, we should learn how to use newer, more dynamic statistical tests, the kind that are customarily used in other fields to attempt forecasts from the data. After all, that is generally the purpose of the data: to estimate the future rather than assigning a historical value to the past.

## Read on

### In print

- Peter Dietz, *Pension Funds: Measuring Investment Performance.*

### Online

- *www.morningstar.com* – the Morningstar website.

# *Politics and Investing*

W hat effects does politics have on economics? How can investors analyze political risks – often across a range of different national political environments – and assess their likely effects on equity returns? After all, financial markets are generally thought to lead economics and economics to lead politics (see *Economic Forecasting*). So there is a direct connection through leads and lags.

One way to think about a global portfolio is as follows. The equity prices of individual firms are in part determined by the past and prospective indicators of their corporate performance, and in part by the nature of the markets and industries in which they compete. But the last and often most significant determinant of share values is overall movements of the stock markets on which they are listed (although it should be noted that recent convergence of the overmarket returns has been attributed to common global banking influence).

These rises and falls are, in turn, influenced by three factors: first, major financial events, notably changes in the level of interest rates; second, major fiscal events, essentially the shifting patterns of revenues, spending and borrowing reflected in government budgets; and third, major political events that could have dramatic effects on both financial and fiscal matters and through them on the future course of the national economy.

For the stock markets of the industrialized and democratic world, often the key political issue is the electoral cycle and how this might affect the business cycle. For example, it has been known for incumbent governments to engineer a boom just prior to an election, and such expansionary policies, aimed at reducing unemployment and taxes, may boost equity markets. After an election, though, as their inflationary consequences kick in and growth turns into recession, they are likely to be followed by contractionary policies, which will generally dampen market enthusiasm.

For example, there is a well-documented *presidential cycle* in US equity markets, which highlights favorable market forces in the fourth year of a presidential term. The suggestion is that political powers favor expansionary policies to attract voters. And then, after the election, regardless of the outcome, markets tend to retrench to compensate for the politically induced pre-election policy.

Political business cycle effects may be tempered by the political color and commitments of incumbent or incoming governments. For example, governing parties of the left have traditionally been regarded as less fiscally responsible than those of the right, and hence less positive for the markets – though there is evidence to the contrary in the United States, where markets have done better under Democratic administrations. What is more, with so many left-of-center political parties practicing or at least promising fiscal conservatism, perhaps a better measure of market prospects is whether a new government – whatever its persuasion – has a working majority, a substantial period in office and a credible reputation on the economy.

Another politically-determined influence on a country's economic prospects, which appears to be increasingly important and may counter the electoral cycle, is the degree of independence of the central bank. These institutions control national monetary policy, primarily through interest rates, and the theory is that the greater their independence, the less room governments have to engineer booms. Recent research seems to confirm that more independent monetary authorities bring about lower inflation, lower interest rates and higher growth. Indeed, the US Federal Reserve now seems to be taking on even bigger chores, such as international monetary coordination, business cycle management and "jawboning."

## *Guru of political analysis: Ed Yardeni*

Most investment economists are also political analysts. Investors like to visit political leaders to learn the course of policy and how it might influence their holdings. Especially in emerging markets, there is a dance of politicians looking for money from advanced countries and investors looking for opportunities for gain greater than in their home markets. And visiting well-publicized government leaders to exchange views on macro-issues is impressive content for reports to committees and clients.

Ed Yardeni, chief economist of Deutsche Bank, may be one of the best in combining economics and politics. His website contains some of the most valuable economic data and his weekly audio telephone meeting for clients is an important visit for people who want to observe a blend of the two disciplines.

Dr Ed, as he styles himself, could be labeled an omnibus economist. Such analysts examine a range of influences on prices, culture, cycles, history, politics and even exogenous events. For example, Dr Ed has been carefully studying the likely economic outcomes of Y2K. He believes that four-decade-old COBOL programming buried deep in computer code and which allocates only two digits for the year 2000 will produce a major economic disruption. His economic peers, who study past economic data for trends and turns, may be skeptical of the value he sees in being interested in an outside factor that might already be anticipated correctly by markets.

## Counterpoint

Politics is usually thought to influence economic outcomes. But is it more often the other way around, with markets leading politics? After all, market declines in Asia from the summer of 1997 preceded political upheavals, and market stability in the United States in the period up until the second half of 1998 seemed to buttress political stability when events might have undermined it.

Economics writer David Warsh of the *Boston Globe* argues that "good markets make for lackluster politics – and vice versa." Asking why voter interest in US presidential and mid-term congressional elections has declined so dramatically since the early 1970s, he concludes that:

> ... *quite simply, economics took over from foreign policy. The nation turned away from the great public issues of the Cold War to pursue private prosperity instead. There was a great inflation in the 1970s; an asset boom in the 1980s; a more widely shared prosperity in the 1990s. More people tended their portfolios. Fewer voted.*

In emerging markets, there are usually greater political risks than those threatened by elections or democratic changes of government. Unrest seems to be a concomitant of economic outcomes below expectations. And while it is true that western-style democracies are not a requirement for prosperity and economic growth, the brief history of most of these markets' international prominence makes investors understandably cautious if willing to exchange greater risk for potentially much higher rewards.

Emerging markets do tend to be less covariant with one another than developed markets: a basket of well-diversified emerging markets, each potentially riskier than its developed market counterpart, may, on aggregate, be less risky. But these covariances can be very unstable. For example, in 1998, emerging markets declined and bond yields increased because of the sense that the two asset classes shared a common need for funds while liquidity was decreasing. Earlier historical analysis did not illuminate these parallel influences.

Political risks in emerging markets include the risk of government default in the case of bonds; the risks of nationalization, stock market manipulation, and unfavorable or inadequate regulatory environments in the case of equities; and the risks of expropriation of assets, exchange controls and other anti-foreign investor legislation, which make it impossible to get capital, profits, interest or dividends out of the country. And such risks are not always limited to emerging markets: a number of countries, the United States among them, have frozen the assets of political enemies, such as Libya, Cuba, Iraq and Iran.

## Guru response

Ed Yardeni comments:

> *I guess I am an old-fashioned political economist. Prior to Keynesian economics, the subject was called political economy. It is unfortunate that the two have been split. It is also too bad that economics was split again into micro- and macroeconomics. Adam Smith carefully explained the advantages of the division of labor. However, the tendency to specialize in narrower and narrower areas of research in politics and economics has been a definite disadvantage. Economists are smarter and smarter about fewer and fewer subjects. They tend to focus only on their narrow field of interest. That makes many of them very uninteresting, and irrelevant.*

## Where next?

A number of organizations like the Economist Intelligence Unit offer subscribers a useful regular summary of national credit risk ratings of emerging markets based on economic and political factors. Looking at a similar sample of emerging markets, the Heritage Foundation, a conservative US consultancy, produces an "index of global economic freedom" in association with the *Wall Street Journal*. This ranks countries on the degrees to which their governments intervene to restrict economic relations between individuals. It covers the gamut of economic affairs, including trade policy, taxation, monetary policy, foreign investment rules, regulation policy, the size of the black market, and the extent of wage and price controls. In the 1998 index, Hong Kong came out on top as the most *free* while North Korea was at the bottom.

While equity market predictions based on economic and political information of this kind will remain fraught with difficulties, these indexes do at least offer a crumb of quantifiable hope to this vital aspect of the game of playing the world's equity markets. Political risks are by no means as easily assessed as a corporate balance sheet, but they should never be forgotten.

As for the economics profession, perhaps the pendulum is starting to swing back the other way towards political economy with the *econ tribe* becoming a little more in touch with the real world and trying occasionally to look at the big picture – certainly once they have jumped through the hoops, such as publishing in the big journals, getting tenure and showing they can do the high-tech theoretical wizardry.

## *Read on*

### In print

- David Warsh, *Economic Principals: Masters and Mavericks of Modern Economics* (Free Press, 1993).

### Online

- *www.boston.com/globe/columns/warsh/* – David Warsh's column in the *Boston Globe*
- *www.eiu.com* – website of the Economist Intelligence Unit
- *www.heritage.org/index/* – website of the Heritage Foundation
- *www.yardeni.com* – Ed Yardeni's website.

# Quantitative Investing

T he essence of quantitative investing is crunching numbers to determine whether a proposed investment or portfolio configuration is worthwhile or appropriate. Anything that can go into a digital computer is fair input. And since computers are mostly digital and linear programs are rigid, *quant* analysis tends to be repetitively structured and rich in reliance on backtesting.

The central themes of quant investing are that history reveals enduring patterns of price behavior, which can be unlocked by statistical techniques; that risk of loss is closely related to volatility, which is related to return; and that management of risk, return, covariance and time frames can be usefully predictable. Part of the attraction of quant tools is cost. All the cost is in setting up the initial framework for analysis, while the incremental cost of each iteration is virtually zero.

Quants often refer to their activity as *disciplined* with the implication that their approach is less personality-prone than others, which rely on qualitative or intuitive judgments to make investment decisions. This is not quite true. Most successful investment managers, whether quant or otherwise, select investment styles consistent with their personalities: they understand the style at its very core, not from the numbers. Indeed, the choice of tools is often artistic, although the repeated application is certainly disciplined or, as some would say, mindless.

## Quant investing guru: Robert Arnott

Quant analysis, initially developed in the world of academia, has had an enormous impact on finance practice in the past couple of decades. This story of the "improbable origins of modern Wall Street" is very well told in Peter Bernstein's book, *Capital Ideas*.

Several coincident factors led to the widespread popularity of quant investing. First, the availability of academic computer time and willing graduate students boosted empirical financial research in the 1950s and 1960s. Second, a cyclical phenomenon of rising markets led to the use of greater degrees of specificity when the returns seemed to be in application rather than new theories. And third, the graduate students trained in North American universities began to assume decision-making posts around the world, sharing common techniques that encouraged the rapid adoption of new securities and global portfolio construction.

Quant practitioners are comfortable moving back and forth across the borders of the investment and academic worlds. They meet at the same meetings. The well-regarded Q group, for example, has held meetings for a generation blending both communities. Their vocabulary is the same and research standards are nearly identical. Academics regularly engage in very well supported research programs funded by investment firms.

Robert Arnott, founder of First Quadrant, personifies the quant investing group. He has academic degrees from the University of California, has written dozens of investment research papers for publication and works tirelessly. His roots are in the University of Chicago and he took his first job as a backroom quant person in a Chicago bank. But he did not stay in the background long. His skill at presenting his own research ideas convincingly to clients and his zeal in work surpassing his peers argued for starting his own firm.

First Quadrant, headquartered in Pasadena, California, has about $26 billion in discretionary assets under management. Its range of investment products is wide since a statistical study of past market behavior reveals the secrets of almost any market. Arnott says:

*We have three elements to our investment philosophy. The first is a pre-disposition toward contrarian investing. The markets don't reward comfort. Secondly, we're quantitative. We try objectively to take emotion out of the investment process. The third element is our use of multi-disciplinary techniques.*

Investment styles are selectively Darwinian in that everyone you talk with is a survivor and can demonstrate that some single mentality has been proven to be correct. Perhaps First Quadrant is best known for tactical asset allocation (TAA). This investment style – which aims scientifically to buy undervalued assets and sell overvalued ones – slides risk up and down according to a pattern, which may be simply stated as deviations from the norm. Regression to the mean is the principal tool of proponents of TAA.

## Counterpoint

All of us now use quantitative tools though many of these tools, introduced a generation ago and in vogue today, are designed for crude mathematics and limited machines. Dean LeBaron, one of this book's co-authors, was an early-days enthusiast for quant investing when it was the counterpoint for one-decision, buy-and-hold investing. As founder of Batterymarch Financial Management, he was an early adopter of academic ideas into investment practice. Now though, when quant investing is the gospel – with a few more agnostics as time goes on – he is less positive.

On the surface, quant analysis is a mechanical application of one or several minds. It is artificial intelligence, which is neither better nor worse than the designer: put some testing device at the end of the process and you have an efficient, automated assembly line. Then you can have a system that is mechanical and learns in a loop, like neural nets and, to a greater degree, genetic algorithms.

But a number of distractions come into the system. One is that it is unclear that the economic hand drives toward profit maximization over whatever time period. The field of behavioral finance is growing (see *Investor Psychology*), making the study of agents – institutional self-interest – respectable, because it uses different terminology.

Another distraction is the noise in the system, such as partly discontinuous time where markets pulse and do not flow in even time units so there is little serial price correlation. When we model, we make simplifying assumptions that try to capture the essence of the real world. We pretend its exactitude for study, understanding and, if we are lucky, predictability, assuming it to be linear as if a few units of one variable have an equal effect on another variable over the full range of measurement or estimation. But the real world is distinctly non-linear, like almost everything else in the social sciences.

And we usually ignore the feedback features of markets in which each moment is a unique and unlikely-to-be-repeated event. If market time is in bursts, it may move from regular to chaotic to random. And market study, more than most, suffers from the implications of the Heisenberg principle: that the results we get are often more subject to the identity of the researcher than to the phenomenon being studied.

Another distraction is that there is so much irrelevant information that we do not know the drivers of results. Engineers know how to deal with signal noise, but investment managers do not. Many pride themselves on working only with clean, accurate data, thinking that careless errors are reduced. But techniques to clean the data must be used sparingly and with full knowledge of what is lost and what is gained. The real world is messy and emergent, never like what just happened, which will never happen completely the same again, with all the ramifications. Real data is inherently dirty; model data is usually scrubbed.

The errors introduced by demanding clean data are many. The foremost is time. To get clean data demands that more time is introduced between the last bit of relevant data collected and the time at which it will be used. And time in markets involves, always, the activity of feedback loops that undoes the value of the measurements we have made.

The second error is competitive. If we wait for clean data, knowing that our competitors do as well, we find the answers from that data just when everyone else does, often in the same manner, increasing the likelihood that we arrive at the same, discounted conclusion.

The third error is sample size. To get clean data, we often discard the suspicious measurements, and these may well include the most advantageous (even if startling) and potentially rewarding insights. There are potential events that are not likely to happen but if they do will have big effects on financial markets. Realistic risk assessment would take account of these large low probability events, and the possibility that they are more probable than we thought – that there are *fat tails*.

And finally, there is synthesis where we study smaller and smaller bits-bytes of data, expecting they will retain their characteristics when put back together into a total system.

Most research contains all of these potential flaws. But the overarching question is why quantitative tools that are almost universal, like back-testing, but with no basis in academic fact are still used? Why are basic academic principles of statistics, multiple tests, reproducibility, rigorous challenge of results hardly ever observed by quant practitioners? The answer is that they are too busy making money the old-fashioned way, promoting their "unique" skills. Perhaps learning comes during periods of prosperity and application during periods of adversity.

What passes for investment research is usually backtesting: if I know now what I should have known then, how good the results would be. Even quantitative backtesting is intuitive *data mining* – determining what patterns exist in a finite sample of numbers. All random number series have a finite beginning and end and patterns can eventually be found – "torturing the data until it confesses to anything." Is it any surprise that looking at historical data always produces wonderful suggestions for investment action, but that application of this same process often produces humbling results? Investment strategies based on hindsight often fail.

Our minds, unconsciously perhaps, are conditioned by the immediate past conditions and project variables we would like to include in our models. So it is not at all surprising when we test, if these conditioned characteristics are included in our tests, we find that investment results would have been superior. And then we make the leap that they are continuous and we can still capture them because we have not consciously data mined. It would be far better to data mine overtly using the best tools and know what we have done than pretend we did not do it at all.

## Guru response

Robert Arnott comments:

> *Quantitative techniques are not magic. They are merely tools for effecting investment ideas and methods with more discipline than traditional qualitative methods. They can be good, indifferent or downright bad, but unlike many qualitative investors, they are* disciplined.
>
> *Quantitative methods are not inherently better than traditional subjective methods. After all, the human brain is a remarkable instrument:*
>
> - *It is an analytic tool, capable of assessing the diverse impact and repercussions of a thousand variables and factors. Quantitative tools tend to break down when weighing more than a handful of variables.*
> - *It is an historical tool, weighing and comparing current market conditions with hundreds of comparison points drawn from history. Quantitative tools can help us draw comparisons only with information in an often narrow database.*
> - *It can interact with other brains. That's called conversation or teamwork. Computers can only interact precisely as and when we instruct them to do so. They are high-speed idiots, even when equipped with so-called* artificial intelligence.
>
> *But, for all of its strengths, the brain comes with excess baggage. We are social creatures craving agreement and company. The capital markets inherently reward the unconventional view. We are creatures of emotion, seeking comfort. The markets inherently penalize the comfortable view. Why? Because the*

*markets price assets to reflect current demand for reward …
and investors demand to be rewarded for discomfort not for
comfort. Market prices are high for comfortable investments
because investors demand less reward for comfortable investments; a lesser demand for reward means a higher current price.*

*The human mind has a strong tendency to focus on recent
history. In essence, we tend to fight yesterday's battle, forgetting
the lessons learned in battles of years gone by. Our short-term
memory is far better than our long-term memory. So, surprisingly, our high-speed idiots can often, but not always, earn us
higher returns than the finest minds in the business world.*

*What good are quantitative techniques? The answer is only
partially better performance. Yes, I do believe that well-reasoned
and well-constructed quantitative techniques may add value. But,
not so much in the United States as they perhaps once did. More
importantly, they can serve as tools to avoid and redress the greatest errors in institutional asset management.*

*What are these errors and what role can quantitative tech-
niques serve to eliminate them? The greatest errors in institutional asset management can be distilled into two words: emotion and slippage. This is evident in the corporate arena, where
we find what might be termed a* clash of cultures. *We know
that the successful corporate culture is one that aggressively rewards success and ruthlessly punishes failures. The successful
investor often follows the opposite pattern, paring back on recent winners and favoring recently disappointing markets.
Quantitative methods can help give us an objective basis for
investing when and where it is frightening to do so. They give
us an objective basis for uncomfortable, hence profitable, investments.*

## Where next?

Just as the failure of Peregrine, the most global and best of the Asian
global firms, signals that the Asian investment crisis is very serious,

the end of an era, so does the near failure of Long Term Capital Management (LTCM), one of the best of the quantitative firms, signal the end of this phase of interest in quant investing. LTCM engaged in what were supposed to be minimal risk investment activities but they made two very low-odds bets, on leverage, both of which hit at the same time.

LTCM made no judgments about the underlying value of the assets it purchased. All its decisions were based on computer models that rigorously excluded any kind of fundamental analysis of companies and currencies. They were only interested in whether the historical relationships between the prices of different assets had changed – not whether they had changed for good reason – on the assumption that you could make money in the future based on what has happened in the past. What is more, they understated the risk of loss by forgetting about large low probability events because their historical data was from a period when these events did not happen.

In doing so, they have reminded us that backtesting and linear investing do not work now at what may be a change point. Instead, we are reminded that we have been in a generation-long period of acceptance of theories and details about investment that ignore major market trends – indexing is one (see *Indexing*), strategy selection by computer is another, trading practices are a third. By emphasizing the details and accepting the theories, one could achieve superior results if the trends remained the same.

But we may have had a turn of the trends now. Linear techniques are being disproved and we have not yet determined which of the non-linear techniques will work and how to do it. Research there is too sketchy to apply. We have left one and we have not yet built the foundation of another.

Aside from the obvious flaws in conventional management, there are some new approaches coming along. The pattern is remarkably similar to developments in physics at the start of the twentieth century when better laboratory equipment found that Newtonian physics failed to explain experimental results. Something was amiss, and two schools emerged: one trying to restate the old work, better and better, and the other to take radical new departures. And from the latter, we have quantum physics. Perhaps we are at the same juncture in investment management 80 years later.

One of the forward-looking technologies offering promise of better science and better results is drawn directly from physics. It is called complexity, sometimes chaos or adaptive systems, evolutionary dynamics and even artificial intelligence, neural networks and genetic algorithms. The problem with these ideas, many of them developed at the Santa Fe Institute, is that although they do not have the flaws of conventional practices, they are fuzzy, usually unsupported by repeatable performance attributes and still undergoing modification. Against the pseudo-precision of old ideas, they seem experimental and flaky. But that is what being on the frontier is all about.

A joke once published in the *Journal of Portfolio Management* made a very profound point. A new researcher, a freshly minted PhD, came to work at a brokerage firm from academia and was told that he would do numbers, problems involving addition, subtraction, multiplication and division – but not to worry, division was not used very much. The point of the story was that what passes for quantitative analysis in the investment arena is frequently static, simplistic and does not meet the rigors of statistical tests that can be used with today's instruments and today's demands.

The new tests are dynamic, often involving complexity analysis, often involving destructive statistical testing to determine the limits, are very demanding of time scales and frequently are so large and so demanding, such as high-frequency analysis, that they can be done only on supercomputers. In today's investment world, quantitative analysis must be the very best, not the most used.

## Read on

### In print

- Peter Bernstein, *Capital Ideas: The Improbable Origins of Modern Wall Street* (Free Press, 1992).

## Online

- *www.fquadrant.com* – First Quadrant's website
- *www.santafe.edu* – website of the Santa Fe Institute
- *mitpress.mit.edu/SNDE* – Studies in Nonlinear Dynamics & Econometrics features the best work of academic quants.

# Risk Management

The complexity of our modern lives and the numerous decisions we are able to take are only made possible by our ability to manage risks – the risk of house fire; the risk of losing a job; the risk to the entrepreneur who invests in a business; the risk to the farmer who plants a crop that will have an uncertain yield and be sold at an uncertain price in several months' time; the risk to the investor in the stock market; and so on.

For each of these problems, society has found solutions. For example, most people agree that house insurance and unemployment insurance increase social well-being. The role of futures markets in insuring farmers against commodity price uncertainty is also understood to increase welfare. Equally, the role of the stock market in enabling the risks of businesses to be shared is now well understood – as indeed is the role of diversification in enabling investors to achieve the minimum risk for the returns generated on their portfolios.

But such widespread public acceptance is almost certainly not true of derivatives, and their role as a means for managing risk through the financial markets is frequently misunderstood. This may, in part, be due to the idiosyncratic nature of the instruments themselves, as illustrated by a number of controversial episodes: the failure of portfolio insurance in the 1987 stock market crash; their misuse in the cases of Barings, Gibson Greetings Cards, Metallgesellschaft, Orange County, California, and Procter and Gamble; and the near failure of Long Term Capital Management (LTCM) whose board included the pioneers of option pricing, 1997 Nobel Laureates for Economics, Robert Merton and Myron Scholes.

Yet these instruments – futures, options and a multitude of variations on these themes – are packages of the basic components of risk: they more than anything else traded come close to the theoretically ideal instruments for the trading of risk. On the one hand, insurance can be a cost borne to eliminate a negative occurrence, accidental or structural, an outcome you cannot tolerate. On the other hand, it becomes a tool to shape a risk-return relationship, unique to each investor, from quite common investment alternatives. Derivatives can turn stocks into bonds and vice versa. And derivatives can pinpoint very precisely specific risks and returns that are packaged within a complex structure.

## Gurus of risk management: Fischer Black, Robert Merton and Myron Scholes

Over the past twenty-five years, financial futures and options have established themselves as an integral part of the international capital markets. While futures and options originated in the commodities business, the concept was applied to financial securities in the United States in the early 1970s. Currency futures grew out of the collapse of the Bretton Woods fixed exchange rate system, and heralded the growth of a wide variety of financial instruments designed to capture the advantages or minimize the risks of an increasingly volatile financial environment. Now these products are traded around the world by a wide variety of institutions.

The quantitative tools which brought derivatives into common use were the invention of the late Fischer Black and Myron Scholes in what is called the Black-Scholes option pricing model. Their sometime collaborator Robert Merton took the work further into a form for everyday application by applying his notions of continuous time relationships in security pricing. Merton's modifications made the leap from the theory to a practical tool.

As Peter Bernstein's excellent books on risk and capital ideas recount, having been rejected by two academic journals, the original Black-Scholes paper was eventually published in the University of Chicago's *Journal of Political Economy*. It is said that the option formula can be derived from the heat transform formula and that while wrestling with the problem, Black was inspired by a conversation after a game of tennis. Apparently, his playing partner, an engineer, saw the analogy with his own field.

Of the three developers of options theory (and its earlier roots date back to work done in 1900 by Louis Bachelier in Paris), two – Black and Scholes – moved full-time into investment practice. Merton moved from MIT to Harvard, a short distance upriver, though he too was involved with LTCM. Thus, the widespread application of academic theory from the early 1970s influenced investments but also the course of the lives of the developers.

The partnership of academia and investments is emphatically illustrated by the integration of derivatives into the everyday work of investment people. Some extracts from the Nobel citation for Merton and Scholes from the Royal Swedish Academy of Sciences provide a useful overview of their work and its many practical applications:

> *Risk management is essential in a modern market economy. Financial markets enable firms and households to select an appropriate level of risk in their transactions, by redistributing risks towards other agents who are willing and able to assume them. Markets for options, futures and other so-called derivative securities have a particular status. Futures allow agents to hedge against upcoming risks; such contracts promise future delivery of a certain item at a certain price. As an example, a firm might decide to engage in copper mining after determining that the metal to be extracted can be sold in advance at the futures market for copper. The risk of future movements in the copper price is thereby transferred from the owner of the mine to the buyer of the contract.*
>
> *Due to their design, options allow agents to hedge against one-sided risks; options give the right, but not the obligation, to buy or sell something at a pre-specified price in the future. An importing British firm that anticipates making a large payment in US dollars can hedge against the one-sided risk of large losses due to a future depreciation of sterling by buying call options for dollars on the market for foreign currency options.*

*Effective risk management requires that such instruments be correctly priced. Black, Merton and Scholes made a pioneering contribution to economic sciences by developing a new method of determining the value of derivatives. Their innovative work in the early 1970s, which solved a long-standing problem in financial economics, has provided us with completely new ways of dealing with financial risk, both in theory and in practice. Their method has contributed substantially to the rapid growth of markets for derivatives in the last two decades. Fischer Black died in his early fifties in August 1995.*

*The Chicago Board Options Exchange introduced trade in options in April 1973, one month before publication of the option pricing formula. By 1975, traders on the options exchange had begun to apply the formula – using especially programmed calculators – to price and protect their option positions. Nowadays, thousands of traders and investors use the formula every day to value stock options in markets throughout the world.*

*Such rapid and widespread application of a theoretical result was new to economics. It was particularly remarkable since the mathematics used to derive the formula were not part of the standard training of practitioners or academic economists at that time.*

*The ability to use options and other derivatives to manage risks is quite valuable. For instance, portfolio managers use put options to reduce the risk of large declines in share prices. Companies use options and other derivative instruments to reduce risk. Banks and other financial institutions use the method developed by Black, Merton and Scholes to develop and determine the value of new products, sell tailor-made financial solutions to their customers, as well as to reduce their own risks by trading in financial markets.*

## Counterpoint

Until the collapse of Barings in February 1995, derivatives were rarely mentioned beyond narrow professional financial circles. At that point, they became infamous, labeled the "wild card of international finance." James Morgan nicely captured their ambiguous role in an article in the *Financial Times*: "A derivative is like a razor. You can use it to shave yourself and make yourself attractive for your girlfriend. You can slit her throat with it. Or you can use it to commit suicide."

There is still some dispute in the academic world as to whether hedging using options is necessarily a good thing. Some argue that our ability to price these instruments unambiguously is primarily restricted to environments in which they are redundant securities and therefore cannot add to welfare. In other words, if we need them we cannot price them but if we can price them we do not need them.

Stephen Eckett of Numa sees dangers in the quest for a *correct* price or value for a derivative. He comments:

> *I think the search for this (apart from all sorts of demand reasons) comes from investors traditionally being able to value their other investments – such as stocks – and being in the mindset to do the same with derivatives. But with the rise of the internet – and high-tech in general – many of those traditional value tools are looking shaky even for stocks.*
>
> *Because of this, I regard the Black-Scholes model as one of the most dangerous inventions of the twentieth century. This is not to blame Black and Scholes obviously: the danger is always in the application. But what happened was that one simple equation – and mathematically, the model is simple – seemed to offer the possibility of quickly "understanding" and controlling derivatives risk. This encouraged thousands of banks to employ bright mathematicians, who had little knowledge of the financial markets but nonetheless started furiously programming their spreadsheets on which billions of dollars were gambled.*

Certainly, it is by no means clear that much of the use of derivatives by non-financial corporations is strictly necessary. Indeed, in some cases, it appears that firms use derivatives not so much for risk management as for trading opportunities – they are selective hedgers, opting not to hedge when they think they are in a winning position, and treating their treasuries as profit centers. Firms as prominent as Procter and Gamble have sustained enormous losses through derivatives, in large part by gambling on the chance of reducing small losses.

Derivatives in their *over-the-counter* form (as opposed to options and futures listed on exchanges) are based on the notion that investments can be designed to fit the investor not the issuer. Thus, you do not take the investor's intention and find the suitable investment, but you make it. And every time you do, you get an investment banking fee. Furthermore, the designer of the derivative instrument has a pricing skill superior to the buyer's so there is a trading fee.

It is also possible that hedging leaves society worse off than it would be if unhedged since it can make markets more volatile than they otherwise would be. During the crash of 1987, for example, a strategy called portfolio insurance, which aimed to use futures to reduce losses in a market decline, was blamed for driving the market down. And the rescue of LTCM by a consortium of banks after its near failure in September 1998 indicates that there were real fears that the liquidation of its positions would threaten the entire financial system. Derivatives flourish in an environment when the ability to pay is optimistic, where the creditworthiness of the chain of issuers is not in doubt. This is clearly a bull market condition only.

Much of the early success of LTCM was a result of the credibility of Merton and Scholes, which attracted heavyweight investors, lenders and trading partners to the firm, and their ideas, which provided potentially profitable trading opportunities. But for all the brilliance of their theory, it was based on "expected volatility," which implicitly assumes that history repeats itself, that the future movements of asset prices will mirror their past movements. Unexpected events in the real world – in this case, Russia's debt default and currency devaluation in August 1998 – can wreak havoc with such models.

In the past five years, a new and extremely important field of asset management has emerged called risk control. At many financial institutions, a risk control manager sits at the center of all of the position managers and asset managers to ensure that the diversification and covariances are in place so that dire results will not occur. But the risk control management process has to be severely challenged with the story of LTCM. Indeed, all the models that are being used for risk control and to buy assets on the basis of small increments using extraordinary leverage must be challenged.

It is far from clear that we have risk control in hand simply by looking at the past and thinking that the correlations are stable. They are not: when you get out to the tails of events, they do not behave like multiples of the means. In such circumstances, risk control by linear standards becomes non-linear and we have disasters like LTCM. Risk control, in the first instance, needs to be challenged, and we may have to go back to such old-fashioned practices as just not taking as much risk of loss.

## *Where next?*

The Nobel citation for Merton and Scholes points out the impact their work has had on the markets:

> *Financial institutions employ mathematicians, economists and computer experts who have made important contributions to applied research in option theory. They have developed databases, new methods of estimating the parameters needed to value options and numerical methods to solve partial differential equations.*

The citation also refers to the extension of options pricing to the world beyond the financial markets:

*Black, Merton and Scholes' contribution extends far beyond the pricing of derivatives. Whereas most existing options are financial, a number of economic contracts and decisions can also be viewed as options: an investment in buildings and machinery may provide opportunities (options) to expand into new markets in the future. Their methodology has proven general enough for a wide range of applications. It can thus be used to value not only the flexibility of physical investment projects but also insurance contracts and guarantees.*

It is said that before Black-Scholes, the government was amazed by what they saw as the stupidity of oil companies. These firms continually paid significantly more than the expected present value of oil when bidding for leases in government auctions. Looked at as options (the oil firms were not required to drill), these payments for the leases were easier to explain. The market managed to price them without the Black-Scholes formula. Indeed, Black-Scholes is only a model: the market still prices some options differently than the Black-Scholes value, and there is little convergence until close to expiry.

MIT's Sloan School is the location of much exciting work on the future of risk management. Professor Stephen Ross, for example, has coined the term *forensic finance* to describe a process he recommends: going back to some of the great disasters of risk management as a *financial pathologist*, and poring over them carefully to find out what went wrong and what lessons we can learn. "Learning the lessons of our past errors is what risk control is all about." Ross writes, "Practicing good risk control, particularly employing serious scenario analysis and stress testing, is just practicing financial safe sex."

And Ross's colleague Professor Andrew Lo (see *Financial Engineering*) is working on the concept of *total risk management*, integrating probabilities, prices and preferences into risk analysis in both the financial and non-financial worlds.

## Read on

### In print

- Peter L Bernstein, *Against the Gods: The Remarkable Story of Risk* (John Wiley, 1996)
- Peter L Bernstein, *Capital Ideas: The Improbable Origins of Modern Wall Street* (Free Press, 1992)
- Fischer Black and Myron Scholes, "The Pricing of Options and Corporate Liabilities," *Journal of Political Economy*, 1973 – the original article
- Bruce Jacobs, *Capital Ideas and Market Realities: Option Replication, Investor Behavior and Stock Market Crashes* (Blackwell Publishers, 1999)
- Andrew Lo, "The Three P's of Total Risk Management," *Financial Analysts Journal*, January/February 1999
- Robert Merton, *Continuous Time Finance* (Blackwell Publishers, 1990)
- Robert Merton and Zvi Bodie, *Finance* (Prentice Hall, 1998).

### Online

- *web.mit.edu/lfe/www* – the website of the Laboratory of Financial Engineering directed by Andrew Lo – includes his paper *The Three P's of Total Risk Management*
- *www.nobel.se* – website for the Nobel Prizes, including the citations for recent economics laureates
- *www.numa.com* and *www.global-investor.com* – excellent derivatives websites and online bookstores run by Stephen Eckett.

**G**oing long an investment asset means buying it in the expectation of a future price rise. *Going short* is the opposite: selling something you do not own in the hope of buying it back more cheaply in the future. Now that financial markets have primacy over hard asset markets, shorting should in principle be as normal an investment strategy as going long – increasing liquidity, driving down overpriced stocks and generally improving market efficiency (see *Market Efficiency*). But as a percentage of the total market, short selling remains small: for example, in 1997, shorting activity was only 1.3% of the total on the New York Stock Exchange (NYSE).

To sell stocks short, investors need to borrow them from willing lenders via a broker. This involves putting up 50% of the short sale price as cash collateral, paying a small fee for the borrowing privilege plus any dividends paid on the stock while the position is open, and setting up a supply of credit, also at some cost. These procedures tend to make shorting more difficult than holding a security long.

Short selling also exposes the practitioner to considerable risk of loss: when you go long, your loss is limited to what you paid for the stock; but when you go short, your losses are potentially without limit as the price at which you can buy back rises ever higher above the price at which you sold. A further risk is that the lenders may recall their stock at any time. In less liquid markets, this creates the possibility of a *short squeeze*, where it is difficult to *buy-in* at any price in order to *cover* the short position.

Why sell short? The obvious answer is to profit from the impending decline of an overpriced stock, an overpriced industry or indeed, an overpriced market. One of the most famous shorting episodes was in 1992 when George Soros (see *Hedge Funds*) sold vast numbers of British pounds prior to sterling's collapse against the other European currencies to which it had been pegged.

Shorting can also provide efficient diversification as well as potentially earning a higher return on cash collateral: your cash continues to earn but you are also making money from the short sale proceeds plus, if you can negotiate it, a share of the interest the broker is saving by using your collateral rather than borrowing from the bank. (However, short sellers, particularly individual investors, do not usually receive the full sale proceeds, though institutions can negotiate to receive some of the proceeds or interest on the proceeds while the short position is open.)

But most short sellers will be investment brokers and bankers hedging other positions: for example, protecting long positions from a market decline with an offsetting short position; or hedging positions that may be quite different from the short position but which are related by covariance. Risk management has become increasingly popular in recent years, even after the disrepute caused by its failure in the late summer of 1998 – and shorting is a prime tool in the risk manager's kit.

## Shorting gurus: Stephen Leuthold and Kathryn Staley

Short selling tends to be counter-intuitive to most investors and, as a result, only a few sophisticated money managers and knowledgeable individuals use it as an active investment strategy (as opposed to a hedging technique). These professional short sellers look for companies with inflated reputations and prices, digging out unfavorable corporate information using a variety of techniques. One such is Steve Leuthold who works out of Minneapolis.

Leuthold employs a program called AdvantHedge, which he describes as "a disciplined quantitative short selling program that is entirely focused on large cap liquid stocks." This means that short-sale candidates must trade in excess of $1 million per day and have a market cap of $1 billion – a universe of about one thousand one hundred stocks. The focus on liquid stocks avoids the problems of *short squeezes* and low trading volumes, which can make covering difficult.

The stocks sold short by the program are selected by a proprietary *Vulnerability Index* based on such indicators as industry group relative strength and fundamentals, performance rating, volume accumulation, insider buying and selling, and earnings disappointments; and including an array of triggers (*short covering disciplines*) to cover, monitor and reduce short positions. The program can be used as a means to offset some market risk without dislodging long-term portfolio holdings; as the short side of a *market neutral* strategy; or in a significant market rally, as an aggressive shorting tool. AdvantHedge is always 100% short in about fifty different issues.

Leuthold is a student of markets, and writes volumes on every aspect of market history and its relationship to the current times. To maintain a distance from the daily market din, he takes frequent, short leaves to concentrate on major trends. And among fellow professionals, he is regarded as one of the most all-encompassing of market strategists (see *Technical Analysis*).

Another noted short seller of US equities is Kathryn Staley. In her book *The Art of Short Selling*, she lays out the four clues she looks for when trying to identify short-sale candidates:

- accounting gimmickry: clues that the financial statements do not reflect the true state of the company's health, with overvalued assets and an ugly balance sheet
- insider sleaze: signs that insiders consider the company a personal bank or are in the process of selling their stock
- a gluttonous appetite for cash
- fad or bubble stock pricing, usually marked by a stellar price rise over a short period.

Staley's methodology can also be applied in the emerging markets simply by substituting the word *country* for *company*. In the dramatic market falls of 1997–8, some emerging market investments were sold off for the very same reason that certain US stocks get dumped: investors discovered that they were shoddily, even fraudulently, run.

Staley also points to what is often the main problem with short selling: being right but too soon. While a company may be overvalued, it may take longer than you expect for its price to fall and, in the meantime, you are vulnerable to margin calls if the price rises as well as the possibility of "buy-in" if the lender wants the stock back. As an old Wall Street rhyme says,

> *He who sells what isn't his'n*
> *Buys it back or goes to prison.*

## Counterpoint

Despite its contribution to market liquidity and efficiency, short selling still has a vaguely disreputable image. Many observers consider it to be "betting against the team," an unsporting or even *un-American* approach to investment, which can lead to severe market downturns. For example, it has been alleged that short selling contributed to the 1987 market crash as part of index arbitrage and portfolio insurance, although the use of derivative securities in such strategies seems to have been far more to blame (see *Risk Management*). And Malaysian prime minister Mahathir Mohamad wanted to make shorting illegal after the 1997–8 collapse of his country's currency and stock market, which he blamed on short sellers.

Part of the US regulatory response to the 1987 crash was the introduction of *circuit breakers* as an attempt to slow downward market movements. These include the SEC's *uptick rule*, which insists that for a short sale to be implemented on the NYSE or the NASDAQ, the most recent price move must have been up. Such tight rules add to the greater costs of shorting than of regular sales or purchases. And these costs have the effect of inhibiting traders with unfavorable information, giving markets an upward bias.

The growth of indexing also increases the costs and dangers of short selling (see *Indexing*). If you short prominent stocks in an index like the S&P 500 because their fundamentals are clearly slipping, you run the risk of losing out if the market rises dramatically since the questionable stocks will be swept along in the overall market fervor. But if you short stocks not in the S&P 500, there is no liquidity. For this reason, rather than shorting, it might be preferable to buy put options or sell stock if you think the market is near its peak.

## Guru response

Steve Leuthold comments:

*The stock market's exceptional rise in recent years has given birth to the concept that we are in a new era of investing, perhaps with the implication that shorting equities in these circumstances is a mistake. But such thinking is just an attempt to rationalize a mania. So I offer some tongue-in-cheek "new definitions for a new era:"*

- *Bear market: when stocks decline for a week.*
- *Major correction: when stocks decline for a day.*
- *Old-timer: a person who knows someone who lost money in the stock market.*
- *Cynic: anyone reminding you stocks can go down.*
- *Conservative: anyone without a margin account.*
- *Diversified portfolio: any portfolio with less than 50% of its assets in technology stocks.*
- *Risk: how much you can lose being out of the market.*
- *Inflation: historical phenomenon that used to adversely affect stocks.*
- *Dividend yield: outdated concept once used in valuing stocks.*

Leuthold adds:

*Few of today's portfolio managers know much about short selling. In what has come to be seen as a permanent bull market, equity shorts and hedging have come to be viewed as unnecessary. Of course, old timers feel the laws of stock market and economic cyclicality have only been suspended, not revoked. I would say that the keys to our relative success shorting stocks in the biggest bull market of all time are the covering disciplines that we rigidly maintain.*

## Where next?

After a long bull market, shorting is tempting, particularly when the market shows all the cultural signs of being in a form where there is universal enthusiasm on the upside, and double digit forecasts are common in the face of news that appears to be worsening.

And yet shorting takes a different mentality from what most of us have. We are almost all products of a period in which markets have gone up for more than several decades. Shorting requires a certain form of tough-minded pessimism. And as indicated above, shorting produces the possibility of infinite loss: you can lose more than you put up, with the potential that the sky is the limit.

So unless one is really psychologically conditioned to this and unless the market has given definite indications that it is in a long downward trend, shorting is probably best left to the absolute pros and the people who give daily attention to the signals.

At the same time, shorting means you need no longer have an optimistic outlook, and thus has understandable attractions for people with a contrary turn of mind or a "gloom and doom" view of the world (see *Contrarian Investing*). While many institutional managers, such as mutual funds, cannot go short, for those who can, it is just possible that it will be the investment skill that keeps them from financial disaster in a bear market.

# Read on

## In print

- Steve Leuthold, *The Myths of Inflation and Investing*
- Steve Leuthold's *Perception for the Professional* – a regular publication of the Leuthold Group
- Michael Murphy's *The Overpriced Stock Service* – a short-selling investment advisory newsletter from Murphy's company, Negative Beta Associates
- Kathryn Staley, *The Art of Short Selling* (John Wiley, 1997).

## Online

- *www.sec.gov* – the SEC's website.

# Technical Analysis

T here are essentially two ways of analyzing investments: fundamental analysis and technical analysis. With the former, investors try to calculate the value of an asset, asking questions like what is the present value of the likely future cash flows I am going to get from it, and how does that compare with its current price. With the latter, they focus exclusively on the asset's price data, asking what does its past price behavior indicate about its likely future price behavior.

Technicians, chartists or market strategists, as they are variously known, believe that there are systematic statistical dependencies in asset returns – that history tends to repeat itself. They make price predictions on the basis of published data, looking for patterns and possible correlations, and applying rules of thumb to charts to assess *trends*, *support* and *resistance levels*. From these, they develop buy and sell signals.

Market timing is a form of technical analysis that aims to identify turning points in the performance of major stock indices. Other methods include filter rules, measures of *relative strength*, line and bar charts, moving averages of prices over various periods, the study of trading volume, aggregate demand and supply analysis and numerous other gauges that measure momentum, valuation, sentiment, leadership or monetary policy.

Technical analysis is based on the assumption that markets are driven more by psychological factors than fundamental values. Its proponents believe that asset prices reflect not only the underlying *value* of the assets but also the hopes and fears of those in the market (see *Investor Psychology*). They assume that the emotional makeup of investors does not change, that in a certain set of circumstances, investors will react in a manner similar to how they did in the past and that the resultant price moves are likely to be the same.

## Technical analysis guru: Walter Deemer

Stock markets have been around for centuries. But technical analysis as a tool for the average investor has thrived over a much shorter period. It was in the late nineteenth century when Charles Dow, then editor of the *Wall Street Journal*, proposed the Dow Theory. This view recognized that it is the actions of people in the marketplace responding to news that cause prices to change rather than the news itself, and that once established a market trend tends to continue.

Since the 1960s, the technical approach to market analysis has been greatly expanded in scope and credibility. But in the US market of that time, market technicians were an arcane group. Mostly, they were introverts dealing in the hen-scratching and wiggles of lines on semi-log charts posted on sliding wallboards in their offices. Managers and analysts would walk into their environments the way one would approach a reader of tea leaves – apprehensive but hopeful.

In those gunslinging days, as they have been called, Walter Deemer was one of a handful of technician superpros. He started at Merrill Lynch in New York as a member of Robert Farrell's department. Then when the legendary Gerald Tsai moved from Fidelity to found the Manhattan Fund in 1966, Deemer joined him. Tsai would consult him before every major block trade, at the start of a time when large volume institutional trading became the norm and the meal ticket for brokers. Deemer, in his *war room*, could recreate market history on his charts and cite statistics the way a baseball fanatic can reach back into any season for parallels and records. He maintained contact with the group of other pros around at that time, who shared their insights with each other in a collegial confidence worthy of the priesthood.

But New York living did not suit Deemer. Not only did he not have room for his ham radio equipment and missed communicating around the world for relaxation, but he also liked the country. So he moved to Boston as the head technician at Putnam Funds. He was still doing the same thing, however: examining the market for its clues of future performance.

While technicians were getting a bad name during markets that mostly went up in a straight line since 1973–4, they adopted a title more suitable to their modern function: market strategists. This label referred to their output, not the fact that they used price instead of company and economic fundamental data for their determinations. If you could win by buying and holding a broad group of stocks as in indexing, why would you need a strategist?

But a handful of strategists persisted in their beliefs and formed a worthy industry group, the Market Technicians Association (MTA). Deemer is a charter member of this group, which continues to share information openly to challenge each other and holds very little back under a proprietary cover.

Currently, Deemer publishes market strategy comment and data from Florida. He has new tools that he did not have forty years ago, a broader sweep of international markets but exactly the same questioning attitude and historical perspective that he has always used. As an early adopter of the internet to communicate with his clients, he produces insights to a very elite clientele, most of whom are portfolio managers. And many other advice givers look to his research for their ideas.

Two market phenomena in 1998–9 provide good examples of Deemer's approach to understanding the market, using history to try to illuminate the future. The first followed the global market turmoil in the second half of 1998, where Deemer looked for a time in the past when the market went down big, followed by a big rally turning speculative in a hurry. The best match he found, prompted by research by fellow MTA member Chris Carolan, is a period when there was a decline of 37% in three months (not all that dissimilar to the late 1990s decline in small-cap stock indexes) and a 97% retracement of that decline in the next three months.

That 97% retracement was very speculative, as a quote from the *New York Times* that was printed just a month after the bottom attests: "Stock exchange speculation is rampant. There is now a greater disregard of relative values than in usual seasons of excitement." The date? 8 December 1873. The market then went down 45% during the next four deflationary years.

The second area in which Deemer has been thinking about historical precedents is the incredible movement in some of the internet stocks in 1998–9 (see *Internet Investing*). He offers the following two cases:

Deja vu # 1
*I recently decided it was time to read* The Money Game *again – particularly the section on* The Kids; *the section that tells about The Great Winfield's solution to the boiling market of 1968: "Kids. This is a kid's market ..." The Kids, you see, were the only ones who could figure out the New Math, the New Economics and the New Market. And what stocks were The Kids buying in 1968? Leasco Data Processing, Data Processing and Financial General, Randolph Computer, Kalvar, Mohawk Data, Recognition Equipment, Alphanumeric, Eberline Instrument, Western Oil Shale and Equity Oil. Ten stocks – none of which are around today.*

Deja vu # 2
*Go back with me to 1983. You're a money manager. You envision, quite clearly, the great PC boom ahead; a boom that is destined to change profoundly the way we do things. What stocks do you buy to capitalize on this great trend? Regrettably, most of the "obvious" candidates, back in 1983, never met the test of time. The "obvious" candidates ranged from IBM, the leading manufacturer of PCs, whose stock was just a market performer for the next two years – and a drastic underperformer for years and years after that, all the way to the PC plays that never made it at all from a longer-term standpoint: plays like Hayes, Prime, Seagate, Tandy, Wang, etc. As things turned out, the two really big winners that came out of the PC revolution were anything but* obvious *in 1983: the company that made the PC's "brains" and the company that made its operating system.*

*Time passes: now you're a money manager in 1999. You envision, quite clearly, the great internet boom ahead, a boom that is destined to change profoundly the way we do things.*

*What stocks do you buy to capitalize on this great trend? Dare I suggest that most of the "obvious" answers to that question will also not meet the test of time? Dare I further suggest that the real answer lies in companies that have locks – and I mean locks – on their particular area of expertise, as Intel and Microsoft did?*

## Counterpoint

Who needs technical analysis? We have had an eighteen-year bull market in the United States and the Dow has gone from 1000 to 9000, doubling in the three years to 1998. How would you possibly want to have a tool, which even if successful, got you in and out of the market? The thing, surely, is to be in – ideally in index funds, which have outperformed most active managers who have tried to do better than the average of other managers or better than the average of the market (see *Indexing*).

Indeed, technical analysis is much derided as hocus pocus. Critics argue that its claims to offer insights into investor psychology are absurd, and that it has less rational basis than astrology or the study of UFOs.

What is more, technical analysis is in effect what is used by quant analysts (see *Quantitative Investing*). For example, Long Term Capital Management's market strategy was based on the assumption that historical price relationships between different assets might change but that they will eventually return to normal.

## Guru response

Walter Deemer comments:

*Technical analysis is one of the most basic parts of the entire investment analysis process, perhaps the most basic of all. The reason: investors don't buy portions of companies; they buy pieces of paper that represent part-ownership of companies – much different things. Technical analysis is the study of all the factors that influence the price of those pieces of paper, and, in aggregate, the stock market. This means that as long as investors buy stocks rather than companies, technical analysis (or* market analysis, *as it is better called) will be, by default, a necessary part of a complete investment analysis process.*

*In recent years, though, the benefits of technical analysis have been shoved into the background by its increasingly short-term focus. The media are partly responsible for this misguided attention. So too are the mushrooming day trader types, who embrace classic technical trendlines and oscillators in their frenetic financial adventures because* normal *investment tools are pretty much useless to them. But investors who focus on long-term technical factors – especially those that anticipate price moves rather than react to them – and who then integrate those factors with all the other inputs at their command are well aware that* technical analysis *adds value to the overall investment process.*

*As far as indexing is concerned, I'll leave it to others to decide whether indexing is "good" or "bad" (although I'm unwilling to concede that the most important stock pickers on Wall Street are the folks who decide – in deep secrecy and with no set rules – what goes into the S&P 500). Like all trends in the financial markets though, the current trend towards indexing to the S&P 500 will ultimately create the excesses that lead to its reversal. The growing concentration of assets in one group of stocks will create relative values in other areas of the market that will, at some inevitable point, cause the pendulum to start swinging the other way. And, since the S&P 500 is* not *the only "index" in the US stock market, one of the biggest investment trends of the next decade is likely to be a gradual but persistent flow of indexed money out of the S&P 500 and into broader stock market indices, especially when performance-oriented pension funds and their consistently-late consultants decide that assets need to be shifted away from a now-underperforming S&P 500 index into better performing broader indices.*

## *Where next?*

Technicians are in the doghouse. And yet, they may have their day. Walter Deemer is one of a number of traditional and extremely good market technicians covering equity markets who have been saying for some time that the US market is getting a little *toppy*. And other technicians like Richard Olsen in Zurich are using very advanced mathematical techniques and high-frequency data to forecast currencies to great effect (see *Foreign Exchange*).

As more and more information becomes available through the internet, the opportunity arises to apply the tools of technical analysis to a huge range of new data. The technical tools available for today's investor are limited only by innovation and historical data. But for the most part, the indicators are not used to forecast stock prices as much as to identify the major market trends and measure risk. It might be said that the true objective of technical analysis is to determine whether or not the ingredients of a healthy bull market are present – and to watch out for possible warning flags before a major decline or bear strikes.

Dean LeBaron, one of this book's co-authors, once went to a fortune teller with friends. The normally dressed seer peered into the tea grounds left at the bottom of his cup and said "you once flew a red airplane into the ground," a fact no one at the table would have known. He followed with other insights from the past and the future. Was it the patterns of the leaves or was he an intuitive student of personalities? It seems likely that the tea was merely the means to occupy time to get the sense of other intuitions.

Technical analysis may also be an intuitive art form. There is an infinite range of data to look at and a sweep of global market history but the sorting is personal to the strategist. The skilled practitioner looks at the tea leaves, mulls over the past and may see into the future. But if you try to convert the art form into a mechanical, repetitive pattern, then the risk is that the art – and the forecast – is lost. Technical analysis looks more repetitive than it is.

The best forecasts are the ones that challenge conventional wisdom. But to do so requires strong conviction and may not be commercially successful unless one presumes to be right 100% of the time. And even in this unlikely event, telling your clients that they are wrong over and over is unlikely to produce high repeat-subscription rates. So a high success rate can be a Pyrrhic victory.

To succeed, the strategist must have a retentive sense of history, mathematics and graphic skills, a skeptical mind, wit and an ability to express ideas that are difficult to imagine. But most of all, fortitude.

## Read on

### In print

- Robert Edwards and John Magee, *Technical Analysis of Stock Trends* (Seventh edition, AMACOM, 1997) – the standard work of technical analysis
- Elli Gifford, *The Investor's Guide to Technical Analysis: Predicting Price Action in the Market* (Financial Times Pitman Publishing, 1995)
- Richard Russell's *Dow Theory Letters* – an example of a technician newsletter
- 'Adam Smith', *The Money Game* (Second edition, Random House, 1976).

### Online

- *www.4w.com/deemer/* – Walter Deemer's website
- *www.olsen.ch and www.oanda.com* – websites of Olsen and Associates
- *www.ifta.org* – website of the International Federation of Technical Analysts
- *www.mta.org* – website of the Market Technicians Association.

# Value Investing

**M**ost investors would claim to buy *value* assets regardless of what they do in practice. After all, it would not be smart to say that your investment choices represent anything else. But value investing is more usually thought of as a particular investment style, in some ways contrarian, but generally as the counterpoint to growth investing (see *Contrarian Investing* and *Growth Investing*).

A caricature of the investment world divides it into value investors – those who buy stocks that have fallen in price in the belief that the rest of the market has missed a bargain – and growth or momentum investors – who buy stocks that have gone up in the hope that they turn out to have been "cheap at any price." Value investors are typically thought of as painstaking, cautious and focused on safe and solid businesses (though value opportunities are often found among smaller cap stocks); while growth investors are portrayed as fun, trend-setting and focused on the prospects for tomorrow's winning companies (often those just recently launched on the market – see *Initial Public Offerings* and *Internet Investing*).

Value investors believe that stock prices are often wrong as indicators of underlying corporate net worth. They dispute the efficient market hypothesis, which suggests that prices reflect all available information (see *Market Efficiency*), and see investment opportunities created by discrepancies between stock prices and the underlying value of the asset. To uncover these opportunities, they use a variety of classic valuation tools, such as price-to-earnings (p/e) ratios, dividend yields and gearing. Typical characteristics of a value stock are a low p/e, a high yield and low gearing.

The man usually described as the world's first investment analyst, Benjamin Graham, who taught the first business school course on fundamental analysis at Columbia University in 1929, was also the father of value investing. Graham recommended that investors either buy and hold a portfolio of undervalued blue chips – what he called *defensive investment* – or, if they are prepared to put a lot of time and energy into careful security analysis, pursue *aggressive* or *enterprising investment*, hunting out bargains where there is a solid *margin of safety* between the price paid for a stock and its *true* value.

In his book *The Intelligent Investor*, Graham describes the benefits of low p/e investing:

> *If we assume that it is the habit of the market to overvalue common stocks which have been showing excellent growth or are glamorous for some other reason, it is logical to expect that it will undervalue – relatively, at least – companies that are out of favor because of unsatisfactory developments of a temporary nature. This may be set down as a fundamental law of the stock market, and it suggests an investment approach that should be both conservative and promising.*

## Value investing guru: Warren Buffett

The modern-day guru of value investing is Warren Buffett, though he dislikes the value/growth dichotomy and seems to have no single straightforward valuation formula. Buffett is one of the most celebrated and successful investors in the world and the returns on his investments over the past three decades have outperformed indexes of the US stock market. How has he done it?

Benjamin Graham wrote that "investing is most intelligent when it is most businesslike," words that encapsulate Buffett's philosophy that the successful investor should buy a business rather than a stock. This means being able to answer three basic questions: is the business simple and understandable? Does it have a consistent operating history? And does it have favorable long-term prospects? Buffett has made most of his money out of sectors he knows intimately, such as media and financial services, and he rarely invests outside this "circle of competence." Knowing the industries, he can then look closely and critically at a company's market standing, earnings potential and management skills to evaluate whether he should invest in its stock.

Buffett buys companies that he likes and understands, *good businesses* in which he can get to know the management and judge their actions in the context of his own experience. "I am a better investor because I am a businessman, and a better businessman because I am an investor," he says.

Is management rational in its financial, operational and capital expenditure policies? Is it candid with the shareholders about performance and does it actively aim to maximize returns to shareholders? And does it resist the institutional imperative to act in its own interests rather than those of the shareholders? Buffett contends that these are all essential questions to ask before investing in a company. And even when proven talented new management comes into a weak company looking to turn it around, you still need to be careful. As Buffett quips:

> ... *when a company with a reputation for incompetence meets a new management with a reputation for competence, it is the reputation of the company that is likely to remain intact.*

It is clear that Buffett's investments have often been more a judgment of the people running a company than the numbers. Nevertheless, there are some powerful and fundamental financial tenets underlying his evaluation of businesses. They include a focus on the measure of return on equity rather than earnings per share, a search for companies with high profit margins, and a check that, for every dollar retained, a company has created at least one dollar of market value. In addition, Buffett calculates *owner earnings*, a company's net income plus depreciation, depletion and amortization, less capital expenditure and any additional working capital.

Using these measures and the company's price quoted on the stock market, Buffett can answer two final questions about a potential purchase: what is the value of the business? And can it be purchased at a significant discount to its value? The critical factor in a successful investment, he contends, is determining the *intrinsic value* of a business and paying a fair or bargain price for it. Opportunities arise when the market forces down the price of a good business or when investor indifference allows a superior business to be priced at half of its intrinsic value.

One principle that is central to Buffett's business analysis is that it does not matter what the overall stock market is doing. You should certainly be psychologically and financially ready for the market's inevitable volatility, and well prepared to see your holdings decline perhaps 50% in value without becoming panic-stricken. But you must also remember that the market is unpredictable and manic depressive, at times wildly excited or unreasonably depressed. Good businesses will not suffer from those moods over the long term.

Similarly, Buffett would argue, there is no point in worrying about the economy and the impact that boom, recession, depression and recovery might have on your portfolio. Again you need to be prepared for the worst: "Noah did not start building the Ark when it was raining." But at the same time, you should be investing only in businesses that can be profitable in all economic environments, concentrating your analysis on the current and potential occupants of your portfolio rather than trying to make macroeconomic forecasts (see *Economic Forecasting*).

Buffett is equally belligerent about how many different stocks the ideal portfolio should hold, the degree to which it should follow the principle of diversification. He is of the opinion that a portfolio should generally be concentrated in a limited number of businesses which the investor can get to know really well. Otherwise, returning to the Old Testament theme, "one buys two of everything and in the end owns a zoo." The short list of equity assets owned by Berkshire Hathaway, Buffett's investment company, reflects this view.

Buffett also believes that the best way to outperform the herd over the long term is to avoid excessive trading of stocks and to reinvest dividends in order to compound gains. Indeed, Berkshire itself has not paid its shareholders a dividend since 1967. In times when many fund managers are constantly changing their portfolio, shifting in and out of a wide variety of stocks and incurring heavy dealing costs, a buy-and-hold strategy can be highly successful.

The important characteristic of such a strategy is that you do not need a lot of good ideas to do well. Brokers are always looking to encourage trading activity in your account. But just a few good decisions made and adhered to are as likely to give you the returns you are seeking, if not better. Buffett thinks the key is patience: "lethargy bordering on sloth remains the cornerstone of our investment style."

And you do not have to be an expert at corporate valuation to benefit from this style of investing. The main thing is to understand the businesses you own or plan to buy. That information can easily be gleaned through their annual reports, the relevant business and financial press and a host of other corporate data, much of which is easily available via the internet.

## Counterpoint

Like beauty, value is in the eyes of the beholder. Critics would say that Warren Buffett does not practice value investing as defined by financial value. What he really does is buy intangible assets, often depressed big names. And his relationship investing, based as it is on extensive personal contacts across US business, hardly makes him a useful role model for the individual investor.

Dominant investors like Buffett have an opportunity to drive a hard bargain. When they are the buyer of last – or nearly last – resort, as should be the case with value investors, they can command special privileges from the companies they are investing in. Buffett has often bought a special class of stock directly from a company, which accords him dividend preference. In return, he has assured management of his continuing voting support (see *Corporate Governance*). This guaranteed proxy voting may have unrecognized monetary value he is able to capture for his shareholders, potentially at a risk to other shareholders in the enterprise. He certainly cannot be seen as a shareholder advocate.

Keynes said if you want to forecast the outcome of a beauty contest, look at the judges, not the beauties. Value depends on stationarity of market factors with the same preferences persisting through time. Since price is generally more volatile than the underlying factors – conventional earnings, dividends, book value, sales or whatever – an attractive statistical relationship of price to these factors is often corrected by nothing more complex than regression to the mean.

Although value proponents ascribe their success to disciplined adherence to enduring truths like p/e, much of their success can be replicated by *negative auto-correlation* or trend reversal. Not only is price more volatile than the underlying financial characteristics, but price may lead changes in those characteristics. Thus, if financial fortunes of earnings are changing, price changes may correctly anticipate those changes and may not be a good indicator of unrecognized investment merit.

A statistician would say that according to standard distribution, there must be someone occupying Buffett's performance slot and it would be someone who had done the right things. But is it a consequence of skill or luck? While Buffett mocks theorists of market efficiency, his superior performance still does not demonstrate that the market is not efficient or that active management will naturally outperform passive strategies like indexing (see *Active Portfolio Management* and *Indexing*).

Value investment tends to work best when the market as a whole is low. There are few guaranteed bargains when the market is highly priced, and with a strongly rising market, growth stocks often rise faster than value stocks. So the late 1990s, with a rampant bull market in the United States and elsewhere, have been grim times for most kinds of value investors. Years of poor performance are eroding the long-term case for value stocks.

In the United States, for example, the S&P 500 beat the Dow Jones Average by eight percentage points in both 1997 and 1998. The Dow has been hit by downgrades from fading industrial and consumer stocks, such as Boeing and Coca Cola, while technology stocks, notably Microsoft, have supported the S&P 500. Economic conditions seem to be powerfully against value investing with falling long-term interest rates increasing the present value of growing revenue streams compared with static ones.

Furthermore, because value stocks tend to be weaker companies in cyclical industries, they are especially vulnerable to an economic slowdown. The assumption that the great companies will always survive and demonstrate their true value, which underlies the classic Graham view of investing, may no longer be true. These days, many leaders of the world's dominant corporations fear that in just a few years' time, their "lunch will be eaten" by competitors they have not yet heard of.

Jeremy Grantham of Grantham, Mayo, Van Otterloo & Co. LLC comments:

> *Value stocks have been bid up to a level where they may not even have an appropriate risk premium far less an excess return. For value investing has always had a hidden but serious risk: the 60-year flood. The so-called price/book effect (and the small stock effect) sound like a free lunch, but in 1929–33, 20% of all companies went bankrupt. They were not the large high-quality blue chips but small* cheap stocks *with low price/ book ratios. To add insult to injury, the data indicates that the best growth managers add more to growth than the best value managers can add to value, probably because the fundamentals and the prices are more dynamic for growth stocks.*

## *Where next?*

Value investing is founded on a variety of security valuation tools. But if you had just a single question to ask of a company or industry – even a country – to determine the market value of a security, what would it be? It should probably be about borrowing capacity: can you borrow, how much and at what price? If you have this information, you need to have very little else. If the issuer of the security concerned can borrow more money at a lower cost than its competitors, then buy it.

The same holds true for a country. Currency of course is a method of borrowing – a representation on paper of the fulfillment of a promise to provide goods and services in the future, very much like borrowing. In the old days, borrowing was fulfilled by completion of a project and then the borrowing was paid off. But that is no longer true; now debt is rolled over and the ability to re-borrow in order to pay off old debt is essential for individuals, companies and countries.

For the tide to turn in favor of the value approach to investing, it is likely that small companies need to come out of their slump of the late 1990s. While value investing is not synonymous with small caps, highly valued markets suggest that value is more likely to be found among smaller companies. But with the contraction of liquidity, diminishing borrowing capacity and quality preference spreads widening, small caps are greatly hurt and seem doomed to continue their bear market.

This also relates to emerging markets – small cap countries – except that the small caps in most emerging markets are local companies with local (rather than internationally trained) management and must borrow at local costs (usually much higher than the international borrowing costs of the large firms in those markets). Following the Asian crisis and its aftermath, the borrowing capacity of the large companies is severely limited and the small ones can get nothing except limited trade finance. Local players tend to speculate in the local companies and international investors in the well-known names. The indexes, mostly made up of large emerging market companies will go up and down now almost entirely on funds flowing from global (US and European) investors, not on fundamentals alone. And the locals will use small stocks for the speculation and trading on inside information (see *Emerging Markets* and *International Money*).

## Read on

### In print

- Benjamin Graham, *The Intelligent Investor: A Book of Practical Counsel* (Reprinted by HarperCollins, 1985)

- Benjamin Graham and David Dodd, *Security Analysis* (1934 edition reprinted by McGraw-Hill, 1997) – the standard work on fundamental analysis, first published in 1934
- Robert Hagstrom, *The Warren Buffett Way: Investment Strategies of the World's Greatest Investor* (John Wiley, 1994)
- Janet Lowe, *Warren Buffett Speaks: Wit and Wisdom from the World's Greatest Investor* (John Wiley, 1997)
- Roger Lowenstein, *Buffett: The Making of an American Capitalist* (Random House, 1995).

## Online

- *www.berkshirehathaway.com* – website with Warren Buffett's annual letters to shareholders in Berkshire Hathaway.

# Venture Capital

T here was a day when the two words *venture capital* would have been an oxymoron for institutional investors. Ventures were for family members or a few rich individuals who wanted to speculate. Capital was for retention or perhaps investment in high-quality, tested equities. Those days, the 1950s, were the aftermath of a depression, a world war and the nagging fear that an inevitable post-war depression would follow. But when prosperity seemed on every corner in the latter part of that decade, a new investment approach was born: venture capital.

Venture capital is essentially the institutionalization of private investment. Wealthy private investors, sometimes called *business angels*, and venture capital companies and funds typically put money into start-ups in their early stages of development in the belief that they offer significant potential to grow substantially and reward investors with exceptional returns over long periods of time.

As private capital, venture investing has become increasingly concerned with business plans – to pass through committees – *burn rates* – the money a start-up is spending in excess of revenues – and exit strategies – a venture capitalist today would never invest without knowing how to get out, either through a buyout or an IPO (see *Initial Public Offerings*). In the mid-1990s in the United States, venture capital would tend to concentrate on late stage companies, those relatively near IPO status. Then came interest in mezzanine financings for an early takeout. And lately, there has been competition to fund high-tech start-ups: aggressive venture capitalists hang out at coffee shops to overhear start-up conversation and jump in to offer money.

## Venture capital guru: Georges Doriot

When venture capital was a new style of investing in the 1950s, the first institutional investor to attract money for it was American Research & Development (ARD) in Boston. This company was the invention of General (ret.) Georges Doriot, a naturalized American who maintained the manner of his native France. He was a senior professor at the Harvard Business School who had served in the American Army during World War II. He returned to his teaching duties convinced that discipline and systems could be applied to investment projects that seemed to defy quantification.

Gen. Doriot, as everyone called him, taught a class called *Manufacturing*, which was a mini-version of what he considered a full MBA curriculum should be. He attracted only top students and demanded that they give his course their highest priority. Students engaged in a major group project of original work, which elsewhere would have been considered a thesis. These projects often resulted in new companies being formed by students following graduation. Federal Express is one of the best known but is far from alone.

Gen. Doriot also served as an active chairman of ARD; the first publicly traded venture capital investor. It was usually the lead investor and did participate with other investors – often, at least at first, the offices of wealthy families. During the 1960s, the ARD portfolio had approximately one hundred positions. It is important to note that only two investments – Digital Equipment and High Voltage Engineering – produced almost all the gains.

There were two lessons about venture investing that Gen. Doriot emphasized. First, invest very carefully but expect that your success ratio will be a tiny fraction of the number of investments. Therefore, run a widely diversified portfolio. Second, prepare to spend time and resources to monitor and nurture your investments during the time you are invested. And his intended investment horizon was perpetual, although his theories suggested that as companies became able to stand on their own feet, ARD should recycle the money elsewhere.

Today, the number of venture capital companies is in the thousands. Venture investing is a worthy subject for business school courses and the field is one of the most popular targets for graduating students. Perhaps influenced by a 50-year business and market recovery, we should not find it unusual for investors to be attracted to venture investing in order to take higher risk in the hope for higher return. Venture investment is now highly specialized with some investing in start-ups; others doing mezzanine investing for companies preparing to raise public market money; others concentrating in particular industries; and still others who tie advice and money in a style that would have been approved by Gen. Doriot.

## Counterpoint

Venture capital firms typically manage multiple funds formed over intervals of several years. These funds usually consist of limited partnerships invested in a number of companies. They generally carry high management fees and offer little liquidity, since investors have to wait until companies in the portfolio go public or are sold to be able to realize their returns.

And many companies in the portfolio may not offer any return: a general rule for the breakdown of returns among venture capital investments is that 40% will be complete losses, 30% will be "living dead," while the remaining 30% may generate substantial returns on the original investment. But while the winners might win big, they often take much longer to emerge than the losers. As William Hambrecht writes:

> In venture capital, the "lemons ripen before the plums"; most funds in their early stages have poor (or sometimes negative) returns as the inferior investments (lemons) take their toll, but after several years, the plums begin to improve returns.

The challenge can be even greater at the height of a bull market with too much money chasing too few great ideas. In a world where timing is everything, the right investment at the wrong moment can be just as disastrous as making the wrong bet. So a venture capitalist can be left with a lot of sleepless nights, even in the best of times.

Internet firms have been the new frontier of venture capital in the late 1990s (see *Internet Investing*). Michael Wolff's book, *Burn Rate*, is a fascinating cultural account of what it is like to be in the internet business today – the financings, the venture capital, the Wall Street deals, and how business and financing get tied together in some ways that are not terribly constructive for the business. But more than that, it is the tempo of the finger-snapping time, which causes so many people such concern about today's market conditions. The book is about a very good idea – the internet – going awry. And it is the process of financing, with its sense of "quick bucks," that is making it happen. It is like reading a mystery: how Wall Street was gulled by those peddling the latest in new technology stocks.

Certainly, it seems difficult to apply the old venture capital rules of strong management, proprietary technology and a small market growing fast to the internet business. Perhaps the widely expected crash in internet shares will force lowered expectations on entrepreneurs and make it easier for venture capitalists to invest in new ideas in Silicon Valley and related hotbeds of high-tech business around the world.

## Where next?

One of the current stars of venture investing is Robert Lessin, chief executive of Wit Capital, the internet-based capital-raising firm started by Andrew Klein (and in which Dean LeBaron, one of this book's co-authors, is an investor). Writing in *Fast Company*, Lessin describes his lessons for anyone considering starting up or investing in an "internet-leveraged" business:

- *Watch the* burn rate: *consider the rate at which a company* goes through money. A good benchmark: a company should spend no more than $200,000 a month. Invest only in companies that can put together a year's worth of capital.

- *Look for creative CEOs: you need chief executives who can react to the changing faces of business. The true entrepreneur can change course at a moment's notice – and succeed. The litmus test: does the CEO think like an artist?*
- *Have an exit strategy: invest only in companies that know the end game. You don't want to run a business. You want to create it. Know when you plan to go public or to sell the business to a larger corporation.*
- *Few assets, few atoms: you want to be as liquid as possible, to own as few assets as possible and to outsource as much of the operation as possible. The premium should be on ideas and dollars. Do as much as you can over the web: finance, distribution, sales, design, supply.*
- *Worship brand equity: look for a strong brand, one that has a stranglehold on its market. Either create a brand or align your start-up with an existing brand that rules its market. Everything rests on the strength of the brand.*
- *The new supreme indicator: the price-to-weight ratio: the less your product weighs relative to its cost, the more secure your investment in the company will be. A computer chip reigns supreme in this regard: it weighs almost nothing but costs a good deal. A silk necktie comes in second. The product doesn't have to be high-tech – but the company that sells and delivers it must be.*

## Read on

### In print

- Andrew Klein, *Wallstreet.Com: Fat Cat Investing at the Click of a Mouse – How Andy Klein and the Internet Can Give Everyone a Seat on the Exchange* (Henry Holt, 1998)

- Michael Wolff, *Burn Rate: How I Survived the Gold Rush Years on the Internet* (Simon & Schuster, 1998).

## Online

- *www.fastcompany.com* – website of the business magazine
- *www.techcapital.com* – website of a leading magazine of technology business and finance
- *www.witcapital.com* – website of the online investment bank launched by Andy Klein.

# James Fraser's Book Bag

## *A Selection of Ten Investment Classics*

O ur contrarian investing guru, James Fraser, runs a publishing house specializing in reprints of investment classics. We invited him to select and comment briefly on ten of his favorites for an "ultimate investor library." All the books are available from Fraser, other booksellers with good investment collections or through online investment books specialist *www.global-investor.com.*

*Why You Win or Lose: The Psychology of Speculation*
Fred C Kelly (Reprinted by Fraser Publishing, 1962)

A successful amateur of the market pinpoints the four greatest enemies to stock market success, and combines eye-opening personal history with observations on the psychological aspects of stock. Easy-to-read primer on those emotions that make us win or lose. Originally published in 1930.

*The Crowd: A Study of the Popular Mind*
Gustave Le Bon (Reprinted by Larlin Corp., 1994)

This masterly analysis of crowd characteristics and psychology is one of the rare books whose message is thoroughly time-tested. More vital today than ever. Indispensable reading on contrary thinking and mass behavior. Originally published in 1896.

*The Battle for Investment Survival*
Gerald M Loeb (Reprinted by John Wiley, 1996)

This book continues to be a practical day-by-day guide that provides experience and wisdom for traders and investors within an ever-changing stock market. The original chapters were written in

1935. The book is a wonderful primer and is worth skimming every few years.

### Reminiscences of a Stock Operator
Edwin Lefevre (Reprinted by Fraser Publishing, 1998)

First published in 1923, this fictionalized biography of Jesse Livermore, one of the greatest speculators ever, remains the most widely read, highly recommended investment book. This is the story of the ultimate *player*, a timeless tale that will enrich the lives – and portfolios – of today's investors. *The Economist* describes it as "a collection of racy tales of topsy-turvy trading and market skullduggery, and of riches won and lost with remarkable sangfroid." It is as timely today as it was 70 years ago.

### Capital Ideas: The Improbable Origins of Modern Wall Street
Peter L Bernstein (Free Press, 1992)

"Bernstein's book is fascinating reading for anyone who wants to understand the financial revolution of the past 20 years," says William E Simon. Fascinating indeed as the author unravels the tale of how the ideas of some *academia nuts*, as they were known on Wall Street, revolutionized the management of the world's wealth and shaped modern finance.

### Extraordinary Popular Delusions and the Madness of Crowds
Charles Mackay (Reprinted by John Wiley, 1995)

"This book has saved me millions of dollars" (Bernard M Baruch). "A case book of human folly" (James Hilton), citing scores of historic manias that led to disaster, notably three great outbreaks of mass investment psychosis: the Mississippi Scheme and the South Sea Bubble in the early 18th century and Dutch tulipmania in the 17th century. Exhaustively documented story of historic disastrous manias is your yardstick for evaluating today's mass trends and fads. Originally written in 1841.

*Art of Contrary Thinking*
Humphrey B Neill (Reprinted by Caxton Press, 1985)

The originator of the Theory of Contrary Opinion answers the question: Contrary Opinion – what is it? With observations on its development and many applications. For anyone seeking to benefit from the contrary approach in analyzing trends. Originally published in 1954.

*Popular Financial Delusions*
Robert L Smitley (Reprinted by Fraser Publishing, 1963)

All the delusions by which investors annually lose billions of dollars are here. The reader will learn to identify those delusions that seek to lure him from his ultimate aim – the protection of capital and the profit that comes from common sense handling of money. Originally published in 1933.

*The Intelligent Investor: A Book of Practical Counsel*
Benjamin Graham (Reprinted by HarperCollins, 1985)

One of America's most respected guides to the stock market, this classic text offers sound principles proven by the success of hundreds of investors for over 35 years. The main objective of the author's philosophy of *value investing* is to develop rational policies that will protect the investor against potential error.

*Common Stocks and Uncommon Profits and Other Writings*
Philip A Fisher (Reprinted by John Wiley, 1996)

The author's investment philosophies, introduced almost 40 years ago, are not only studied and applied by today's finance professionals, but also regarded by many as gospel. Fisher is one of the pioneers of modern investment theory. His book was considered invaluable when first published in 1957 and is a must read today.

## *Read on*

### In print

- Leo Gough, *25 Investment Classics: Insights from the Greatest Investment Books of All Time* (Financial Times Pitman Publishing, 1999)

Charles Ellis, *Classics* (Dow Jones-Irwin, 1989) – the first volume of a series on investment ideas.

### Online

- *www.global-investor.com* – Stephen Eckett's online investment bookstore.

# Future Focus I:
## Ten Key Investment Issues

A list can never be complete or fully comprehensive and *The Ultimate Investor* is no exception. There are, of course, numerous investment ideas and in focusing on the thirty we have discussed, we have had to omit several that could easily have been included. So here are brief discussions of ten more issues in investment, which we think might be worth exploring in greater depth for the future.

## Valuing intangibles

The so-called knowledge economy is making asset valuation an increasingly difficult process. Easily measured corporate assets, such as plant and equipment, are declining in importance while less tangible assets, such as brand names, technology, software and the skills and commitment of the workforce, are becoming more important. This is making even general judgments about the *intrinsic value* of a business very difficult.

Traditional accounting measures the financial impact of what has happened. And it nearly always relies on money transfers to establish a value transfer. But increasingly, with customers, competitors and alliances changing roles, money does not capture every important event. Often knowledge transfers, market access, product integration and personnel assignments are more important than a notation on an income statement.

Today, we have no systematic way of measuring these transfers, which are critical in a knowledge economy. We now have to find ways of valuing intangibles. Techniques to do so are being prepared and we shall see common usage in years to come.

## Ethical investing

Proponents of ethical investing advocate that businesses should be socially and environmentally responsible. For example, John Elkington, a consultant on issues of sustainable development, argues that companies should now pursue a *triple bottom line* of economic prosperity, environmental protection and social equity. Ethical funds avoid investing in industries such as tobacco, alcohol, drugs and arms dealing, or companies that flout health and safety regulations, use animal testing or operate in oppressive regimes.

Ethics used to be a cyclical phenomenon. After a business expansion and bull market followed by a decline, there is usually a resurgence of interest in ethics and principles, especially in business. And when there is easy money to be made, the principles are forgotten, and in the aftermath, we all say: "How could we not have thought of whatever it was that we should have been doing to take care of other people and not exploit the conditions?" A strange thing is happening now: interest in ethics is picking up during an expansion. Business schools are relaunching ethics courses, universities are making a big push to teach ethics to undergraduates, and professional associations are developing ethical guidelines. But ethics is extremely simple: just ask somebody what have they done, at their own sacrifice, to benefit the interests of others.

## Insider trading

Even some hard-core believers in market efficiency will concede that company directors trading in their own shares tend to beat the market. This suggests that some people are more plugged in than others and that the key to active investing might be to follow smart insiders or, better perhaps, to follow companies with smart greedy insiders: companies whose directors own a lot of stock and are buying more. Certainly, that is the implication of a book by Michigan finance professor Nejat Seyhun on how to make use of investment intelligence from insider trading.

The conventional regulatory response to insider trading has been to try to keep the market fair by preventing insiders from trading during corporate blackout periods and making government officials use blind trusts. So while the United States considers itself the model of disclosure in financial affairs, information known by insiders is kept out of the market by our archaic rules. Perhaps we should instead be encouraging insiders to get their information priced into the market by trading whichever way they wish, revealing their insider status though perhaps not necessarily their identity.

## Agency

Agency issues tend to be forgotten in bull markets. But there is an ever-present phenomenon of people engaged in generally high-priced services – like investment managers, brokers, consultants – acting in their own interests rather than those of the fiduciaries they should be serving. Usually, the mistakes or omissions are fairly minor – high expenses; a limousine when a subway would do; wasted meetings; soft dollars, where institutions tolerate higher commission charges than do the more tight-fisted retail customers using electronic brokerage for their own accounts; and slow innovation, because it is so much fun making money the old-fashioned way.

This is really the edge of ethics. It is not out-and-out dishonesty. Rather, it is the avoidance of putting somebody else's interests ahead of your own. It is a field of academic study, which should be pushed more by the various industry groups that hold out their standards of high ethics.

## Models

Models are developed on the basis of history and while they may be quite sophisticated, they frequently prove to be useless or wrong. The problem is that they depend on the assumptions that the past is the prolog to the future, that all information is captured by the model period, and that no simplifying assumptions predetermine the outcomes. Models will operate slavishly, continuously doing whatever is instructed by an embedded algorithm. They can be marvelously elegant – and tend to become more so with time as they incorporate yet more initial conditions. But they are dumb: they do not learn but depend on the learning of the model builder.

Instead, we should be using forward-testing and simulations, understanding how the assumptions selected for modeling will determine outcomes. Simulations are often messy, fuzzy and seemingly counter-intuitive. Similar initial conditions can produce differing results. The inter-relations are complex and chaotic. Instead of neat one-to-one correlations of the components, simulations act as a whole with every part moving at once.

But simulations more nearly act as humans do: learning from the past and getting smarter in the future. Combined with complexity engines that do not guarantee a specific outcome from every event, you can play through business possibilities. We can train ourselves and do forward-testing rather than relying on the historical accidents of backtesting.

## Risk

The conventional view of risk is that the long term is less risky than the short term because there is regression to the mean: if we wait long enough, economic balance will return. There is also the notion of a built-in equity premium: after a fifty-year period of expansion, we take it for granted that equities will produce higher returns because they have in the past – and we think it is because they have higher degrees of risk.

But there is a strong academic view that says risk may compound in the long run, and that you do not necessarily have regression to the mean. Rather, you can have deviations from the mean over long periods of time and things may get worse. There are economics of increasing or decreasing returns; and momentum and expectations may create their own trends. Are we prepared for the time when risk produces lower returns for equities? Or that risk itself, on closer examination, is something other than volatility but rather risk of loss and risk of being knocked out of the game?

## Time

We are raised to think of time as absolutely immutable, a steady object: time goes on. Economists and investment people, for example, know that time is the x-axis, with equal units all the way across, and that time flows continuously. And we wear wristwatches that click at a steady rate. But this assumption is wrong and it builds errors into our system. Time comes in packets, quanta, bunches of information, at irregular rates. Time means different things to different analysts. Some market events on particularly significant days are more important than ten years of market data.

We should look at time with a great degree of skepticism and search for new tools in dealing with it. High-frequency analysis is one way to take time out of the equation and look at it as a complete variable. We will make better forecasts if we treat time as discontinuous, not continuous. For example, we might guess that events will compress as impending events are discounted faster than before. But events outside the markets will probably not happen much faster than before. So if markets react faster, we should have a quick discounting response to the hints and then long periods of frustrating dullness – a pulsating, quantum burst market with long pauses.

## Diversification

Conventional investment wisdom says that diversification is good. If risk (volatility) is equivalent to return and we know how to increase risk, all we have to do is mix assets that are uncorrelated to increase aggregate (portfolio) returns and reduce risk. Alphas, betas and R-squared are all part of the analyst lexicon. Close to the means, these measures seem to be quite stationary over the time periods we have studied them.

But an alternative complexity-based view suggests that past correlation tells us little about *stress* times. The factors that determine values are non-stationary and combine in different ways. The evolutionary history of markets is unlikely to combine in the same way each time. And when they part, the results may appear chaotic.

## Causality

Investment people frequently confuse coincidence with causality. With any two sets of finite data, we can find correlations which will satisfy a statistical test. Once we find those correlations, especially if they are plausible, we tend to enshrine them as causality, cause and effect. We assume that the very conditions that produced those circumstances, coincidences perhaps, in the past can be projected into the future where conditions can be entirely different. Even if they were the same, the result might not be the same in a complex adaptive system. And once we project into the future, we further attribute leads and lags that are quite predictable – or rather, we think they are predictable – and ascribe those to the system that we have produced.

It is a tissue of assumptions, of implausibility, and produces a result that is highly prone to flaws, failures and excuses. We even go on to be prescriptive in the cause and effect, to say that if we do this, that will happen. For example, we say if interest rates are increased, that will make the stock market go down. This is not necessarily true if the market interprets that move in entirely the opposite way, perhaps as an indicator of a very strong economy. So it is not a one-to-one relationship. There are new tools that are very infrequently used and which do not promise as much: fuzzy data, high-frequency data, adaptive systems, simulations. We should look at those as being at least more honest than what we do now.

## "What's the market doing?"

In trying to diagnose the health of markets, it is difficult to find conditions in past practices that fit today's circumstances. Perhaps it is because we are looking for physical conditions when we should be looking for mental conditions as a precedent for today's market conditions. Today's markets in the United States are manic depressives, with violent swings of euphoria and depression without any connection to a sense of reality. Manic depression is not a curable disease, except in the extreme, but it can be controlled with Prozac and other anti-depressants.

Or perhaps the market is a nuclear reactor. A nuclear reactor is absolutely necessary for the economy around it but not the other way around. The economy does not drive the nuclear reactor, except over the very long run. And the nuclear reactor has to reach a very delicate, critical balance within a critical mass to run. But not so much that you generate, in fact, a runaway meltdown, as happened in Chernobyl.

We may be running into a particular hot spot in this nuclear reactor of the market within the area of technology stocks. Normally, you put down some safety rods to absorb some of the reaction. But the last time we did that in this reactor, in early 1998, it generated a global credit crunch and we pulled the safety rods out very quickly. Now, we have no tools with which to dampen down the market so we are concerned by the lack of a safety device. We do not want to have the radioactivity distributed throughout the air as sometimes happens in the case of a nuclear accident, and indeed we do not want to have to encase this market in a coffin of glass.

Finally, we have a very odd paradox today between the theoretical conditions of markets and our abilities to implement market strategies. On the one hand, markets seem remarkably like those of the 1870s when there was oversupply of goods and a noticeable satiation on the part of consumers as an aftermath to the US Civil War. Prices went down, commodity prices declined and markets were very volatile, much more than seemed warranted by the economic conditions.

Many of today's conditions seem like that period of the late 1800s. And yet, today's technical implementation of markets is like the coming century: markets are global; they are instantaneous; they are accessible; they are cheap. The individual rocket power of the free market forces vastly exceeds that which can be marshaled by central bankers and treasuries. They are powerless and must simply look on to see what happens when markets move, thereby affecting economies and trade in their aftermath.

## Read on

### In print

- John Elkington, *Cannibals with Forks: The Triple Bottom Line of 21st Century Business* (Capstone Publishing/New Society Publishers, 1997)
- Robert Reilly and Robert Schweihs, *Valuing Intangible Assets* (McGraw-Hill, 1998)
- Nejat Seyhun, *Investment Intelligence for Insider Trading* (MIT Press, 1998).

### Online

- *www.fortuneinvestor.com* – a website with extensive information on potential investments, particularly featuring details on directors' dealings in the stocks of the companies they manage.

# Future Focus II:
## Ten Key Global Issues

tewart Myers, finance professor at the Sloan School at MIT, likes to say that there are always ten problems in finance that are intractable. If one is solved, another comes in, perhaps because our ten fingers are a handy counting device. We can apply this unit-of-ten circumstance to other walks of life too. In almost any field, it seems there are always ten burning questions, issues for which there are no clear answers. Different observers will assign different weights to the factors and come up with different opinions. Some will be solved, some will just wither away and others will stay. We briefly discuss ten issues here that we think are of global significance and all of which may have implications for our investment futures. What are your ten?

## Twin peaks

The world is undergoing a sharp polarization across economies, clustering into the very rich and the very poor, while the middle-income class of countries is vanishing. What is more, the emergence of these *twin peaks*, as London School of Economics professor Danny Quah describes the phenomenon, applies not just to economies but equally to people within individual societies. Note, for example, that the world's 225 richest individuals – of whom 60 are Americans – have a combined wealth of over $1 trillion. This is equal to the total annual income of the poorest half of the world's population.

The mission of reducing the gap between the *haves* and *have-nots* is vital. Aggregate growth is not continuing because the have-nots have said "enough." According to the 1998 United Nations report on world income disparity, global capitalism based on the model of the past fifty years is being rejected by the majority of the world's population. We might say that a two-generation period is not enough, but the world is deciding that it is. Government is taking control in Asia, often at the provocation of the IMF; Russia has repudiated, at least in official statements, the consequences of *bandit capitalism*; and China, never a model democracy, has confirmed that its path of "capitalism with a socialist face" is the right way in launching a trillion dollar public works program. There are major structural problems that unbridled capitalism, best personified in Russia but evident elsewhere, including political campaign financing in the United States, will not solve.

## Information divide

Boundaries, chasms, barriers are forming in American society that may produce very severe clashes in the future. Widening income inequality is one and it has been gaining momentum over the last twenty years. But there is also the financial gap between those with access to the financial system and the serfs without. People who have access to financial instruments – savings accounts, mutual funds and the like – are doing much better than those who do not. This gap is also widening further although a market decline may have an impact there.

There is also an information gap. Access to computer skills, the ability to self-learn and have access to the world's knowledge through the internet helps a certain group of people educate themselves, adapt themselves to new skills and new climates. But those without fall behind. Computers enable the *haves* to have more and, without them, the *have-nots* are left out. In combination with the poverty divide and the financial divide, the information divide may produce circumstances in the future, which could provoke very sharp cleavages in the American economy and elsewhere.

## Comparative disadvantage

We have all been raised to understand comparative advantage in economics, whereby through globalization and free flow of capital, each of us learns to pursue our own best specialty. And by combining all of these separate agents, we produce the best results because everybody does what they can do best based on their circumstances, skills and intelligence. What we do not understand is comparative disadvantage, where those people who are not only below the poverty line, but below the financial line – the financial world does not reach them – and below the information line – the free flow of information does not reach them – become an increasing social drag, which must be taken care of.

So now we may be entering a world of comparative disadvantage where, for social purposes, we must support those skills that are not the best, perhaps through negative tariffs or subsidies. They may be the most local or the most political. But such actions could be a vital response to the rising tide of nationalism around the world, which is replacing the global movement of the last generation, and the unrest on the part of populations, who are concerned that the apparent prosperity has only benefited the few, not the many. Society as a whole must carry the burden.

## Free trade

Who really is in favor of free trade? It is a nice phrase but the answer is any country representing those industries that are the most productive, the most prosperous and would benefit most. The United States is in favor of free trade for financial services, for example, but it is not in favor of free trade for agricultural goods. And while the United States has been, in principle, a global supporter of multilateral trade negotiations, especially through the World Trade Organization, it usually resorts to bilateral, specific negotiations with trading partners with whom it has an adverse trade balance, especially those in Asia. It is prepared to undermine the overall notion of free trade and say that, specifically, when we get into periods of instability, we have to solve problems on a case-by-case basis. This is not going to help global trade.

The United States also engages in vigorous anti-dumping, for example, against Russian steel companies and African agricultural products. Yet it is happy to dump education, selling it around the world at below the cost of producing it in the United States by offering scholarships and fellowships to bring in the best students. So, free trade comes wrapped in prosperity and it is a very industry-specific prosperity at that, rather than a general proposition.

## Connectivity

One of the essential features of this era is the extraordinary amount of connectivity that we have – on a personal level, corporate level, governmental level. We are able to intertwine almost everything that we do in ways we have never been able to do before. We have benefited from comparative advantage, in that each of us has become a specialist at something and we can produce that something for other people better than they can for themselves. But no longer are we generalists, no longer can we survive by ourselves. As such, we are enjoying the benefits, but exposed to the risks also, of increasing returns, which has become the new economics.

We have a global financial interconnectivity that we have never had before. We have a common banking system, the capacity for money to flow electronically around the globe, instantly, in unrestrained amounts, and with no transparency. We have a common educational system for business people, based largely on the American model. We have the notion that Adam Smith's unrestrained capitalism for the individual produces the best common good. And we even have a common desktop, the English language.

But when one of our global members gets into trouble, whether Korea, Indonesia, Russia or Brazil, the others feel, perhaps quite rightly, that a major rescue package at any cost must be contained. It is rather like a patient with a potentially contagious disease. But it seems the only way to stop it is to put the diseased patient back into the population. The way you would normally take care of a diseased patient is by quarantine.

## Nuclear race

At the end of the Cold War, we thought that nuclear bomb technology was finished. But despite the propaganda campaign to say that nuclear weapons are no longer useful, we have demonstrated that they are the most useful things of all. India and Pakistan received a slight slap by joining the nuclear club, but then it turned into a pat. Both used *blitz* timing, in a public relations sense: if you want to do something bad, do it quickly, get it over with and then appear contrite.

Another example of the value of nuclear weapons is Russia, which has received economic aid of billions of dollars every year since the Soviet break-up. Ukraine, in similar circumstances, received almost nothing, but it gave up its nuclear weapons to Russia at the behest of the United States, voluntarily. Other countries with nuclear capabilities that are at the fringes – Korea, Egypt, Israel, Iran and Iraq – will all want to cross the line. Even in Latin America, Brazil and Argentina might too.

So the nuclear race is on. The club is important to be a member of – not for political expansion, but for economic purposes. It is a high-return business.

## Terrorism

Terror – the empowerment of individuals to destroy, with a purpose or not – is a force that we have no idea how to stop. We know that individuals can be empowered to use simply terrible weapons, and there is no particular form of protection that we have for that. And not necessarily just external terrorism, but internal, the most insidious of all. We have seen that cropping up around the world where leaders have been assassinated by their own people. We may see more with more tremendously devastating suitcase-sized weapons.

But should we try to combat terrorism through a war of explosions or a war of intelligence? Perhaps disclosure might work. Terrorists work in the dark. They engage in activities where they are always in a clandestine environment. What they cannot stand is to be exposed. And yet, that is exactly what we should do: disclose who they are, what their connections are, who deals with them and who helps them. Typically, their supporters radiate out, including bankers, industrialists, shippers – all helping terrorists, either intentionally or otherwise.

## Weightlessness

Economic value – whatever it is we are willing to pay money for – used to be concentrated in big physical things like steel girders, huge cars and heavy wooden furniture. All this has changed. We are now living in what economics journalist Diane Coyle calls the *weightless world*, a place where value lies predominantly in products with no physical presence: things like software code, genetic codes, the creative content of a film or piece of music, the design of a new pair of sunglasses, the vigilance of a security guard or the helpfulness of a shop assistant.

The size of the advanced industrial economies has grown more than threefold in the past fifty years – but the literal weight of economic output has barely climbed at all. As a result of a phenomenal series of advances in computer and telecommunications technology, our economies are growing bigger but not heavier, increasingly miniaturized, "dematerialized" or weightless. The best example is the microchip in a musical greeting card, which contains more computer power than was on the entire planet in 1945.

This is not to say we have lost out appetite for physical goods – clearly, this it not true. Rather, as a result of both new technologies and increasing prosperity, the share of the value of goods created by materials is minimal compared with the research, design and marketing that have gone into them. The fundamental natural resource of the weightless world is human creativity and intelligence.

## Language

The internet has changed language in ways that are permanent. The old ways will never come back. Capital letters are going out of use as most computer programs are case-insensitive. We now put links in our writings, hot links to other sites and other programs, somewhat like footnotes, but as an active part of our writing. Our writing is more conversational. It is quick, not necessarily following the old grammatical rules. And it incorporates multi-media devices and graphics. We have returned to working with words and graphics together.

And we have wonderful new tools. Not only do we have spell-check and grammar-check programs in Word, we also have a secret weapon tucked in there called auto summary, which can condense writing down to any size that we wish. We can also get translations through such programs as Babelfish and LanguageForce, which tries to cope with some of the more exotic languages. These programs are somewhat primitive, but clearly they will get it right eventually and make sense of the whole thing. "The art of readable writing" will never be the same.

## Games and simulations

We used to look at children playing computer games and thought they were wasting their time. But we were wrong. In fact, they learn an enormous amount because they are right inside the game, working on strategies. These games were the forerunners of business-type simulations and the spreadsheet revolution that started with VisiCalc, went on to Lotus 1-2-3, and is now coming to complicated 3-D sight maps. Simulations and these types of spreadsheets are coming together to portray business graphically and in a way that is just as realistic as the flight simulator is to a pilot.

Games are devices for learning, devices for testing and devices for recording alternatives that might have occurred in history but actually did not. Games need to have reward systems and penalty systems and they need to have meaningful scenarios. But they can be forward-testing, rather than merely looking at history; and they can be a way of practicing for a variety of alternatives that may occur in the future but have not occurred in the past.

## Read on

### In print

- Diane Coyle, *The Weightless World: Thriving in the Digital Age* (Capstone Publishing/MIT Press, 1997).

### Online

- *econ.lse.ac.uk/staff/dquah* – website of Danny Quah, inventor of the concepts of twin peaks and weightlessness
- *www.babelfish.com* and *www.languageforce.com* – websites with language translation tools
- *www.deanlebaron.com* – website of one of this book's co-authors, featuring a daily video commentary on global issues
- *www.un.org* – website of the United Nations
- *www.wto.org* – website of the World Trade Organization.

# AIMR's One Hundred Top Websites For Investment

T his directory of some of the best websites for investors was compiled by the Association for Investment Management & Research (AIMR) as part of their first live "webcast," *Using the Internet for Investment Research* by Dean LeBaron and Paul Turner. It is reproduced here by kind permission of AIMR.

## Introduction

The internet has taken the world by storm and the investment profession has not escaped the onslaught. The internet will change how investment professionals work: how they research investments; how they search for information; and how they communicate with other professionals. The information available on the internet today for investment professionals is vast and growing by leaps and bounds every day. This directory can only be a snapshot of a fast-moving train.

The title of the directory is somewhat misleading. First, there are more than one hundred websites profiled. Second, selecting the *best* websites is by definition subjective. A site useful for one person may be of little value to another. It is more accurate to say that this publication contains about 125 useful sites selected from literally thousands on the internet. It will be useful for investment professionals with some knowledge of the internet, who want to use the internet as another tool in their professional arsenal. And it will be useful to many individual investors too.

The directory covers most investment areas, including information about equities, bonds, money markets, currencies, futures and options, macroeconomic information and so on. One caveat:

the internet is changing daily. Sites described will change over time or may disappear altogether. Web addresses may change. Usually, sites that change their address will often leave a forwarding one, just like the Post Office. The web version of this list is updated periodically to reflect changes:

*www.aimr.org/aimr/knowledge/seminars/webcast/top_100.html*

I hope investment professionals and others find this publication to be a useful tool.

Paul Turner<br>
Director of Educational Technology<br>
Association for Investment Management & Research

## Associations

*Association for Investment Management & Research*
www.aimr.org

AIMR is the leading professional organization providing global leadership for investment professionals worldwide. With over 30,000 members in more than 85 affiliated societies and chapters in over 79 countries around the world, AIMR sets the highest standards in education, ethics and advocacy for investment professionals, their employers and their clients.

*Association of Mutual Fund Investors*
www.amfi.com

The Association of Mutual Fund Investors (AMFI) is a research organization dedicated to helping its members beat the stock market through its mutual fund investment systems.

*The Bond Market Association*
www.psa.com

Legislative/regulatory issues; market practices; conferences, research, reports, statistics, search facility.

# Banks and Investment Companies

*JP Morgan*
www.jpmorgan.com

Extensive site with a variety of information about JP Morgan's products and services.

*Morgan Stanley Dean Witter*
www.ms.com

Extensive information for global investors.

*Wells Fargo Bank*
www.wellsfargo.com

This is a comprehensive online banking site that includes automatic bill payment and special services such as ordering foreign currencies and traveler's checks online. This site offers a good sense of what is possible in online banking.

# Brokers

## Discount

*Charles Schwab*
www.schwab.com

Extensive resource for investors from the discount broker.

## Full-service

*AG Edwards*
www.agedwards.com

AG Edwards is a full-service brokerage firm with a century-long commitment to investor success.

*Merrill Lynch*
www.ml.com

Full-service broker.

*Prudential Securities*
www.prusec.com

Full-service broker. Site provides: fundamental research, industry reports, online trading, real-time market data, stock quotes.

## Online

*Ameritrade*
www.ameritrade.com

Online brokerage.

*Currency Management Corporation*
www.forex-cmc.co.uk

A UK-based online trading firm, specializing in derivatives trading.

*Datek*
www.datek.com

Online brokerage.

*Discover Brokerage Direct*
www.discoverbrokerage.com

This site offers real-time quotes, instant account updates and portfolio management along with online trading.

*DLJ Direct*
www.dljdirect.com

DLJ Direct is the online brokerage of Donaldson, Lufkin & Jenrette.

*E-Trade*
www.etrade.com

E★TRADE Group Inc. is an online broker. E★TRADE also offers a range of portfolio management tools and access to company research, market analysis, news and other information services.

## Directories

*Dow Jones Business Directory*
bd.dowjones.com/index.asp

Dow Jones Business Directory provides resources about business information on the web. The Directory is published by Dow Jones & Company Inc., the world's leading publisher of business news and information in every form of media.

*Global Investor Directory*
www.global-investor.com

This directory contains various types of information, including: a Global Investor Directory, a resource for financial sites and services; a Market Performance service that compares the performance of the world's major markets; Finance netWatch, which looks at the latest developments in finance on the net; information about ADRs, with a complete listing of international ADRs issued in the United States. The service can create a customized portfolio monitor.

*Hoover's Online*
www.hoovers.com

Online site for the Hoover's Company directory. Includes free and subscriber-only information about 12,000 companies; 2700 in-depth reports; custom searches; stock screening; information about IPOs, cyberstocks, industry snapshots and employment information.

*Invest-o-rama*
investorama.com

Huge resource for information. Includes a directory of investing resources with over 7000 entries in 75 categories, each with a brief description; a complete directory of public companies with websites, with over 4500 links; a portfolio tracker; stock research that features 75 direct links to information about a specific stock; and technical charts with customizable parameters.

*Yahoo*
www.yahoo.com

One of the most popular internet directories.

*Yahoo Finance and Investment Index*
www.yahoo.com/Business/Finance_and_Investment

The finance and investment index of the Yahoo internet directory.

## Megasites

*Armchair Millionaire*
www.armchairmillionaire.com

An extensive information and educational site for personal investors.

*IDD Information Services of Dow Jones*
www.idd.net

This is an umbrella site for financial services, including: Smith Barney Wall Street Watch; daily market information; information from the New York Institute of Finance Center; and general articles on equities/funds.

*Investor Home*
www.investorhome.com

Lots of useful information and links. Contains a very useful collection of finding tools, such as search screens from Yahoo and other search engines, stock analysis tools, etc.

*Investors Edge*
www.irnet.com

Operates Stock Point, a general information service for investors, with a wide range of investment information.

*InvestTools*
investools.com

Huge site for personal investors, with information including: links to extensive research reports from Zack's, Standard & Poor's and others; news from Reuters Worldwide Corporate News Wire; extensive charting; quotes; investment newsletters; portfolio tracking and account management.

*Microsoft Investor*
investor.msn.com/common/welcome.asp?

Huge site with variety of information for the individual investor.

*OSU Virtual Finance Library*
www.cob.ohio-state.edu/dept/fin/overview.htm

A huge site, with links to every conceivable subject in the areas of finance and investment.

*Pathfinder*
www.pathfinder.com/welcome

Pathfinder is Time's umbrella site for: Fortune, Hoover's Business Profiles and Money. The site offers general information on personal finance and investment.

*PAWWS Financial Network*
pawws.com

PAWWS Financial Network is a comprehensive internet investment resource. It features integrated portfolio accounting, securities and market research tools, real-time quotations, and online trading.

*Smartmoney Interactive*
www.smartmoney.com

Smartmoney Interactive, developed from *Smart Money* magazine, is a large, general-purpose site for the individual investor.

*Stockmaster*
www.stockmaster.com

Extensive investment information, including personal portfolios, news, SEC filings, detailed quotes, earnings histories and more.

*Thomson Investors Network*
www.thomsoninvest.net

A large site with a variety of information for individual investors.

*Wall Street Research Net*
www.wsrn.com

This site contains a wealth of information about particular subjects, as well as references to hundreds of other sites. It is a gateway site.

## Search Engines

*Copernic*
www.copernic.com

A software product that searches ten other search engines at a time. Copernic saves searches for future reference.

*DailyStocks*
www.dailystocks.com

Daily Stocks is a search engine that uses extensive links to other sites. Includes quotes, charts, news, SEC filings, research reports, earnings estimates, magazine articles, fundamentals, 10K and 10Q filings and other similar information.

*Excite*
www.excite.com

One of several excellent search engines. Excite also includes a Business and Investing channel, which includes links to a huge variety of investment-related information.

*FinanceWise*
www.financewise.com

FinanceWise is a search engine that focuses specifically on financial-only content. FinanceWise indexes sites with content of interest to the financial world. Every topic, from risk management to syndicated finance and equities is indexed in depth, with the contents of each site evaluated by FinanceWise's editorial staff before sites are allowed into FinanceWise's search index.

# Exchanges

*American Stock Exchange and NASDAQ*
www.amex.com and www.nasdaq.com

Sites for the American Stock Exchange and NASDAQ with extensive information, including information about the most active companies traded, listed companies, options and derivatives, SPDRs & WEBS, etc.

*List of World Exchanges*
db.axone.ch/FinanceWatch/ExchangesByCountry.cfm

A 'mega-list' of world exchanges.

*The Chicago Board of Trade*
www.cbt.com

Site for the Chicago Board of Trade, with detailed information about futures, options, commodities, etc.

# Financial Research

## Bonds

*Bloomberg – International Yield Curves*
www.bloomberg.com/markets

Information about bond performance, both US and global, including international yields. Also includes equity indexes and currency information.

*JP Morgan*
www.jpmorgan.com/research

Daily updated information on government bond indices, Emerging Markets Bond Index plus currency indices and other information about bonds.

## Company research

*DailyStocks*
www.dailystocks.com

Daily Stocks is a search engine that uses extensive links to other sites. Includes quotes, charts, news, SEC filings, research reports, earnings estimates, magazine articles, fundamentals, 10K and 10Q filings and other similar information.

*First Call Corporation*
www.firstcall.com

First Call Corporation, a division of Thomson Financial Services, is a source of real-time, commingled research, earnings estimates and corporate information serving the worldwide financial community. The information distributed by First Call originates from the world's leading brokerage firms, investment research firms and global corporations. Services include, among others: FIRST CALL Notes, for real-time, electronic delivery of commingled morning meeting comments, intraday research broadcasts and special equity notes from more than 250 top brokerage and investment research firms worldwide; FIRST CALL Research Direct® offers clients real-time, electronic access to more than 500,000 commingled full-text research reports – including all text, charts, graphs, color and formatting – from more than 190 leading brokerage firms worldwide.

*FreeEdgar*
www.freeedgar.com

Offers free SEC company filings in a more accessible form than is available directly from the SEC.

*Hoover's Stock Screener*
www.stockscreener.com

Hoover's stock screening database.

*Morningstar.Net*
www.morningstar.net

This is the popular Morningstar website, with extensive stock and mutual fund research and screening information.

*Motley Fool*
www.fool.com

A popular site for investment education, portfolio management, news and advice about personal investment.

*Public Register's Annual Report Service*
www.prars.com

The Public Register's Annual Report Service (PRARS), is America's largest annual report service. Company financials, including annual reports, prospectuses or 10k's on over 3,200 public companies are available without charge to the investing public.

*Quicken Financial WebSite*
www.quicken.com/investments

A one-stop shop of financial information. Includes, among other information, investment, savings, loan, retirement and insurance information.

*Standard & Poor's Index*
www.stockinfo.standardpoor.com

Standard & Poor's Equity Investor Services provides investors with extensive information about companies, industries and equity markets, including the well-known S&P stocks reports.

*Stockmaster*
www.stockmaster.com

Extensive investment information, including personal portfolios, news, SEC filings, detailed quotes, earnings histories and more.

*Telestock*
www.teleserv.co.uk/stock

TeleStock provides finance information as well as 'day old' online quotes of major US and European shares, options and commodities.

*Zacks Investment Research*
www.zacks.com

Extensive site featuring Zack's popular investment analysts' reports.


## Charting/Technical analysis

*Big Charts*
www.bigcharts.com

BigCharts offers free online access to charts, reports, indicators and quotes on over 50,000 US stocks, mutual funds and major market indexes. BigCharts is constructed with several proprietary bolt-on financial applications and is powered by Concerto's proprietary Financial Media Server (FMS).

*Decision Point Market Timing & Charts*
www.decisionpoint.com

Decision Point is an information and educational source for technical analysis and stock market timing. Includes extensive free technical analysis materials, including: daily charts; quick technical analyses of stocks, mutual funds and industry groups; historical charts; commentary; analysis; daily coverage of funds, including BUY and

SELL Signals and Strength Analysis; daily relative strength rank-ing and weekly charts of 102 Industry Groups and 12 Market Sec-tors.

*Online calculators*
www.global-investor.com/dir/g-calcs.htm

Calculators for the following types of information: Commissions Calculators, Options, Convertible Bonds, Warrants, Fixed Income Yield Calculators, Statistics, Present/Future Value, Deposit Cal-culators, Loan Payments, US Savings Bond Calculators, General Personal Finance, Retirement.

*Stock Market Timing*
www.firstcap.com

Stock Market Timing is a short-term, top-down technical approach to trading the stock market. It is intended for investors and traders who are not satisfied with the buy-and-hold forever approach to investing. It is a methodology that seeks to reduce market risk by recognizing the underlying market trend and then by trading with the trend of the market, long or short. The site includes analysis of the direction of both the stock and bond markets; market evalua-tions, a list of stocks with favorite technicals.

*Stock Smart*
www.stocksmart.com

Extensive investment information for stocks, markets, and returns, and has *active* (and fast) bar charts for its market watch, mutual fund watch, and industry watch, including software for technical analysis.

## Real-time data

*DBC Online*
www.dbc.com

A provider of real-time market data to individual investors, provided by Data Broadcasting Corporation.

*Quote. Com*
www.quote.com

Quote.com provides financial market data to internet users. This includes delayed and real-time current quotes on stocks, options, commodity futures, mutual funds, and indices, for US and Canadian markets. Quote.com also provides real-time business news, earnings forecasts & reports, market analysis & commentary, including analyst upgrades and downgrades, fundamental (balance sheet) data, annual reports, intraday & historical charts, weather information and company profiles.

## Currency information

*Bloomberg Markets*
www.bloomberg.com/markets

News and detailed information about currency rates, including a table of US Dollar rates with selected key cross rates, as well as information about stocks, rates and bonds, currencies and commodities.

*CNN Financial Network*
cnnfn.com/markets/currencies.html

Includes table of US Dollar rates updated around the clock and other currency information.

## Depositary receipts

*American Depositary Receipts*
www.global-investor.com/adr/index.htm

This site includes an extensive database of over 2,000 ADRs from all over the world.

## Futures, options, derivatives

*Chicago Mercantile Exchange*
www.cme.com

The Chicago Mercantile Exchange site offers information about futures and options contracts traded on the CME's trading floors, including currencies, interest rates, stock indexes and agricultural commodities. The site includes news, electronic trading and educational resources, including online simulated trading, and a EuroFX Resource Center.

*Finance.wat.ch*
finance.wat.ch

Finance.wat.ch offers information about futures/options contracts; financial education/training resources; a glossary explaining derivative instruments; and various reports and papers on derivatives and risk management; and guided tours of finance on the internet.

*INO Global Markets*
www.ino.com

Global information about futures and options.

*MarketPlex*
www.cbot.com/mplex

MarketPlex is located at the Chicago Board of Trade and is an umbrella site for a collection of futures-related services, technical charts, research reports, select articles from journals, access to subscription MRI service, daily charts/data, and access to MJK closing prices for commodity exchanges worldwide.

## High-tech companies

*Hoover's Online*
www.hoovers.com/features/industry/internet.html

An information source for internet-related stocks, this site features free in-depth profiles of more than 100 public internet companies, plus news, industry information, stock quotes, charts and daily market information on the cyberstocks.

*High-Tech Investor*
members.home.net/mathewi/investone.html

Extensive resources for high-tech companies; also includes a collection of links to other sources.

*Silicon Investor*
www.techstocks.com

Extensive information from a virtual company about high-tech stocks.

*CMP Net*
www.techweb.com/wire/finance

The "technology news site," this site focuses on news about high technology companies and has a company news search engine.

## Macroeconomic research

*Yardeni's Economics Network*
www.yardeni.com

Dr Ed Yardeni is Chief Economist and Global Investment Strategist of Deutsche Bank Securities in New York. Dr Yardeni's site offers a wide variety of information, including country reports, industry reports and so on. Information categories include: macroeconomic information; economic analysis and forecasting; economic reports; economic research studies; charting information; and a Y2K Reporter.

## Mutual funds

*Fidelity Investments*
www.fid-inv.com

Primary site for Fidelity Investments. Offers account access, stock analysis tools, educational materials, etc.

*Mutual Funds Interactive*
www.brill.com

Extensive information about mutual funds, including: market analyses; mutual fund recommendations; features; educational articles; search facility and other resources; and even a *toolshed* for mutual fund investors.

*Mutual Funds Interactive*
www.fundsinteractive.com/toolshed.html

Partnering with Lipper Analytical Services, Value Line and Data Broadcast Corporation, and including links to BigCharts, Zack's and Edgar-Online, to offer useful tools for mutual fund investors.

*Mutual Funds*
www.mfmag.com/start.htm

Extensive information about Mutual Funds. Most information is available only to subscribers, however.

*Quicken Financial WebSite Mutual Funds*
www.quicken.com/investments/mutualfunds

Offers extensive mutual fund finding tools, including profiles by Morningstar and Value Line, and a useful "Quick Fund Finder" by Morningstar.

*Vanguard Securities*
www.vanguard.com

Extensive site from the mutual fund company, with a wealth of information for individual mutual fund investors, including brokerage services and online access for employees with 401(k) plans. Includes variety of educational materials.

## Software/Tools

*Brightline*
www.ragm.com/brightline

Market simulation from Robert AG Monks.

*Microsoft Agent*
www.microsoft.com/workshop/imedia/agent/default.asp

An example of the evolving area of voice recognition software.

*Olsen & Associates*
www.olsen.ch

Olsen is a world leader in advanced forecasting technology for the financial markets with operations in Zurich and London. The Olsen

Information System is a family of decision support tools for the foreign exchange markets. A Currency Converter at *www.oanda.com/converter/classic* offers exchange rates for 164 currencies.

*UltraHal*
www.zabaware.com

Intelligent assistant software. "Bring Out the Person in your PC."

*Visible Decisions*
www.vdi.com

3-D interactive – user-controlled – visualization that can handle massive amounts of financial data.

## Global Information

*Emerging Markets Companion*
www.emgmkts.com/index.htm

The Emerging Markets Companion provides a convenient window into the emerging economies of Asia, Latin America, Africa and Eastern Europe. It provides an integrated view of global economic and political events, market activity, and investment strategies.

*Fidelity International*
www.fid-intl.com

Fidelity offers a number of financial products and services designed specifically for people from certain countries or regions. These products or services are not available outside their region.

*Institute for Commercial Engineering*
www.fe.msk.ru

A Russian site that includes the Russian exchange; REDGAR, Federal Commission on Securities and the Capital Market. It may be viewed in Russian and, partially, in English.

*Interactive Investor*
www.iii.co.uk

Interactive Investor is an umbrella site for information about IFAs, UK unit trusts, investment trusts, PEPs, and offshore funds, with pages maintained by fund managers. It also offers a news service with the following journals: *Financial Adviser, Product Adviser, Investment Adviser and Offshore Financial Review.*

*JP Morgan*
www.jpmorgan.com/research

Daily updated information about emerging markets, including its Emerging Market Outlook.

*Morgan Stanley Capital International*
www.ms.com/msci.html

Extensive information for global investors.

*TeleStock*
www.teleserv.co.uk/stock

TeleStock provides finance information as well as "day old" online quotes of major US and European shares, options and commodities.

## Government/Regulatory Agencies

*Internal Revenue Service*
www.irs.ustreas.gov/prod/cover.html

Extensive site for the US IRS.

*SEC Edgar Database*
www.sec.gov

Extensive financial filings from companies.

# News/Publications

## Discussion forums

*Stock Club*
www.stockclub.com

Discussion of stocks, mutual funds and other financial information.

## News

*Bloomberg*
www.bloomberg.com

Extensive information site for the Bloomberg financial service.

*Briefing.com*
www.briefing.com

Briefing.com delivers analysis of important news affecting stocks and bonds. Includes analysis of individual stocks and the factors that will affect value tomorrow. Offers free and paid subscription levels of information.

*Business Wire*
www.businesswire.com

Business Wire (BW) disseminates financial and product news releases, photos, advisories and features from large, medium and small companies and organizations worldwide.

*CNBC*
www.cnbc.com

Extensive business and investment news, includes links to CNBC Europe and CNBC Asia.

*CNN Financial Network*
www.cnnfn.com

Extensive information resource, featuring: news, market information, a link to Quicken's financial network with information for investors, global information, currency conversion, and links to a wide variety of business resources, including tax, consumer credit, company sites, mutual funds and other information.

*Inside China Today*
insidechina.com

News about financial and investment issues in China.

*Pensions & Investments*
pionline.com

Online site for this well-known publication for investment professionals.

*PointCast*
www.pointcast.com

PointCast is the "Internet's All News All-the-Time Network," a software-based information service that uses streaming technology to bring personalized data to the desktop.

*Reuters*
www.reuters.com

Extensive business and financial news.

*ZD Interactive Investor*
www.zdii.com

Investment news from Ziff-Davis.

## Publications

*Barrons Online*
www.barrons.com

Online version of the popular financial publication.

*Business Week*
www.businessweek.com

The online version of the business publication. Free information includes a Daily Briefing, with business news, analysis, Q&As and commentaries; alerts to key economic reports and meetings. Business Week Plus includes online-only content arranged by topic, including Best Business Schools; Business Books Online; The Computer Room; Enterprise Online (for small business); Investors Central; Mutual Fund Corner; and Personal Business Network. The site also includes a banking center, with money and credit information and links to useful financial sites; a tool chest for investors, including a personal portfolio tracker, historic stock information and more. As with most online publications, this site includes a "search and archives" section.

*Forbes*
www.forbes.com

Online version of the business publication, with extensive additional information about business and finance. It has all the features, including a search engine, quick quotes, and a handy "digital tool home" menu.

*Fortune*
cgi.pathfinder.com/fortune

Online version of the business publication.

*The Hulbert Financial Digest*
www.hulbertdigest.com

The most renowned digest reviewing over 160 investment newsletters and the 450 portfolios they recommend.

*Investors Business Daily*
www.investors.com

Online version of the investment publication.

*Money.com*
www.money.com

Online version of the publication.

*TheStreet.com*
www.thestreet.com

*TheStreet.com* is an online financial publication that provides news and reporting.

*The Pristine Day Trader*
www.pristine.com

A newsletter and online information service that focuses on daily stock recommendations for active traders.

*USA Today – Money*
www.usatoday.com/money/mfront.htm

Business and finance news from the online version of the newspaper.

*Wall Street Journal Interactive Edition*
interactive.wsj.com

Internet, subscription-based edition of the *Wall Street Journal*.

## Webcasting

*Wall Street Forum*
www.wallstreetforum.com

Wall Street Forum "webcasts" industry presentations, analysts' conferences and other events.

© 1999 Association for Investment Management and Research

# Index